The Ultimate Improvement Cycle

Maximizing Profits through the Integration of Lean, Six Sigma, and the Theory of Constraints

BOB SPROULL

CRC Press
Taylor & Francis Group
Boca Raton London New York

CRC Press is an imprint of the
Taylor & Francis Group, an **informa** business

A PRODUCTIVITY PRESS BOOK

CRC Press
Taylor & Francis Group
6000 Broken Sound Parkway NW, Suite 300
Boca Raton, FL 33487-2742

© 2009 by Taylor & Francis Group, LLC
CRC Press is an imprint of Taylor & Francis Group, an Informa business

No claim to original U.S. Government works

International Standard Book Number-13: 978-1-4200-9034-5 (Hardcover)

Library of Congress Cataloging-in-Publication Data

Sproull, Robert.
    The ultimate improvement cycle : maximizing profits through the integration of lean, six sigma, and the theory of constraints / Bob Sproull.
       p. cm.
    Includes bibliographical references and index.
    ISBN 978-1-4200-9034-5 (hardcover : alk. paper)
    1. Business logistics. 2. Production management. 3. Six sigma (Quality control standard) 4. Theory of constraints (Management) I. Title.

HD38.5.S63 2009
658.4'013--dc22
                                                  2009002289

Visit the Taylor & Francis Web site at
http://www.taylorandfrancis.com

and the CRC Press Web site at
http://www.crcpress.com

Contents

Preface

When I first began my career in a manufacturing environment, I knew nothing about the inner workings of a manufacturing facility. I knew that you had to process customer orders, order raw materials, create a production schedule, process them into a finished product, and deliver them to a customer in a timely manner, but I was unaware of the intricacies involved in doing all this.

I was taught that if I maximized the efficiencies and utilizations of each individual operation, I could maximize the efficiencies and utilization of the entire system—that the key to reaching global optimization was by achieving local optimums. I was taught that every operation was equal in value, and that the key to increasing profits was to reduce the amount of money required to operate each individual process. In so doing, I was taught that manpower was expendable, so that it was okay to lay off excess manpower. I was also taught that inventory was needed to protect all of the steps in the process so that if you had downtime, you could use inventory to continue running. Besides, inventory was viewed by cost accounting as an asset, so how could it possibly be bad?

As I continued learning, I began to realize that some of what I had taken as being the gospel was, in fact, bogus! In the years that followed my initial stint at a manufacturing plant, I began to better understand the different roles of groups within a typical company and how they impacted the success of the company. I learned that processes do not always produce a product according to a plan, because of downtime and quality problems. I began to realize the impact and influence that leadership can have on an organization, and how performance metrics invariably influence the behaviors of the resources within the organization. I have been at it for many years now and have come to several conclusions that apply to all manufacturing companies, some of which are shared by the various mentors and leaders who shaped and influenced my career, and some of which directly contradict what I learned from them.

In hopes of not offending too many cost accountants, the first and perhaps the most important conclusion is my belief that cost accounting influences the behaviors of many manufacturing organizations in very negative ways. I had always been taught that if you were able to minimize the cost of each individual operation, the total system would operate at minimal cost. I had also been taught that the total cost of each operation is directly proportional to the cost of direct labor for each operation, and that the total cost for the system minus the raw material cost is proportional to the sum of direct labor costs. But I soon realized that maximizing the efficiency and utilization of each operation did not result in optimization of the total system at all. In fact, I learned that maximizing the efficiency of all operations served only to create mountains of inventory. I learned that inventory is not an asset at all because it actually has a carrying cost associated with it. But more importantly, excess inventory increases the effective cycle time (C/T), which decreases an organization's ability to ship product on time. I also learned that inventory tends to hide other problems. I learned that cutting the cost of each individual operation does not result in the system cost's being minimized. In fact, many times, in an attempt to minimize the cost of individual operations, companies make drastic cuts in operating expense (OE) and labor that are too deep, thus causing motivational, quality, and delivery problems.

My second conclusion is that in every organization, there are only a few (and most of the time only one) operations that control the rate of revenue generation, and hence the profits. All processes are composed of constraining and nonconstraining resources, and the key to improvement is focusing on the operation that is constraining throughput (TP). Attempts to improve nonconstraining resources usually result in very little improvement, from a system perspective.

My third conclusion is that variability is the root of all evil in a manufacturing process. Variability in product characteristics, in process parameters, and in processing times (P/T) degrades the performance of a process and of a company. The presence of variability degrades a company's ability to effectively plan and execute scheduled production, increases operational expense, and decreases the chances of producing and delivering product to customers when they want it and at the cost they want to pay. Because variability is so devastating, every effort must be made to reduce it as much as possible.

My fourth conclusion is that excessive waste exists in every process, and until it is identified and removed, real process improvement will not happen. Although there are many forms of waste, the most obvious—and perhaps the two most debilitating—are the wastes associated with waiting and overproducing. Waiting and overproduction both work to lengthen the overall C/T.

My fifth conclusion is that how people and organizations are measured significantly dictates their behavior. If, for example, a company measures operator efficiency and values high efficiency in every step in the operation, the organization will have high levels of inventory, low values of quality, and a high incidence of late or missed shipments. As a corollary to this, maximizing the efficiency of an operation that is limiting TP is mandatory to maximizing revenue and profits.

My sixth conclusion is that most companies do not know how to focus and leverage their improvement efforts in the right area. Many companies have embraced Lean, Six Sigma, or a combination of the two and, in so doing, have practically attempted to solve world hunger by struggling to improve every operation. When this happens, the efforts become diluted, and improvements become protracted to the point of frustration. Both of these initiatives work well if only they are focused in the right area of the organization.

My seventh and final conclusion is that organizations that fail to involve their workforce typically do not succeed in the long run. Everyone in the organization needs to know the goals of the company and how they are doing relative to these goals. But even more importantly, everyone must be permitted to contribute to these goals. After all these years, it is apparent to me that shop floor workers have a vast array of information and ideas, both of which must be harvested.

Unfortunately, many of the companies with which I have been involved do not practice what I have learned. Many companies still use ineffective performance metrics and outdated accounting systems. Many companies fail to recognize and capitalize on the constraints that exist within their systems. Many companies still do not appreciate that waste and variability encumber their processes, and that the participation of the general workforce is needed to make them successful.

As a consultant, I have been able to study the inner workings of many companies in many types of industries, and I have discovered a better way to make the most of your precious resources. Not only do I have an idea of why you may have failed to achieve an acceptable and sustainable return on your improvement investment, but I have a solution for you as well. The solution is not revolutionary, but it is innovative. What I have to offer you is a way to make certain that your improvement effort is focused in the right place, at the right time, using the right methods and tools, with the right amount of resources to deliver the maximum amount of return on your improvement investment. This method addresses the problems associated with cost accounting, variation, waste, and performance measurements. But most of all, it focuses your organization on the right area to optimize your TP, OE, inventory, revenues, and margins.

I know, I know: You have heard it all before. You have heard the same declaration from experts in Total Quality Management (TQM), Just in Time (JIT), Six Sigma, Theory of Constraints (TOC), Lean, and all the others, but I believe once you see the simplicity and logic behind what I term the Ultimate Improvement Cycle (UIC), you will be motivated—and maybe even inspired—to move forward with it. UIC is based upon the basic principles associated with

Lean, Six Sigma, and the TOC, but it is unique in that it capitalizes on a time-released formula for use of the key tools, techniques, principles, and actions of all three initiatives focused on the right area. It does not require any more resources than you currently have available, but it does provide the focus needed to achieve maximum resource utilization, which translates into maximum ROI. Using this method will provide you with a self-funded improvement effort that will sustain itself.

The genesis behind UIC is based upon many years of analysis of both failures and successes using Lean, Six Sigma, and TOC as stand-alone improvement initiatives. The TOC reveals interdependencies that exist within your operation and focuses your efforts on the constraining operation. Although TOC provides the necessary focus, Lean works to simplify and free the constraint of unnecessary waste, as well as increase the TP of your total system. As Lean is doing this, Six Sigma removes variation and defects, while working to sustain the improvements.

My analysis has revealed a common thread between successful initiatives, no matter whether they were based on Lean, Six Sigma, or TOC models. The key to success is the leverage point, or where the improvement efforts were focused. Although eliminating waste (Lean) and reducing variation (Six Sigma) are both critical components of all successful improvement initiatives, where these efforts are focused will determine the ultimate impact on a company's bottom line. By integrating Lean, Six Sigma, and TOC into a single improvement cycle, I have developed a recipe that will maximize your ROI, cash flow, and net profit (NP).

I think you will find this book, *The Ultimate Improvement Cycle: Maximizing Profits through the Integration of Lean, Six Sigma, and the Theory of Constraints*, to be both stimulating and thought-provoking, but more importantly, it will provide your organization with a road map for maximizing the use of your resources to achieve more bottom-line improvement than you ever imagined possible. I am convinced that *The Ultimate Improvement Cycle* is the definitive improvement strategy going forward, and I am confident that if you follow the guidelines I have developed, your company will not only survive in this new global economy, but it will also flourish.

One final thought. Although my targeted audience for this book was manufacturing, UIC works equally well in any environment where processes exist. This applies to businesses such as Maintenance, Repair and Overhaul (MRO), hospitals, engineering companies...virtually every industry where maximizing TP translates directly into revenue and bottom line improvement!

Acknowledgments

Writing this book would not have been possible without the many opportunities I have been given over the years—those that gave me the chance to witness, firsthand, both good and bad, weak and strong, and dynamic and apathetic leadership. I have been fortunate enough to have been able to develop my craft by witnessing what works and what does not work, what fails and what succeeds. I dedicate this book to all the great (and not so great) leaders I have been fortunate enough to work with. Both groups of leaders—and I am certain each knows which category he or she falls into—demonstrated to me the right way and the wrong way to run a manufacturing organization. To both groups, I am forever grateful!

Introduction

Before I get into the details of UIC, it is important that you have a good understanding of the goals of each individual initiative—in terms of the key principles, tools, and methods—if each were a stand-alone improvement initiative. This introduction provides that background, for your review.

Lean Principles, Tools, and Methods

Lean manufacturing is a whole-systems approach that focuses on identifying and eliminating non-value-added activities within a process. Lean, as an improvement initiative, attempts to involve everyone in the organization in a quest to eliminate any and all forms of waste, everywhere in your enterprise.

Lean's objectives are to use less human effort, less inventory, less space, and less time to produce high-quality products as efficiently and economically as possible, while being highly responsive to customer needs and demands. Lean thinking starts with a conscious effort to define value in very specific terms through constant dialogue with customers.

So just exactly what is value? Surprisingly, value is not always an easy thing to define. James Womack and Daniel Jones, authors of *Lean Thinking—Banish Waste and Create Wealth in Your Corporation*, tell us that "part of the reason value is hard to define for most producers is that most producers want to make what they are already making and partly because many customers only know how to ask for some variant of what they are already getting. They simply start in the wrong place and end up at the wrong destination." Womack and Jones further explain that another reason firms find it hard to get value right is "that while value creation often flows through many firms, each one tends to define value in a different way to suit its own needs."[1] The basic definition that I have always used for value is whatever the customer feels good about paying for. Customers know what they want, when they want it, where they want it, the price they are willing to pay, and the quantities and varieties they want while demanding exceptional quality. The bottom line is that if you do not give customers all this, they will simply go elsewhere. So if customers are questioning why they should pay for something, it simply is not value. Why should a customer pay for things like excess inventory or defective product? At the end of the day, value clarifies itself.

Lean manufacturing is generally recognized as one of the most effective business improvement strategies in the world today, but many Lean initiatives are either failing or stagnating. Given Lean's focus on the complete elimination of waste everywhere within an organization, the list of potential wastes becomes mind-boggling: mistakes that require repair or modification; production of items that have not been ordered or that nobody wants; transportation of products within a facility that travel great distances to get from one process step to another; idle time of one process step created by downtime at another, or just differences in P/T; defective or scrap materials—the list could continue indefinitely. And, for many companies, the list of activities that *do* create value—or those steps that are said to be *value-added*—would probably not fill a single page. When most companies calculate the ratio of value-added to non-value-added activities in their processes, they are shocked, surprised, and maybe even embarrassed. This phenomenon makes Lean seem a bit overwhelming.

Seven Categories of Waste, Plus One

Taiichi Ohno, a Toyota executive and intense opponent of waste, was the first to identify and classify seven different categories of waste with corresponding examples, as follows:[2]

- **Overproduction:** Producing items for which there are no orders. That is, making too much, too soon, or too often than is required by the customer. Overproduction generates other wastes, like overstaffing, storage, and transportation costs, because overproduction always results in excess inventory.
- **Waiting (time on hand):** Workers having to stand around waiting for parts from upstream process steps, tools and supplies that they need to process the parts, or instructions on how to process the parts; equipment downtime; defective products from internal and external suppliers; inspections results; and even information are all considered waste. The waste of waiting accounts for the highest amount of non-value-added time in almost all processes.
- **Unnecessary transport or conveyance:** Having to transport raw material, work-in-process (WIP), or finished goods over long distances, or moving products in and out of storage or between process steps is the third waste. Unless the product being produced proceeds uninterrupted from

one step to another, and when it gets there is *not* stacked or shelved, it is considered unnecessary transport or conveyance.

■ **Overprocessing or incorrect processing:** Having unnecessary or unneeded steps or extra effort within a process adds little or no value. This includes overworking or overinspecting a part, in an attempt to make it "perfect," when perfection is not required by the customer.

■ **Excess inventory:** Any part or supply that is in excess of one-piece flow through the manufacturing process is also considered waste. This includes excess raw material, WIP, or finished goods that cause excessive lead times, obsolescence, damaged parts, transportation, or storage costs. In addition, inventory hides problems like defects, machine downtime, flow problems, and so on.

■ **Unnecessary movement:** Any motion of operators, tooling, or equipment that adds no value, such as looking for parts or supplies, stacking and unstacking of parts, walking to get something, reaching, unnecessary twisting and turning, and so on.

■ **Defects:** Production of products that results in repairs or scraps, replacement production, reinspection, or late deliveries, or that requires extra inspection, sorting, scrapping, downgrading, or replacement, creates waste.

■ **Creativity:** This recently added eighth category treats wasting people's creativity—not fully utilizing employees' or, more explicitly, operators' brain power, creativity, and experience—as another waste to eliminate.

The Five Principles of Lean

From the 10,000-foot view, implementing Lean typically follows the below five steps (or principles):

1. Define value from the customer's perspective.
2. Identify the value stream, which is all the actions required to bring products from a concept to a detailed design to an order to delivery of products. Womack and Jones state that "value stream analysis will almost always show that three types of actions are occurring along the value stream: Many steps will be found to unambiguously create value; many other steps will be found to create no value, but to be unavoidable with current technologies and production assets; and many steps will be found to create no value and to be immediately avoidable."[3] Translated, these three actions are value-added, non-value-added but necessary, and non-value-added. For the non-value-added steps, Lean requires eliminating them immediately.

3. Once value has been defined and precisely specified and the value stream analyzed with obvious non-value-added steps removed, make the remaining (value-creating) steps flow. In this step, the focus is on maximizing value by producing only what is needed in the shortest time possible with the fewest resources needed.
4. Pull to customer demand by producing only at the rate of customer orders, and no more. In other words, do not overproduce.
5. Pursue perfection by empowering employees with waste elimination tools to create a culture of continuous improvement.

Basic Lean Building Blocks

In order to better understand how and why Lean works, it is a good idea to also understand the basic Lean building blocks. These are the basic tools, techniques, and methods that are used during a Lean implementation, which include:

- **5S:** A five-step procedure aimed at fashioning workplace organization (WPO) and standardization, with each step starting with the letter S. The five S's originated in Japan and are (with the English translation): *seiri* (sort), *seiton* (straighten), *seison* (shine), *seiketsu* (standardize), and *shitsuke* (sustain).
- **Visual controls:** The assignment of all tools, parts, production procedures, performance metrics, orders, and so on in plain view so that the status of a process step can be understood in thirty seconds or less. Typically, one might expect to see things like andon lights or different-colored flags that indicate the process status at a glance.
- **Standardized work:** A physical description (often including photos) of exactly how to perform each job according to prescribed methods (developed with operator assistance), with the absolute minimum of waste.
- **Cellular layout:** The layout of a process (machines, materials, supplies, and people) performing different operations in a tight sequence (a manufacturing cell).
- **One-piece flow:** The flow of product through a sequence of process steps that pass one piece at a time, with few interruptions, backflows, scrap, rework, or accumulated inventory.
- **Quality at the source:** Quality is the responsibility of the person producing the product, with inspection and process control done at the source by the operator, prior to passing the product on to the production step.
- **Quick changeover:** Being able to change tooling sets or fixtures rapidly, to permit the production of multiple products in small batches on the same equipment.

- **Pull and kanban:** A system of production and delivery instructions sent from downstream operations to upstream operations that is done after a signal, usually in the form of a small card (a kanban), is given.
- **Total Productive Maintenance (TPM):** A series of maintenance methods that ensures process equipment will always be available when needed, for as long as it is needed, with minimal amounts of downtime.

Six Sigma Principles, Tools, and Methods

The first book I read on Six Sigma included a quote that drove home what Six Sigma is all about. Harry and Schroeder told us something about the power of measurements with the following:

> We don't know what we don't know.
> We can't act on what we don't know.
> We won't know until we search.
> We won't search for what we don't question.
> We don't question what we don't measure.[4]

These words, although elegant and simple, deliver a compelling message to all of us about first questioning, searching for answers, and then measuring to find the answers. The fact is, if you do not measure, you simply will not improve. This is the powerful and dynamic message of Six Sigma: you can make calculated guesses and assumptions based on experience, but without hard data, conclusions are based on insufficient evidence. Or maybe a more simple message is this: without data, you are just another person with an opinion.

Identifying Core Processes and Key Customers

The first step in the Six Sigma road map is the identification of core or primary processes and key customers. As a rule of thumb, most companies have four to eight essential core processes that represent the backbone of how the company functions. These typically include customer acquisition, order administration, order fulfillment, customer service and support, new product/service development, and invoicing and collections. If you consider each of these in the context of the goal of the company to make money now and in the future, and although they all contribute, each could also be a system constraint. For example, if you were producing a product and shipping it according to order rates, but were not receiving the revenue in a timely manner, invoicing and collections could be the operation that is constraining or restricting your organization's revenue stream.

Or maybe your order fulfillment process is preventing you from moving closer to your goal.

Six Sigma uses "projects" to make improvements, and these projects can be located in any of the core processes or support processes, or even external to the company. Peter Pande, Robert Newman, and Roland Cavanaugh, authors of *The Six Sigma Way—How GE, Motorola, and Other Top Companies Are Honing Their Performance*, list three criteria for understanding what will qualify as a Six Sigma project:[5]

- There is a gap between current and needed/desired performance.
- The cause of the problem is not clearly understood.
- The solution is not predetermined, nor is the optimal solution apparent.

These three criteria may appear logical, but only if they are applied to performance issues or problems within the operation that is constraining your organization. At the risk of sounding redundant, any action taken in operations outside the constraint operation, or that process step that is limiting TP, is a wasted use of valuable resources. And although you might move closer to your goal, your rate of movement will be much slower than it could or should be.

Sigma Levels

One of the key teachings of Six Sigma is the concept of sigma levels that, in a nutshell, refers to the quality level of the product produced or service delivered. Quality is measured and tracked as defects per million opportunities (DPMO). In Table 1, Harry and Schroeder estimated the cost of quality as a percent of sales for each level of sigma. Harry and Schroeder believe that a typical corporation operates at a three to four sigma level, with DPMO levels ranging from 66,807 down to 6,210. They also believe companies that operate below three sigma usually do not survive, because their cost of quality prevents them from being competitive. The concept of measuring processes on the basis of defective product (or service) is an important one because even a shift from 4 sigma to 4.5 sigma represents a big improvement to the bottom line. Harry and Schroeder further explain that "the improved quality that results will translate not only into cost reductions but into increased sales and quantum leaps in profitability."[6] Although I agree, in spirit, with the comment regarding increased sales and "quantum leaps in profitability," I would add that Harry and Schroeder's comment has this impact only if the improvement efforts are focused in the constraint operation. However, if your operation already has excess capacity, clearly an improvement in your product's quality level could be leveraged to improve your ability to land new orders, and therefore new revenue.

Table 1   The Cost of Quality

Sigma Level	DPMO	Cost of Quality
2	308,537 (noncompetitive companies)	Not applicable
3	66,807	25–40% of sales
4	6,210 (industry average)	15–25% of sales
5	233	5–15% of sales
6	3.4 (world class)	<1% of sales

The Eight-Step Six Sigma Methodology

When Harry and Schroeder introduced their Six Sigma methodology, there were eight steps in their process:

1. (R) Recognize functional problems that link to operational issues.
2. (D) Define the processes that contribute to the functional problems.
3. (M) Measure the capability of each process that offers operational leverage.
4. (A) Analyze the data to assess prevalent patterns and trends.
5. (I) Improve the key product/service characteristics created by the key processes.
6. (A) Control the process variables that exert undue influence.
7. (S) Standardize the methods and processes that produce best-in-class performance.
8. (I) Integrate standard methods and processes into the design cycle.

Somewhere along the way, these eight steps have been distilled into the familiar DMAIC methodology that you now see in most texts.

Statistical Tools

The real power of Six Sigma lies in its disciplined structure and use of statistical tools, techniques, and methods. In 1925, H. G. Wells wrote: "The time may not be very remote when it will be understood that for complete initiation as an efficient citizen of one of the new great complex worldwide States that are now developing, it is as necessary to be able to compute, to think in averages and maxima and minima, as it is now to be able to read and write."[7]

Wells was clearly a visionary—he saw statistics as being a basic skill in the future. And now, more than eighty years later, what separates Six Sigma from other improvement methodologies is the use of statistical analysis tools and techniques to translate operational data into usable decision-making information. I agree with Wells and believe that the training provided by many of the Six Sigma Black Belt certifications is now a business imperative.

Although statistical tools and techniques are vital, they can be overused to the detriment of many improvement initiatives. In fact, many companies have experienced information overload and analysis paralysis, whereby there is a failure to launch into solutions. That is, companies sometimes spend so much time analyzing data that their improvement initiative never seems to get off the ground, or if it is launched, there are too many equally rated problems, and participants end up drowning in a sea of data. Companies must always guard against trying to collect and analyze more data and information than they need to in order to make improvements to their process. For this reason, six simple tools (and a seventh that is a bit more complicated) are critical to master and use. They are as follows:

- Run charts
- Pareto charts
- Cause-and-effect diagrams
- Causal chains
- Control charts
- Check sheets

Each of these six simple tools plays a valuable role in the improvement process, and as such, each has a distinct purpose. The run chart serves several important purposes. First, it provides a history of where the process or product variable has been, where it is operating right now, and where it could likely be in the future. When changes are made to the process, the run chart lets you know the impact of changes, and from a problem-solving perspective, being able to relate changes to shifts in the response variables you are attempting to improve is invaluable. By recording the changes that you are making or have made directly onto the run chart, you get a visual presentation of the impact of the change. Pareto charts serve a much different purpose than run charts in that they help you identify, focus on, and prioritize the defects and problems that offer the greatest opportunity for improvement. By seeing things in priority order, you have less of a tendency to squander your resources. Cause-and-effect diagrams help you organize potential causes of defects and problems, while causal chains facilitate the logical dissection of problems by continuing to ask *why* until you arrive at potential root causes of the problem you are attempting to solve. Control charts provide you with the opportunity to identify sources and types of process variation, help you reduce process variation, let you know whether or not your processes are in a state of statistical control, and then allow you to predict what future results might be. Check sheets help you pinpoint where on the object the problem or defect is occurring.

A more complicated tool is design of experiments (DOE), which really is not difficult but is perceived to be. Because many people believe the statistics involved in DOEs are too advanced for them, they tend to shy away from using this tool. The reality is that with the statistical software that exists today, and in particular Minitab 15, DOEs are relatively straightforward to design, run, and analyze. Minitab even has a feature that explains in very simple terms the purpose of each step of the DOE process and how to interpret the results of the study. (If this sounds like an endorsement for Minitab 15, you are absolutely right. As I write today, I can state that of all the statistically based software on the market today that I have used, Minitab 15 is clearly the most user-friendly one available, and I highly recommend it!) At any rate, DOEs are an important part of your improvement initiative and will help you identify which factors and interactions are most responsible for creating defects and excessive variation. DOEs also facilitate the optimization of your process and corresponding response variables. Every successful improvement tool kit must contain DOEs.

TOC Principles, Tools, and Methods

TOC suggests that all systems are comparable and analogous to a single chain or to chains linked together to form a network. Every chain has one weakest link. When force, in the form of tension, is applied to it, the chain will break exactly at its weakest link. If you are using a chain rated up to 5 tons to tow an economy car, you will have no trouble doing so. If you try to use that same chain to pull a large and heavy truck, either it will pull the back end of your car off or the chain will break at its weakest link, whichever point is weaker. Thus, the chain is limited by its weakest link.

TOC applies this chain analogy to manufacturing organizations in that an organization's success is determined by its weakest link. In other words, the TP of the process is determined strictly by the operation that is constraining it—the bottleneck or system constraint. The constraint can be either physical or policy related, and it can be either internal or external to the organization. For example, if the capacity of the facility is less than the demand (i.e., number of orders), the constraint is internal to the organization. If, on the other hand, the capacity of the facility is greater than the demand, the constraint is external.

Two types of constraints impede the progress of an organization: physical constraints and policy constraints. *Physical constraints* are usually easier to locate and break, because you can physically see the effect they are having on a system's TP. *Policy constraints*, on the other hand, are insidious and somewhat sinister. They are lurking in the dark, just waiting to be found; if you do not know how to find them, you will never be able to break them.

Goldratt's Five Tools

Dr. Eli Goldratt introduced us to TOC through his highly successful and widely read business novel, *The Goal*, the purpose of which was to find ways of dealing primarily with policy constraints. The following five tools make up what Goldratt refers to as the TOC *thinking process*:[8]

- The *current reality tree* (CRT) begins by identifying UDEs and works backward to identify a few root causes or a single core problem.
- The *conflict resolution diagram* (CRD) is used to resolve hidden organizational conflicts that usually perpetuate chronic problems.
- The *future reality tree* (FRT) allows you to verify that the actions you want to take to resolve the conflict will produce the desired outcome and helps you identify any potential adverse new consequences of your actions.
- The *prerequisite tree* helps to identify both what might keep you from doing what you want to do and the best way to overcome any obstacles.
- The *transition tree* helps you develop the necessary steps to implement your new course of action as well as the rationale for each step.

Mastering these five tools will help you identify policy constraints, resolve conflicts, and break those constraints.

Goldratt's Five Focusing Steps

In *The Goal,* Goldratt outlines his five focusing steps (reviewed in a bit more detail in Chapter 1). After articulating the goal of the organization, you must do the following:

1. Identify the constraint (the thing keeping you from your goal).
2. Exploit the constraint (make sure it is doing something unique and is doing what it should be doing).
3. Subordinate and align all other processes to the exploited constraint.

4. Elevate or permanently increase the capacity of the constraint.
5. Repeat the first four steps continuously.

The first four of Goldratt's five focusing steps can be consolidated into three, as follows:

1. Determine *what* to change.
2. Determine *what to change to.*
3. Determine *how to cause* the change.

What to change is the constraint. Knowing what to change requires that you identify the constraint that is in line with the first of the five focusing steps. *What to change to* requires that you become very creative, and because you are working at the system level, any change you make will have an impact on the components that make up the system. The changes made here will demand breakthrough and out-of-the box thinking that is difficult for many organizations. H. William Dettmer[9] has provided us with two simple questions that will help:

■ Will this change really deliver the results you want?
■ What adverse side effects can you expect?

The answers to these two questions provide a validation that the proposed changes are the right ones. Dettmer explains that this step is a consolidation of steps 2 and 4 of the five focusing steps (*exploit* and *elevate*).

Once you have determined and validated what to change to, you must now decide *how to cause* the change. In other words, you are now faced with the most difficult task of all: breaking the policy constraint. As Dettmer explains, ideas are not solutions; they have to be converted into effective actions. Again, Dettmer provides us with three questions:

■ What obstacles stand in the way of your implementing this bright idea?
■ How do you overcome these obstacles?
■ What must you do—and in what sequence—to turn your ideas into reality?

Answering these three questions is rudimentary to making effective change of any kind.

Four Levels of Response

Dettmer tells us that when the system is not performing as it should, there are four possible levels of response:

- Do nothing and hope that the problem either resolves itself or goes away.
- Make minor changes to or tweak the system.
- Make major changes, such as reengineering the system.
- Throw out the existing system and start over with a new one.

Most company executives do not opt for the first response because they were hired to and are evaluated on their ability to make improvements to the system. The fourth response, throwing out the existing system and starting over, usually is not a viable option for most executives because starting over requires time and money. So executives are typically left with making some minor and major changes. For minor changes, they see some kind of continuous improvement initiative as the answer (e.g., Lean and Six Sigma), but what happens many times is that they end up cherry-picking the tools of the initiative instead of adopting the entire initiative as a business strategy. For large changes, reorganizing is usually what happens. Many times, there is not much thought going into it, but because they believe that change itself will improve business, they just jump in and do it.

Thoughts on Constraints Management

There are several final thoughts on the subject of constraints management that I want to share with you. Constraints management is based upon four assumptions about how systems function (note that many of these thoughts are also articulated by Dettmer):

- Every system has a goal and a finite number of necessary conditions that must be satisfied while trying to achieve the goal. In order for efforts to be effective in improving system performance, there must be a clear understanding and consensus between all members of the organization about what the goal and necessary conditions are. This assumption is completely congruent and harmonious to the principles of both Lean and Six Sigma.
- The sum of the system's *local optima* (e.g., efficiency) does not equal the global system optimum. The most effective systems are never achieved by maximizing the efficiency of individual system components, but by recognizing that the system is made up of a series of interconnected and interdependent processes that interact with each other. To a certain extent, this assumption is incompatible with the basic principles of Lean, because Lean advocates attacking all processes to eliminate waste. Although I do believe this approach is necessary, it is more a question of timing. That is, to immediately seek out and eliminate waste across all operations is, in my opinion, the wrong approach. This approach results in short-term

gratification and in some measure explains why some Lean initiatives fail.

■ Very few variables limit the performance of the total system at any one time; there is usually only one weakest link in the system at a time. Lean does not recognize the need to focus on constraints as a starting point, while Six Sigma only passively mentions them. And if the constraint is policy related, neither seeks to eliminate or modify the constraint to improve TP.

■ TOC believes that all *negative symptoms* (UDEs) observed within a system are related to a few core problems. In other words, most of the organizational problems you observe can be traced to a few root causes that, if eliminated, will eliminate most of the negative symptoms.

Keep in mind that nonconstraint operators and processes will be forced, at times, to work at less than their maximum. As a result, they will sometimes sit idle, which Lean identifies as non-value-added waste. Companies often see this as an opportunity to reduce OE, typically in the form of layoffs. The fastest way to demotivate your workforce is to involve them in improving TP, and then turn around and lay them off to gain short-term OE reductions. Don't do it!

In addition, the selection of incorrect performance metrics can be a key driver of failure in improvement initiatives. One metric commonly used in manufacturing companies is resource (i.e., operator or equipment) efficiency. Efficiency measures how well a resource performed relative to an established standard. In real terms, it measures output relative to standard output for a particular resource. Because many supervisors, managers, and executives of these companies are measured and evaluated based on how efficient their operations are, they behave accordingly. That is, they attempt to maximize efficiency at every step in the process and generally overproduce what is needed or even produce what is not needed, just to achieve higher levels of efficiency. Even worse, they will reduce the size of their workforce through layoffs. The only place where efficiency or utilization makes any sense at all is at the constraint operation. My advice to companies that are using efficiency as a metric is this: Before you attempt to implement any TOC-based improvement initiative, abandon this metric in all nonconstraint operations. How your people behave is dictated by how you measure them. If you do not have the courage or fortitude or guts to do so, look somewhere else for an improvement initiative, because you will not do well.

Once you have identified a physical constraint within your system, never let the constraint operation sit idle. This means that you must always have acceptable product available when it is needed, and that unplanned downtime must be eliminated or at least minimized. If you do not have a preventive maintenance

(PM) program in place, it is a good time to implement one, especially in your constraint operation.

Constraints do not go away permanently; they just move. Just as soon as you break one constraint, another will emerge to take its place, so be ready. As you complete cycle after cycle of the UIC, it is entirely possible for a constraint that had previously been broken to reemerge as a constraint. The good news is that if you have gotten to this point, your TP has probably improved dramatically, and your profits are probably higher than they have ever been.

One final note: Most of the negative symptoms (UDEs) that you see within an organization or system are interconnected and caused by only a few core problems. If you can find them, define their interconnectedness, and eliminate them, life will be so much easier.

Throughput Accounting (TA)

Goldratt analogized the concept of a chain to organizations and explained that failing to identify and strengthen the organization's weakest link, or system constraint, will not strengthen the global system. Similarly, attempts to improve nonconstraint operations will not necessarily translate into significant organizational improvement. It is kind of like a professional baseball team signing free agent sluggers, when the real constraint is in pitching. They can score lots of runs, but in the end, if they cannot hold the other team to fewer runs than they score, they will never win a pennant.

According to Dettmer and Goldratt, TOC is based upon the fact that there is a common cause for many effects you observe at the systemic or organizational level. TOC envisions a company as a system or a set of interdependent relationships, with each relationship being dependent on others in some way. The global system performance is dependent upon the combined efforts of all the relationships within the organization. In addition, there are disruptions and statistical fluctuations (variability) that interfere with the production and delivery of products to the next process step that ultimately impacts delivery to the customer.

Every for-profit organization has the same two goals, to make money *now* and to make money in the *future*. Therefore, every action or decision taken by an organization must be judged by its impact on the organization's goals. This, of course, implies that before you can do this, you must first define the goal and then determine how you are going to measure or judge your decisions and actions.

A system's constraint was defined by Goldratt as anything that limits the system from achieving higher performance versus its goal. So how should you measure and judge your performance? Because the goal of the organization is to make money now and in the future, doesn't it make perfect sense that at least some of the performance measurements you choose should be money based? For example, two metrics that you could use are NP and ROI. Goldratt explained that in order to judge whether an organization is moving toward its goal, three questions must be answered:

- How much money is generated by your organization?
- How much money is invested by your company?
- How much money do you have to spend to operate it?

In order to answer these questions, Goldratt created his own version of accounting, commonly referred to as TA, and developed the following performance measurements:

- **Throughput (TH):** The rate at which the system generates "new" money through sales of its products or even earning interest at a bank. TH represents all money coming into a company minus what it pays to its suppliers or vendors. So, TH = P − TVC, where TH is throughput, P is the price/unit of product, and TVC is the totally variable costs, like raw material costs, sales commissions, or any costs associated with the sale of a product.
- **Investment (I):** The money the system invests in items that it plans to sell (such as inventory).
- **Operating expense (OE):** The money spent on turning investment (inventory) into TH, including labor costs, supplies, overhead, and so on.

TH is not considered TH until new money enters the company by producing and shipping product to customers. Anything produced that is not shipped is simply inventory, which costs a company and is not considered TH. Accordingly, Goldratt defines NP and ROI as follows:

$$NP = TH − OE$$

$$ROI = (TH − OE) \div I$$

With these three measurements (TH, I, and OE), Goldratt reasoned that organizations are able to determine the impact of their actions and decisions on the company's bottom line NP and ROI. Intuitively, then, the best actions and decisions are those that increase TH while simultaneously reducing inventory and OE. In reality, I have always believed that the final judge as to whether or not an action or decision is a good one should be its impact on ROI, because all three measurements are involved in the calculation.

Comparison of Lean, Six Sigma, and TOC

This brings us to an important question: Why have so many Lean, Six Sigma, and TOC initiatives failed? Some authors have stated that the Lean and Six Sigma philosophies are at odds with or contradictory to TOC. Still others have suggested that Lean and Six Sigma are only complementary to TOC. It is my belief, however, that Lean and Six Sigma are essential ingredients for the success of TOC. By the same token, success in Lean and Six Sigma initiatives is driven by adopting TOC as the basis for improvement, because TOC supplies both the focus and leverage points needed for true improvement. It is my contention that all three initiatives, when implemented in concert with each other (as presented in UIC, which is the subject of this book), represent the best possible strategy for maximizing revenues and profits. These three initiatives form a symbiosis whereby they not only coexist but actually benefit from each other's presence. In fact, they form UIC and act as a guide for maximizing profits.

Seeing the Symbiosis

Table 2 draws a comparison between Lean, Six Sigma, and TOC by summarizing their principal activities, defined methods, primary area of focus, and objectives. Look at the principal activity of each initiative, and you will see that they are all complementary—not independent, as some have suggested. The primary deliverables of each initiative cover the entire gamut of improvement: fewer defects, less variation, less waste, faster cycles, and improved capacity. Aren't these all the things you want out of an improvement initiative? Finally, the financial impact of these three initiatives (reduced OE, reduced inventory, and increased TH and revenue) all translate into big profits. Problems and processes are each contained within any system and potentially add intrinsic value to the system, if you can capitalize on them.

UIC: Why the Integration Works

In addition to the financial case made for integrating these three improvement methodologies, there are other rational and logical reasons why such

Table 2 Comparing Lean, Six Sigma, and TOC

	Six Sigma	*Lean*	*TOC*
Principal activity	Reduction of variation and defects	Elimination of waste	Management of constraints
Defined method	1. Define 2. Measure 3. Analyze 4. Improve 5. Control	1. Define value 2. Identify the value stream 3. Make value flow 4. Pull to customer demand 5. Pursue perfection	1. Identify the constraint 2. Exploit the constraint 3. Subordinate everything else 4. Elevate the constraint 5. Go back to step 1
Primary focus	Defining and solving problems	Improving processes	Systems optimization
Primary objective	Reliability and predictability	Simplifying processes	Defining and applying the right focus
Primary deliverable	Fewer defects and less variation	Less waste and faster cycles	Improved capacity
Financial impact	Reduced OE	Reduced inventory and OE	Increased TH/revenue

an integration works so well. In attempting to answer which of these three initiatives a company should use, Steven W. Thompson presents an excellent summary of the fundamental elements, strengths, and weaknesses for each improvement initiative.[10] In doing so, Thompson has inadvertently (or perhaps purposely) answered the underlying question of why the three improvement initiatives should be combined and integrated rather than choosing one over the other.

The first four columns in Table 3 reflect the summary of Thompson's comparison (i.e., the initiative, fundamental elements, strengths, and weaknesses). I have added a fifth column, "Counterbalance," that demonstrates how the strengths of one initiative counterbalance or compensate for the weaknesses of the others. By comparing the weaknesses and strengths of each of the three initiatives, you see that all the weaknesses of each individual initiative are neutralized by one or both of the strengths of the other two. This is such an important point for those companies that have experienced implementation problems for any of the three individual improvement initiatives done solo.

Let us look at several examples. Note that weakness 1 in Lean (may promote risk taking without reasonable balance to consequence) is counterbalanced by Six Sigma strength 3 (the focus on reduction of variation drives down risk and improves predictability). One thing you know for certain is that as you reduce variation in your process, you reduce risk, and your ability to predict future outcomes improves dramatically. This is the cornerstone of statistical process control (SPC), which means that risks can be minimized if you rely on this Six Sigma strength to do so.

Lean weakness 2 tells you that you may not provide sufficient evidence of business benefit for traditional cost accounting. This weakness is countered by both Six Sigma strength number 2 (the data gathering provides strong business cases to get management support for resources) and TOC strength number 4 (provides direction on appropriate simplified measures).

Lean weakness 3 states that Lean has a limitation when dealing with complex interactive and recurring problems (uses trial-and-error problem solving), and this is countered by Six Sigma strength 1 (the rigor and discipline of the statistical approach resolves complex problems that cannot be solved by simple intuition or trial and error) and TOC strength 3 (distinguishes policy versus physical constraints). One of the Six Sigma tools that permit you to solve complex interactive and recurring problems is DOE, which identifies significant factors that cause problems and insignificant factors that do not. TOC strength 3 helps you in two ways: First, if the problem you are facing is a policy constraint, you use TOC's CRT to identify it, and second, use the evaporating cloud to solve it. Both of these strengths will compensate for this weakness in Lean.

Now let us look at one of the Six Sigma and TOC weaknesses and see how they are compensated for by other strengths. For example, look at Six Sigma weakness 2 (the heavy reliance on statistical methods by its very nature is reactive, as it requires a repetition of the process to develop trends and confidence levels). This weakness is offset by Lean strength 2 (directly promotes radical breakthrough innovation) and Lean strength 3 (emphasis on fast response to opportunities). Likewise, TOC weakness 3 (TOC's inability to address the need for cultural change) is offset by Lean strength 4.

Table 3 How Lean, Six Sigma, and the TOC Counterbalance Each Other

Initiative	Fundamental Elements	Strengths	Weaknesses	Counterbalance
Lean	The cause of poor performance is wasteful activity. Lean is a time-based strategy and uses a narrow definition of waste (non-value-adding work) as any task or activity that does not produce value from the perspective of the end user. Increased competitive advantage comes from ensuring every task is focused on rapid transformation of raw materials into finished product.	1. Provides a strategic approach to integrated improvements through value stream mapping and the focus on maximizing the value-adding-to-waste ratio. 2. Directly promotes and advocates radical breakthrough innovation. 3. Emphasis on fast response to obvious opportunities (just go do it). 4. Addresses workplace culture and resistance to change through direct team involvement at all levels of the organization.	1. May promote risk taking without reasonable balance to consequence. 2. May not provide sufficient evidence of business benefit for traditional management accounting. 3. Has a limitation when dealing with complex interactive and recurring problems (uses trial-and-error problem solving).	1. Six Sigma strength 3 2. Six Sigma strength 2 and TOC strength 4 3. Six Sigma strength 1 and TOC strength 3

Table 3   How Lean, Six Sigma, and the TOC Counterbalance Each Other (Continued)

Initiative	Fundamental Elements	Strengths	Weaknesses	Counterbalance
Six Sigma	The cause of poor performance is variation in process and product quality. Random variations result in inefficient operations, causing dissatisfaction of customer from unreliable products and services. Increased competitive advantage comes from stable and predictable processes, allowing increased yields, improving forecasting and reliable product performance.	1. The rigor and discipline of the statistical approach resolves complex problems that cannot be solved by simple intuition or trial and error. 2. The data gathering provides strong business cases to get management support for resources. 3. The focus on reduction of variation drives down risk and improves predictability.	1. Statistical methods are not well suited for analysis of systems integration problems. I can calculate sigma for a product specification, but I am not sure how to establish sigma for process interactions and faults. 2. The heavy reliance on statistical methods by its very nature is reactive, as it requires a repetition of the process to develop trends and confidence levels. 3. The strong focus on stable processes can lead to total risk aversion and may penalize innovative approaches that by their nature will be unstable and variable.	1. Lean strength 1 and TOC strength 2 2. Lean strength 2 and Lean strength 3 3. Lean strength 2

TOC			
The cause of poor performance is flawed management technique. Systems logic is used to identify constraints and focus resources on the constraint. The constraint then becomes the management fulcrum.	1. Provides simplified process and resource administration through a narrow focus on the constraint for management of a process as well as improvement efforts (exploitation). 2. Looks across all processes within a systems context to ensure that limited resources are not overbuilding nonconstraint capability (the local optimization problem). 3. Distinguishes policy vs. physical constraints. 4. Provides direction on appropriate simplified measures (TH, inventory, and OE).	1. Overemphasizing exploitation of the constraint may lead to acceptance or tolerance of wasteful nonconstraint tasks within the process. 2. If the underlying process is fundamentally inadequate, no matter how well managed, it may not achieve the goals and objectives. 3. Does not directly address the need for cultural change. TOC change process is very technically oriented and fully acknowledges the need for TQM and other improvement methods.	1. Lean strength 1 and Six Sigma strength 2 2. Lean strength 2 3. Lean strength 4

In the same way, if you compare all the weaknesses in Lean, Six Sigma, and TOC to the strengths found in the other initiatives, the three initiatives not only complement each other but actually *rely* on each other. Thus, in addition to the demonstrated financial benefits of this symbiotic trilogy, you now see evidence from a logical perspective as to why they should be implemented in unison as a single improvement strategy.

Liker and Meier, when discussing why the Toyota Production System is so successful, tell you, "A sporadic removal (of waste) will yield pockets of improvement, but the system-wide benefits that Toyota enjoys are achieved by following a cyclical method of continuous improvement."[11] I completely support Liker and Meier's contention, and it is precisely the reason I believe UIC is the indispensable "cyclical method of continuous improvement" of the future. Like the Toyota Production System, UIC delivers system-wide benefits that result in maximum TH at minimum inventory levels and OEs.

The UIC Integration Is Easier Than It Seems

You may be saying to yourself, "Is he crazy? I can't do even one initiative right, let alone all three at the same time!" Although this may be a concern of yours at the moment, the reality is that by integrating Lean, Six Sigma, and the TOC, life becomes much easier on the shop floor. Because you are typically limiting your focus on only one operation at a time (i.e., the constraint) and not attempting an enterprise-wide improvement initiative, you will have:

- Fewer resource allocation problems
- Fewer problems to solve at any one time
- Fewer amounts of waste to remove at any one time
- Less organizational chaos and disorder
- Products that flow through your operation much more quickly and more efficiently
- A rate of revenue generation that improves dramatically
- More motivated employees
- Faster ROI
- Much more impressive bottom-line results

Chapter 1

The Lean, Six Sigma, and Theory of Constraints (TOC) Improvement Cycles

Perhaps you are attempting to implement Lean, Six Sigma, or TOC. If so, my experience is telling me that you are having difficulties, perhaps after a brief burst of success. You may be attempting across-the-board improvements to your entire enterprise, only to find that your resources are stretched to the limit. Perhaps you are expecting significant bottom-line improvement, but you just do not see it. You are trying to do the right thing, but you are having problems and need help.

What I have to offer you is a way to focus your efforts on the right areas without stretching or stressing out your resources—a way to maximize your margins. UIC will not only guide your improvement efforts but also sustain your gains and provide a focus for new improvement efforts. UIC is the focus of this book, but before I go into detail on UIC, I describe the improvement cycles of Lean, Six Sigma, and TOC. Then, in Chapter 2, I introduce UIC, which combines the best of these three improvement initiatives. The remaining chapters in this book flesh out the ideas summarized in Chapter 2.

Reviewing the Current State of Improvement Initiatives

For-profit organizations exist ostensibly for two purposes: to make money *now* and to make money in the *future*. Making money now requires organizations to relentlessly remove needless sources of waste and variation so that their products and services are not only profitable but are also consistently delivered on time and at the right price.

But to sustain these profits (that is, to make money in the future), organizations must continually reinvent themselves. What worked yesterday and today probably will not work tomorrow or next year, so change is necessary. The good news is that it is much easier to manage change than it is to react to it. Because products or services have such short half-lives these days, change must not only be expected, but also be passionately pursued and embraced. But what is it that you should be changing? That is the question this book attempts to answer.

Knowing what to change, what to change to, and how to implement change are the determining factors for how successful an organization will be in the future. In fact, in an effort to reinvent themselves, many organizations have attempted improvement initiatives like Lean manufacturing and Six Sigma, but they have failed to achieve the positive results they expected or at least hoped for. These companies then become disillusioned and either abandon the initiative altogether (backsliding to their old, more comfortable way of doing business) or use bits and pieces of the improvement strategy.

Reviewing the Data

The Lean Enterprise Institute (LEI) conducts annual surveys[12] on the subject of how well Lean implementations are going. Considering the last three surveys (2004, 2005, and 2006), the results do not paint a rosy picture. In fact, the LEI reported in 2004 that 36 percent of companies attempting to implement Lean were backsliding to their old ways of working. In 2005, the percentage of companies reporting backsliding had risen to almost 48 percent, while in 2006, the percentage was at 47 percent. With nearly 50 percent of companies reporting backsliding, we are not looking at a very healthy trend, especially when you consider the amount of money invested in the initiative. Add to this what Jason Premo of the Institute of Industrial Engineers reports: "A recent survey provided some shocking results, stating that over 40 percent of Lean Manufacturing initiatives have hit a plateau and are even backsliding, while only 5 percent of manufacturers have truly achieved the results expected."[13]

In the case of Six Sigma initiatives, the results have been more impressive, but not as impressive as they could or should be. Celerant Consulting carried out a Six Sigma survey in 2004, generating responses from managers across all business sectors, and although the results of the survey were more positive than negative, there were several problems that did surface:[14]

- The survey suggests that most businesses new to Six Sigma often find that running effective projects has been a significant challenge, with Six Sigma projects often quoted as taking four to six months or even longer to complete.
- Poor project selection is a key area where many businesses still continue to struggle. Industry experience suggests that about 60 percent of businesses are currently not identifying the projects that would most benefit their business.
- There is a shortage of good Master Black Belts. Across the survey, the ratio of Master Black Belts to Black Belts is 1 to 18. This creates pressure on the leadership of the most challenging projects and the capacity to train and develop others.

Asking the Right Question(s)

Based on my experiences in a variety of organizations and industries, the disappointing results coming from Lean, and sometimes from Six Sigma, are directly linked to failing to adequately answer the question "What to change?" or, worse yet, failing to ask that question at all. Deciding what to change cannot be done in a happenstance or chance manner. It must be addressed logically at the strategic, tactical, and operational levels after careful deliberation and analysis. The roots of this disillusionment are manifested in ill-advised efforts wasted on local improvements that fail to achieve global (or system-wide) improvement.

But even if an organization successfully considers and visualizes *what* to change, many times that same organization will fail to rightfully answer the question of *what to change to.* It is one thing to change your way of doing business, but you had better make sure that what you are changing to makes sense strategically. So how do you know what to change to? In today's world there seem to be so many choices regarding improvement initiatives, so surely one of these will work, right? Not so fast.

Even if an organization is successful in determining what to change and what to change to, there is still the question of how to make the change happen. No matter how well conceived an improvement initiative is, how the change is executed plays a tremendous role in the success or failure of the change. Establishing and implementing a sustainable improvement initiative requires selecting the right area to focus on, what the content of the improvement initiative should look like, carefully planning and developing a step-by-step execution plan, total support and buy-in from the leadership, and sincere collaboration with and involvement from the employees who make the product or deliver the service.

Why Lean and Six Sigma Fail

The question of why these stand-alone or integrated improvement initiatives have not lived up to their advanced billing is not always simple to answer. It could be that the projects or processes selected to focus on were ill-conceived, or it could be that their vision of the future was flawed. It could be that implementation plans were not well planned and executed or, worse yet, never developed. But let me be clear: The reason for failure is not the initiative itself. The failure is not because Lean, Six Sigma, Lean–Six Sigma, and TOC are not good improvement initiatives. It is really a question of planning, execution, focus, and leverage.

In fact, after having witnessed the remnants of failed initiatives, it is pretty clear to me that many of these initiatives fail for two primary reasons. First, the *scope or size* of the initiative is well beyond the capability of the available resources. The second reason is that companies generally fail to recognize their *leverage points*.

Failing to Focus

Instead of developing a strategically focused and manageable plan, many companies try to solve world hunger instead of focusing on the areas of greatest payback. Many companies attempt to use these improvement initiatives across the board and end up making very few sustainable improvements. Many Lean initiatives attempt to drive waste out of the entire value chain, but management is disappointed that the predicted waste reduction does not impact their bottom line to the extent that they had hoped. Many Six Sigma zealots attempt to drive all forms of variation to lower and lower levels and, again, are disappointed that the variation reduction alone does not result in significant bottom-line improvement.

Part of the problem with failed Lean and Six Sigma initiatives is that many companies simply have too many ongoing projects that drain valuable resources needed for the day-to-day issues facing many companies. Knowing what to do next can also be confusing to managers who have reached the saturation point and are not able to distinguish which projects are vital or important and which ones are not. The economic reality that supersedes and overrides everything else is that companies have always wanted the most improvement for the least amount of investment. Attacking all the processes and problems simultaneously, as part of an enterprise-wide Lean–Six Sigma initiative, quite simply overloads the organization and does not deliver an acceptable ROI in many cases. In addition, some companies cherry-pick which Lean and Six Sigma tools to use instead of thinking of them as part of the overall improvement strategy.

Failing to Recognize a Leverage Point

Although the implementation problems I have discussed thus far certainly impede progress, in my opinion, there are other reasons initiatives have failed in many companies. So again, I ask, why are many Lean and Six Sigma initiatives failing to deliver their promise of significant profit increases to many companies?

Take a look at the Lean improvement cycle in Figure 1.1. You begin by defining what value is, and then identify the entire value stream. You then make value flow without interruptions and let customers pull value from the producer. Finally, you relentlessly pursue perfection, making your processes less and less wasteful. A true Lean implementation will definitely produce a better process as long as it is done correctly, but this is sometimes a big if.

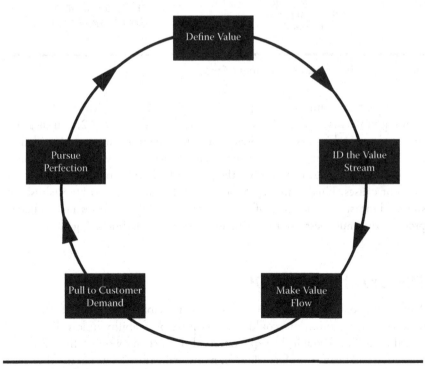

Figure 1.1   Lean Improvement Cycle.

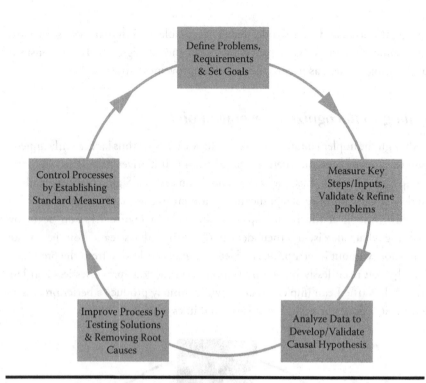

Figure 1.2   Six Sigma Improvement Cycle.

The Six Sigma improvement process in Figure 1.2 shows that step 1 is about defining problems and requirements and setting goals. In step 2, you measure the key steps and inputs and validate and refine the problems you identified in step 1. In step 3, you analyze pertinent data to develop or validate your causal hypotheses. In step 4, you improve the process by testing solutions and removing root causes. Finally, in step 5, you control your processes by establishing standard measures. Like Lean, if done correctly, Six Sigma creates a much better process with much less variation, but again, this is sometimes a big if.

The Drawbacks of TOC

And what about TOC? Has it failed as well? Eli Goldratt, author of *The Goal*, believed that organizations could not maximize profitability unless they maximized their TH through the exploitation of the system's weakest link. But like Six Sigma and Lean manufacturing, for many companies TOC has not delivered the huge rewards predicted by Goldratt. Some believe that the reason for this failure is strictly a question of poor planning and execution. Still others believe that TOC is not an improvement initiative at all.

Theoretically, the implications of TOC to improvement initiatives can be profound. From a TA perspective, reduction in inventory (one of the benefits of Lean) has a functional lower limit of zero, and once you have reached zero inventory, there is none left to harvest. Lowering inventory can lead to substantial dollars, but it is a one-time occurrence. Operating expense (OE) reduction, the favorite of many Lean and Six Sigma aficionados, also has a functional lower limit, but when this lower limit is surpassed, further attempts to reduce it can actually debilitate an organization.

TH improvement, on the other hand, has no upper limit. Even if the productive capacity of the organization exceeds the number of customer orders, the market becomes the constraint, so lead time and cost reductions can be used to generate more sales. It is important to remember that if you have excess capacity, as long as your new product cost covers your cost of raw materials and you have not added excess labor to achieve this excess capacity, the net flows directly to the bottom line. Of course, all three of these actions (TH increases, inventory reductions, and OE reduction) have a positive impact on NP and ROI. Think about this: If there were no constraints in a company, wouldn't their profits be infinite?

What TOC Is

TOC's process of ongoing improvement is a direct result of always focusing your efforts toward achieving the system's goal. In order to achieve this focus, Goldratt developed a five-step process toward that end:

1. *Identify* the system's constraint(s).
2. Decide how to *exploit* the system's constraint(s).
3. *Subordinate* everything else to the above decision.
4. *Elevate* the system's constraint(s).
5. If in the previous steps a constraint has been broken, go back to step 1, but do not allow inertia to cause a system constraint.

Figure 1.3 is a graphic illustration of TOC improvement cycle, with the four major steps included. By making this cyclic representation, we automatically assume that once a constraint has been elevated, it will be broken and a new constraint will take its place. Let us look at each of these individual steps in a bit more detail, with the help of Goldratt and Dettmer.

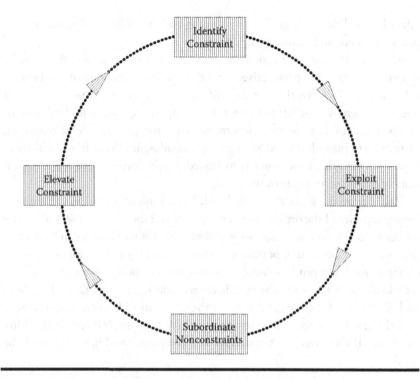

Figure 1.3   Theory of Constraints Improvement Cycle.

Identify the System Constraint(s)

Just as a chain has a weakest link, there will always be a resource of some kind that limits the system from maximizing its output. In order to improve the system's performance, it is imperative that you locate the weakest organizational link and focus your improvements there. There is a logistical *value chain* of mutually supporting processes and operations in every company or manufacturing facility. Included within this value chain is the organization's weakest link that limits the performance of the total organization. It may not be obvious to you, but when you are looking for a starting point in any improvement initiative, it should always be the system's constraint simply because it offers the greatest opportunity to increase profits in a relatively short period of time. Whether your constraint is a flow problem, a quality problem, a capacity problem, or a policy problem, it should be identified as the area on which to focus your efforts. This first step answers the question "What should you change?"

Decide How to Exploit the System's Constraint(s)

Once you have identified the restrictive link in the organizational chain that is limiting TH, you must decide how to take advantage of or squeeze the most out of it. For example, if the constraint is one of the steps in a manufacturing process that is limiting the output of the entire process (a bottleneck), you must take all necessary actions to improve the rate at which parts flow through this bottleneck. If you do not increase the rate through the bottleneck, TH will not increase. It is really that simple. By increasing the flow of product through the constraint, you automatically improve the system TH, which translates into more revenue and more bottom-line dollars. This second step answers the question "What should you change to?"

Subordinate Everything Else to the Above Decision

This is one of the most important steps in terms of resource utilization, with "resources" meaning nonconstraint operations, people, and so on. The nonbottleneck resources should work only at the same pace as the constraint operation—neither faster nor slower. If the nonconstraints are permitted to run faster than the constraint, the result is excess in-process inventory and prolonged C/T. If they are permitted to run slower than the constraint, the output of the constraining operation may be jeopardized, as would the organization's TH.

This subordination step is where most companies attempting to embrace and implement TOC have failed. Your organization must be totally committed to subordinating all other resources to the constraint operation or you will not realize all the potential TH gains (and profits) that you could or should. This step begins to answer the question "How do you make the change?"

Elevate the System's Constraint(s)

If the actions taken in steps 2 and 3 do not break the constraint, you will be forced to take other actions on the constraint itself. These actions could include using additional shifts, using additional overtime, adding additional resources (e.g., equipment or people), or, as a last resort, radically changing the process through automation or a new product or process design. Although this step and step 3 answer part of the question "How do you make the change?" they do not provide enough insight as to what might be done.

If in the Previous Steps a Constraint Has Been Broken, Go Back to Step 1, but Do Not Allow Inertia to Cause a System Constraint

The aim of the first four steps of TOC is focused on breaking the organizational or system constraint. Once you have accomplished this, you must now guard against backsliding, which could result in the constraint's becoming a constraint once again. For this reason, you must always develop some type of control that serves as an alert to guard against any kind of reversion to old ways.

What TOC Is Not

So what does TOC have to do with either Lean or Six Sigma, or vice versa? The answer to this question is, quite simply, everything. It is my belief that the key to successful Lean, Six Sigma, and TOC implementations, in terms of maximizing TH and ROI, is to ensure that your company's efforts are focused on the right area of the business. TOC provides this focus. In other words, the right area of focus is always the system constraint.

Yet although TOC provides the needed focus, Six Sigma and Lean provide the tools needed for improvement. In effect, you need to use Lean, Six Sigma, and the TOC together in order to improve your business. These three together form UIC, which is the focus of the remainder of this book.

Chapter 2

Introducing the Ultimate Improvement Cycle (UIC)

As discussed in Chapter 1, the major difference between the Lean, Six Sigma, and TOC improvement initiatives is simply a matter of *focus* and *leverage*. Although Lean and Six Sigma implement improvements and measure reductions in inventory and OE as well as increases in TH, TOC focuses up front on TH and looks for ways to achieve higher and higher levels. The only way to increase TH is to focus on the operation that is limiting it.

UIC combines all three initiatives into one. The net effect of UIC is greater TH, coupled with reductions in OEs and reductions in inventory costs. All three financial profit components move in the right directions at a faster rate than if you had attempted any of the three as stand-alone initiatives.

Please keep in mind that I am not challenging the validity of Lean, Six Sigma, or TOC. I am simply presenting what I believe is a better approach for all three initiatives. All three initiatives are vital pieces to the improvement pie, and I believe this amalgam of the three is a better approach to improvement than each being pursued in isolation as stand-alone initiatives. With the failure rates of all three initiatives being as high as they are, it seems to me that combining forces is intuitively a better approach.

Debra Smith, explaining the benefits of using TOC improvement tools and techniques, says: "In research sponsored by the Institute of Management

Accounting that studied 21 companies in both Europe and North America, we found this payoff to be the case in nearly all the companies examined. Numerous studies have substantiated the quick and relatively painless superiority of TOC as a process of ongoing improvement to manage production."[15] But TOC by itself simply will not maximize a company's ROI to the same degree as the fusion of Lean, Six Sigma, and TOC, which I call the UIC. Yes, TOC does drive TH up, but Lean and Six Sigma bring additional rigor and discipline, in order to sustain these gains, as well as offer key tools and techniques for reducing waste and variation.

In what I consider a very compelling study, Pirasteh and Farah present some very revealing statistics relative to a study performed in a "global electronics contract manufacturer" that compared the financial impact of implementing Lean, Six Sigma, and a combined TOC, Lean, and Six Sigma approach.[16] In this study, eleven plants applied only Six Sigma, four plants applied only Lean, and six plants applied UIC. This was a somewhat double-blind study, in that none of the plants knew that a comparison of results was being studied. A "plant" in this study was defined as a production facility that was fully capable of prototyping, designing, producing, and distributing customer products located in various regions in the United States. In total, there were 101 projects completed over a two-year period, with the results validated by company controllers and senior management.

Although there are some significant differences in the Pirasteh and Farah model when compared to the UIC that I have developed, the models are close enough to translate the findings in this study to similar results that I have achieved. In fact, the Pirasteh and Farah process improvement methodology "delivered consistently higher cost savings to the company.... Specifically, its application resulted in a contribution of 89 percent of the total savings reported. Six Sigma by itself came in a distant second with a 7 percent contribution to company savings; followed by 4 percent from stand-alone Lean applications."[17] Figure 2.1 is a graphical representation of the savings contribution from each of these three methodologies. Think about it. Eighty-nine percent of the total improvement came as a result of combining Lean, Six Sigma, and TOC.

UIC

If you were to combine the best of all three improvement initiatives into a single improvement process, what might this amalgamation look like? Logic would say that you would have an improvement process that reduces waste and variation, but primarily focusing in the operation that is constraining TH. Figure 2.2

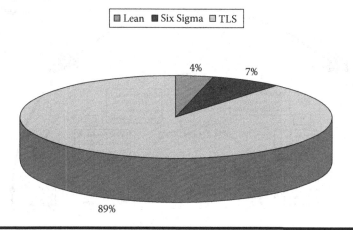

Figure 2.1 Percent Savings Contribution by Initiative.

shows the UIC that combines the power of Lean, Six Sigma, and TOC improvement cycles to form a more powerful and profitable improvement strategy. The UIC improvement cycle weaves together the DNA of Lean and Six Sigma with the focusing power of TOC to deliver a powerful and compelling improvement methodology. All the strategies, principles, tools, techniques, and methods contained within all three improvement initiatives are synergistically blended and time released to yield improvements that far exceed those obtained from doing these three initiatives in isolation from each other.

The UIC is not simply a collection of tools and techniques but, rather, a viable and practical manufacturing strategy that focuses resources on the area that will generate the highest ROI. The UIC is all about focusing on and leveraging the operation or policy that is constraining the organization and keeping it from realizing its full potential.

By combining Lean, Six Sigma, and TOC, UIC forces us to take several steps, as discussed in the following sections.

Identify, Define, Measure, and Analyze the Process

The actions in steps 1a to 1c serve to characterize the process value stream by identifying which step is limiting the full potential of the process (the constraint operation), defining value, pinpointing the potential sources of waste, and locating and measuring potential sources of defects and variation. There will be a compelling urge to make changes during this phase, but resist this temptation! In this phase of the improvement cycle, you are simply trying to define, analyze, and understand what is currently happening in your process. Taiichi Ohno used

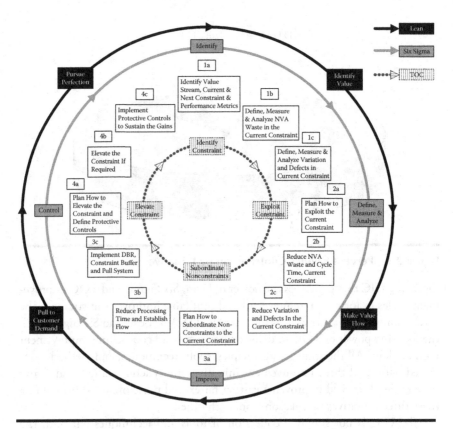

Figure 2.2 UIC.

a technique known as "standing in the circle," which emphasized going to the process to observe and understand. It was not uncommon for a person to have been left standing for eight solid hours or more before Ohno was satisfied that he or she had seen the waste in the process and the reasons why the waste exists. During this *standing in the circle exercise*, I believe it is best to simply acknowledge that the waste exists without trying to eliminate it just yet.

By the same token, you are also looking for sources of variation within the process. What is preventing your process from being consistent and stable? Keep in mind that the next phase deals with stabilizing the process by reducing both waste and variation in the constraining operation. So it is important, for now, to remember that you are simply trying to understand what is happening in your current process and, more specifically, in your constraint operation.

Although you will be focusing your attention primarily on the operation that is limiting your TH, because the upstream and downstream process steps could be contributing to this limitation, they must be observed as well. For example, if an upstream process consistently stops the flow of product to the constraint, you cannot ignore it. Conversely, if a downstream operation is consistently losing constraint output to scrap, it cannot be ignored, either. In both cases, the result would be less than optimal TH.

Create Stability

Before any process can be improved, there must be a focused plan developed or improvement efforts will be disjointed. In steps 2a to 2c you are attempting to simultaneously stabilize and improve your process. What does stabilize actually mean? Quite simply, stabilizing means that you are attempting to make your process more predictable, reliable, and consistent. In this sense, the actions in steps 2a to 2c serve primarily to reduce waste and variation within the constraint operation so that a new level of consistency and reliability is achieved. What you observe in the analysis phase will form the basis for your plan to achieve stability. It is important to remember that true and lasting improvement will never occur unless and until the process is consistent and stable over time. You will use a variety of tools and techniques during this phase of the Ultimate Improvement Cycle to accomplish this end. In order to achieve improved process flow, you must be patient and deliberate when reducing waste and variation.

Create Flow and Pull

The actions in steps 3a to 3c are intended to optimize flow. Flow in this phase includes the flow of materials, information, and products through the process. Although you are seeking to create flow, creating it will also bring to the surface any problem that inhibits it. So, in order to sustain flow, you must stop and solve these problems. Because of your past experiences, you might be tempted to fix these problems on the fly, but do not do it. You must begin to view problems as opportunities for long-term improvement and not as a failure.

Control the Process to Sustain Gains

The actions in steps 4a to 4c serve to both increase constraint capacity, if you need to, and ensure that all the changes made and improvements realized will not be squandered. What a shame it would be to make big improvements that you cannot sustain. Sustaining the gains is a hallmark of great organizations.

The Objectives of UIC

UIC accomplishes five primary objectives that serve as a springboard to maximizing revenue and profits:

■ It guarantees that you are focusing on the correct area of the process or system (i.e., the constraint operation) to maximize TH and minimize inventory and OE.

■ It provides a road map for improvement to ensure a systematic, structured, and orderly approach to ensure the maximum utilization of resources to realize optimum revenue and profits.

■ It integrates the best of Lean, Six Sigma, and TOC strategies, tools, techniques, and philosophies, to maximize your organization's full improvement potential.

■ It ensures that the necessary, up-front planning is completed in advance of changes to the process or organization so as to avoid the "fire, ready, aim" mindset.

■ It provides the synergy and involvement of the total organization needed to maximize your ROI.

If you are seriously committed to following the steps of UIC, in the sequence illustrated in Figure 2.2, I am convinced that you will see bottom-line improvements that far exceed what you have experienced using stand-alone initiatives. Just like any new initiative, it requires the entire organization's focus, discipline, determination, and a little bit of patience. This is new territory for you, so follow the path of least resistance that I have provided for you—it truly does work.

Accomplishing Each Step of the UIC

So just how do you accomplish each of the steps in UIC? You do so by using all the tools and actions that you would use if you were implementing Lean and Six Sigma as stand-alone improvement initiatives, but this time, you focus most, if not all, of your efforts primarily on the constraint operation. Figure 2.3 lays out the tools and actions you will use and perform at each step of the UIC. As you can see, there are no new or exotic tools that I am introducing. Instead, in creating UIC, one of my objectives was to keep things simple, and I think you will agree that the tools I have laid out are all basic and time tested.

.   For example, in step 1a, you are creating a simple current state value stream map (VSM) to analyze where the excess inventory is, what the individual

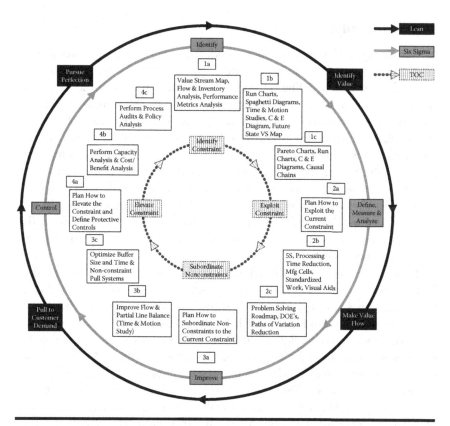

Figure 2.3   UIC Tools and Actions.

processing times (P/T) are, and what the cycle times and the overall lead times are within the process. You use this tool to identify both the current and next constraint. You are also looking at the current process, information flow, and performance metrics to make certain that the metrics stimulate the right behaviors, and that they will in fact track the true impact of your improvement efforts.

Likewise, in steps 1b and 1c, you will be analyzing your process by using simple tools like Pareto charts, run charts, spaghetti diagrams, time and motion studies, cause-and-effect diagrams, and causal chains. Keep in mind that these are by no means the only tools you can utilize, but just a few of the more common ones. In each phase of the UIC, you will use tools to perform the tasks at hand; all the subsequent chapters of this book explore these tools and actions in a bit more detail.

Step 1: Identify

In the first step of UIC, I have combined identification of the value stream from the Lean cycle, identification of performance metrics from Six Sigma, identification of the current scheduling system used to schedule the plant, and identification of the current and next constraint from the TOC cycle. In some respects, this first step is the single most important one, because it forces you to view and evaluate the entire value stream to locate the area, policy, or process step (the system constraint) that is preventing you from reaching your full financial potential. The first step focuses resources where they will do the most good and is the basis for continuous improvement. In addition, you need to not only measure your progress toward improvement, but also reinforce your efforts. To this end, you need to select performance metrics that drive the right behaviors. The metrics you choose can actually motivate behaviors that are counter to what you are trying to accomplish.

Lean teaches you to first identify and map the value stream as it exists today. A value stream is defined as all the actions, including both value-added and non-value-added ones, that are required to receive the order, schedule it, obtain necessary raw materials, produce it, and deliver it to the customer. A VSM helps you to see and understand the flow of material and information as a product or service makes its way through the value stream. Included in the VSM are methods for receiving orders, methods for communicating information about production requirements (i.e., scheduling system), the locations and amount of inventory, the current processing and cycle times for all process steps, the distance traveled between process steps, and so on. All this information will be used to facilitate the identification of the current constraint, which will become the focal point of your improvement activities.

Without this focusing step, it is possible to make improvements in both quality and productivity that end up having minimal impact on bottom-line profits because they may be in nonconstraint operations. It is important to understand that unless you improve the total system TH, any improvement in a nonconstraint is just really an illusion. It is an illusion because people mistakenly believe that improvements anywhere in the process will translate to system-wide improvements. If you are not careful, you may end up building excess or unneeded inventory somewhere in the process and inflating cycle times. At the end of the day, this excess inventory serves only to increase costs (i.e., holding or carrying costs, unneeded labor to produce it, and so on) and jeopardize due dates at the expense of revenue gains. This misplaced or misguided focus is one of the primary reasons why many improvement initiatives fail.

It should be said that there are other things to consider when attempting to identify the constraint operation or system constraint. According to Standard and Davis, "Often bottlenecks are not obvious. Although the most straight-forward way is to look for excessive WIP, there are many other reasons why WIP might accumulate between processes."[18] Standard and Davis give, as an example, that a performance measure, such as equipment utilization or man-power efficiency, might encourage production of items regardless of whether or not a downstream operation needs them. In this case, your constraint might be the performance metric itself!

Standard and Davis also tell you that bottlenecks tend to wander around the factory because of things like product mix and even managerial decisions. An example of this is a decision to run large batches of product so as to avoid or minimize the perceived setup costs, when in reality reduction in setup times (and costs) can be minimized through the application of SMED or rapid changeover techniques. The point here is that when attempting to identify the constraint operation, you must also search for and analyze the real reasons why the constraints exist. If there is excessive inventory, you must determine why it exists before you take actions to reduce it. Keep in mind that simply reducing inventory without understanding the root cause for its existence could be disastrous.

Note: One of the primary reasons companies have excess inventory on hand is to compensate for hidden problems—a kind of safety net, if you will. For this reason, some people advocate a radical inventory reduction to force the problems to the surface, but I adamantly disagree. The reason I disagree with this strategy is because most organizations are not prepared to tackle the problems that have been covered up for so long. As inventory is reduced, these problems will surface, and if the organization is not prepared for or capable of solving these problems, not only will improvements not happen, but chaos will reign. You will get there eventually, but for now, do not worry about excess inventory.

You will notice in this first step, step 1a, that I am recommending that you identify not only the current constraint, but also what you believe could or would be the next constraint, once the first constraint is broken. Why do I recommend identifying the next constraint in this first step? Because in too many instances, companies attempting to implement TOC and constraints management fail to look forward and predict where the next constraint will be. As you identify the current constraint, ask yourself the following question: What will be the effect, or where will the next constraint be, when I break the current constraint? You must remember that when you break your current constraint, another will appear almost immediately, and unless you prepare in advance, you will spend needless time searching for something that you probably could have predicted in advance. In addition, the apparent gains in TH when the current constraint is broken will be limited by the TH of the next constraint. In so doing, you can begin planning and identifying resources that will be needed when the next constraint appears. You can use the VSM that you created to assist with the identification of the next constraint you will be dealing with. You will usually be looking primarily at where the inventory is and how long it takes a part to pass through a process step (i.e., P/T).

Also included in step 1a is the need to review the current method that you employ to schedule production within the plant. Why is this an important thing to know? The fact is, there is a right way and a wrong way to schedule a production facility. If you schedule it the wrong way, you will see excessive amounts of inventory, extended lead times, and late delivery dates. If you schedule it the right way, your TH, inventory, and OEs will be optimized, and you have a much better chance of delivering products on time.

In steps 1b and 1c of the improvement cycle, you are attempting to define, measure, and analyze non-value-added waste and variation in the current constraint. It is important to understand that in this step, you are interested only in defining, measuring, and analyzing the waste and variation that exist, not removing them yet. Some will argue that unnecessary waste and variation should be removed immediately, but I disagree. In my opinion, it is this compulsion or urge to do everything right now that causes some companies' improvement initiatives to fail. Effective waste elimination and variation reduction are not effective without a systematic plan that ties together both steps 1b and 1c. You want waste and variation to be attacked concurrently to ensure that any changes associated with reducing waste (i.e., Lean) are not interfering with changes related to variation and defect reduction (i.e., Six Sigma), and vice versa. Too many companies are engaged in the "fire, ready, aim" scenario that typically results is chaos, confusion, and sometimes even competition between the two initiatives.

Using the tools of Lean (e.g., waste walks, time studies, spaghetti diagrams, and flow diagrams), you identify all existing forms of waste (e.g., downtime, unnecessary travel time, wasted motion, inventory, and equipment changeover time), but for now, do so only within or in front of the constraint. Waste in nonconstraint operations is certainly important, and you are not ignoring it forever, but remember that you are focusing your resources on improving only the constraint right now, because the constraint dictates the system's TH, and TH, above all else, dictates profits. Notice in steps 1a to 1c that you are using the elements of the typical Six Sigma road map (DMAIC) to evaluate your improvement options.

It is my belief (and that of others like Goldratt and Dettmer) that improving TH provides the opportunity for maximum return on your investment. Figure 2.4 is a graphical comparison of TH, OE, and inventory as they relate to profitability contribution. I have not attempted to insert numbers into each piece of the profitability pie simply because it is situation dependent—that is, it is dependent upon the current state of the process, company, or organization

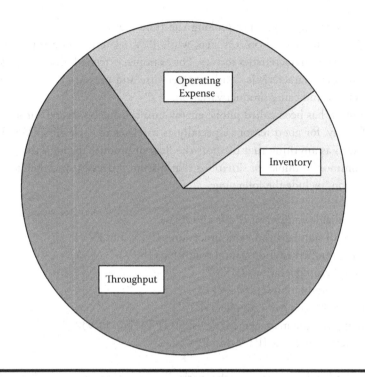

Figure 2.4   Profit Margin Contributions.

you are improving. But generally speaking, the order in which these three profit components impact profitability is TH (by a wide margin), inventory, and then OE. For any given company, however, depending on the circumstances, OE and inventory could be reversed, but it is clear that TH is king.

In step 1c, your efforts are aimed at defining, measuring, and analyzing variation and defects in the current constraint. Like step 1b, you are interested only in defining, measuring, and analyzing the sources of variation and defects, but not acting upon them just yet, for the very same reason you are not yet acting on sources of waste. You want to maximize the utilization of your human resources, and you simply will not do that effectively without taking the time to develop an attack plan. Thus, in this step, you use the Six Sigma tools and techniques (e.g., Pareto charts, run charts, check sheets, cause-and-effect diagrams, and causal chains) to identify the sources of variation and defects within the constraint operation.

Recall that there are two types of variability you are interested in: processing time variability (PTV) and process and product variability (PPV). Sources of PTV are those things that prolong the time required for parts to progress through each individual process step, while PPV relate to those variables that cause the part's characteristics to vary. For example, extruded product thickness is the product characteristic, while temperature and pressure are the variables that fluctuate and cause product variation.

Variation has been called public enemy number one by several authors and, quite frankly, for good reason, especially as it relates to cycle time. Variability can be seen as anything that disrupts the flow of product through the process. Some common examples of situations that disrupt processes, and therefore create variation, include the following:

- Unreliable equipment (PTV and PPV)
- Lack of standardized work procedures (PTV and PPV)
- Uncontrolled environmental conditions (PPV)
- Long setup operations (PTV)
- Large production lots (PTV)
- Late deliveries from suppliers (PTV)
- Inappropriate management decisions (PTV and PPV)
- Defective product (PTV and PPV)

Standard and Davis suggest that variability encumbers the factory because it leads to congestion, high inventory, long lead times, and many other operational difficulties. According to Standard and Davis, the importance of reducing variability is highlighted by the tremendous impact it has on the entire manufacturing operation, so if you are able to reduce it, there are direct and immediate benefits, which include:[19]

- Shorter P/T (time through an individual process step)
- Shorter cycle times (time through an entire process)
- Shorter lead times (time from order to delivery)
- Lower WIP inventory
- Faster response time (to customer changes)
- Lower cost (less rework and scrap)
- Greater production flexibility (single machine producing multiple products)
- Higher quality (competitive advantage)
- Better customer service (happier customers)
- Higher revenue (more dollars to the bottom line)
- Higher TH (higher capacity)
- Increased profit (more revenue, fewer costs, and less inventory)

Keep in mind that simply reducing variability (i.e., by implementing Six Sigma) will not impact this impressive list by itself. The key to realizing these improvements is by focusing on the right area, with the right manufacturing strategy, using the right tools and techniques at the right time, and then making the right decisions. All these can be accomplished by following the structured approach of UIC.

Step 2: Define, Measure, and Analyze

In step 2a, you formally develop your plan on how to exploit the current constraint, and as such, you spend time developing the specifics of your attack plan. Your plan will include what to attack, when to attack it, and how to attack it, identifying the resource requirements and understanding how your actions help you move closer to your goal of making more money now and in the future. Your plan will include identifying sources of waste and how best to eliminate them, understanding the priority order of which defect problems to resolve, eliminating chronic downtime problems, reducing process variation, and reducing processing and cycle time variation. In so doing, you will use all the Lean, Six Sigma, and TOC tools and techniques at your disposal, but remember that step 2a deals exclusively with the *development* of your improvement plan and not the *execution* of it.

The central theme of UIC is the main focusing steps from TOC: identify, exploit, subordinate, and elevate. (The continuous arrows highlight the realization that improvement is a never-ending, ongoing effort, which is Goldratt's fifth step.) In steps 2b and 2c, your objective is to execute your improvement plan, and in so doing, you will be reducing non-value-added waste, variation, and defects in the current constraint. You are now taking definitive actions by executing the plan you developed in step 2a. Because you want these steps to complement each other, you will carry them out in a concurrent manner. The plan that you developed in step 2a will guide you through these two steps and will provide you with not only an automatic TH gain, but also reductions in operating and inventory expenses. In these two steps, you should see many things happening in the constraint operation. Examples include:

- All forms of waste being removed
- Variation (PTV and PPV) being reduced
- Defects being reduced or eliminated
- Processing and cycle times being shortened
- Lead times being reduced
- Manufacturing cells being developed
- Standardized work methods being developed

- Process controls being implemented
- Error-proofing devices being added to the process
- Changeover times being reduced
- Travel times and distances being shortened
- Downtime being reduced
- On-time delivery being improved

The impact of these improvements will translate into more productive capacity in the constraint operation, which will then be converted into improved TH, higher revenues, and increased margins. Remember, all this will be taking place primarily in the constraint operation for now, unless an upstream process is starving the constraint operation or a downstream process is scrapping the constraint's output. It is absolutely imperative that there is constant and synergistic collaboration between the resources focused on the waste reduction activities and the resources focused on the variation and defect reduction activities, because both sets of resources will be making process changes that could impact each other's activities.

I cannot emphasize the communication piece enough. If yours is a company in which Lean and Six Sigma are being implemented by the same person, you will automatically consider all changes together. But if they are being done by two groups, they must communicate. Planning is critical to the success of the improvement initiative, so proposed changes should be fully discussed up front before they are actually implemented, and this dialogue should take place in step 2a if the proposed changes are known.

Before going any further, I want to reinforce an important point regarding improvements in nonconstraint operations. Because the constraint operation dictates the TH rate of the plant (or a specific process), you must do everything possible to protect the output of the constraint operation. Protection, in this sense, includes problems occurring both in downstream operations that could be negatively impacting your total TH (e.g., scrap, rework) and in the upstream processes that could starve the constraint. It would make little sense to make significant quality improvements in the constraint operation, only to have the constraint products scrapped in a downstream nonconstraint process step. Likewise, it would equally make little sense to make P/T reductions in the constraint operation only to have the constraint starved by an upstream process. For this reason, part of your analysis and action plan must also include downstream and upstream opportunities if they are seen as potential threats to the constraint. Remember, TH is not achieved unless new money enters the company, so if you are losing or scrapping even a single product in a downstream operation, your TH and corresponding profits will be limited by the amount of the loss. The same can be said of an upstream process starving a constraint due to unplanned downtime, quality problems, and so on.

So far, your improvement initiative has identified your value stream, the area of focus within the value stream, and waste and variation improvement opportunities, and you have begun implementing improvements that ultimately will increase your system TH. In order for your efforts to be considered successful, you must be making decisions and taking actions that move you closer to the realization of your goal of making more money now and in the future—that is, simultaneously increasing TH, while reducing inventory and OE.

In this step, you will also be implementing a new scheduling system referred to as *drum-buffer-rope* (DBR). If you have read *The Goal* and Goldratt's Boy Scout analogy, you will immediately recognize and understand the meaning of this name.

- The *drum* is the schedule for the resource with the most limited capacity, the constraint.
- The *buffer* is the protective device (a combination of parts, capacity, and time) used to protect the constraint from starvation.
- The *rope* is constraint management's safeguard against overproducing at the nonconstraint operations. In effect, it is a material release schedule that prevents work from being introduced into the system at a rate faster than the consumption rate of the constraint.

In this step you will design the correct DBR system to ensure that you do not starve the constraint, assembly (if assembly uses product from the constraint), or shipping.

Step 3: Improve

To this point, you have dealt only with your constraint operation, but you cannot forget about your nonconstraint operations. Because of what you know about TOC, you know that you must not continue producing product at a rate that exceeds your constraint operation. In step 3a, you plan how to subordinate nonconstraints to the current constraint, and in so doing, you must now effectively slow down, limiting your nonconstraint operation's output to the same rate as your constraint operation. Otherwise, you will continue building inventory in front of your constraint, beyond your safety buffer. Subordinate in its simplest form means that you will produce product at the same rate as the constraint operation, no slower or faster.

According to Debra Smith, "Mastering step three, subordination, is the key to succeeding with TOC. Mastery of step three is dependent on a methodology of aligning measures, performance objectives, strategies, and policies to support maximizing ROI. ROI is centered on understanding the interdependencies of the constraining resources and the rest of the organization."[20] I could not agree more with Smith, as subordination is beyond a doubt one of the keys to the success of any TOC-based improvement initiative.

Like step 2a, step 3a of the UIC is a planning step, in that you must evaluate the nonconstraints and look for opportunities where you might be able to offload some of the work from the constraint to one or more of the nonconstraints. You will look upstream and downstream for these opportunities, so you must be very thoughtful and methodical as you develop this plan. In doing so, however, you must exercise caution in this step because you must make certain that you do not turn a nonconstraint into a constraint, and you could, if you are not careful. In addition, contrary to what many production managers believe, having a perfectly balanced line (i.e., all cycle times equal) is not necessarily a good thing (see Chapter 9).

In addition, you are attempting to establish one-piece flow within your process to ensure the steady flow of work into and out of the constraint. Because you have already implemented work cells in step 2b, in essence you may have already begun using elementary one-piece flow, but in this step, you formalize it. Your plan will include an analysis of current constraint and nonconstraint cycles and P/T, telling you where you might be able to move work away from the constraint; how best to move the work; how best to create flow; how to establish a constraint buffer, an assembly buffer, and a finished goods buffer as well as a buffer replenishment system; what your resource requirements are; how to address your training needs; and how to best time all of the proposed moves.

At this point, you might be wondering why you did not perform this step of the cycle sooner. There are two reasons. First, my belief is that because you know that the capacity of the constraint operation will improve as a result of your waste and variation reduction actions completed thus far, you should wait until your new constraint capacity and P/T are known. The second reason is that the next step in the improvement cycle could radically change the time in the constraint, and hence the capacity.

In step 3b, you will focus your efforts on reducing P/T and improving flow by executing part of the plan you developed in step 3a. You have analyzed your upstream and downstream nonconstraint workloads; decided what work, if any, can be safely moved away from the constraint operation; developed or proposed redesigned process steps to accommodate the unloading of constraint work; estimated the new P/T for both nonconstraint and constraint operations; and estimated the impact on flow and TH. If you did your homework correctly, you should breeze through this step and move on to step 3c. Remember, the planning for this step had already been completed in step 3a.

In step 3c you will optimize the constraint, assembly, and finished product buffer and refine your DBR scheduling system based on any problems you may have encountered in step 2b. You will analyze your new data on compliance to schedule and, if need be, make any corrections necessary to improve compliance. The buffer in front of the constraint operation, sometimes referred to as a *WIP cap*, is your protection for the constraint operation in the event that one of your upstream nonconstraints could unexpectedly have downtime. Keep in mind that your buffer is not necessarily product. In fact, most of the time your buffer will simply be a measure of time—that is, instead of having excess product available, your production schedule will dictate when and how many parts to produce so that you never starve your constraint.

The assembly buffer is a buffer of nonconstraint parts in front of assembly, assuming the constraint part is required in assembly. The finished product buffer is your protection for on-time delivery to customers. In this step, you need to recalculate the size of your protective buffers, taking into account the speed of the upstream nonconstraints, the historical downtime associated with the nonconstraint operation, buffer penetration rate, and so on.

The important thing to keep in mind is that your nonconstraints have *sprint capacity*, that is, the capacity to produce product at faster rates than your constraint operation; thus, if an upstream nonconstraint operation experiences downtime for some reason, when it begins producing again, it should still have the ability to produce product at a fast enough rate to resupply the constraint buffer before the constraint buffer runs dry. Assuming you calculated the size of the buffers correctly and designed the DBR system correctly, the constraint will be protected from ever sitting idle.

Step 4: Control

In step 4a, you develop a plan for how to elevate the current constraint (if this step is needed) and define appropriate protective controls. The premise here is that, if in the previous nine steps, you have not broken the constraint (i.e., increased the capacity of the constraint), you may have to acquire more resources and even spend money to do so. Spending money, in this context, simply means that you have to add additional resources, by adding additional labor, additional time (i.e., overtime or additional shifts), additional equipment, or a combination thereof to break the constraint. Based upon my experience, if you have to elevate the constraint, you are talking only about minimal labor increases without spending money on new equipment, but in reality, sometimes you do have to spend. Sometimes, any labor increase can be achieved with overtime or additional shifts. However, in the event that you must spend money, you must do so under control, only after performing a detailed analysis of constraint P/T, and only by adding labor or equipment that is needed for the constraint to satisfy the needs of the market. Because your objective is to break the current constraint, you must be mindful that any labor increase may only be temporary, so having a flexible workforce facilitates this increase.

Also included in this step is an analysis of what type of protective controls you must develop to protect the improvements and not lose the gains you have already made. Many times just a simple audit of the process is enough to ensure that you maintain the gains. Other times, a simple control chart of TH or P/T is sufficient. One thing you learned from the TOC is that once a constraint has been broken, you must never allow inertia to cause a system constraint. What inertia refers to is that within any organization, in the course of attempting to break the constraint, you sometimes develop specific rules or policies, so you must not fail to review these rules and policies to ensure their applicability is still relevant. If it is not, get rid of them. Without doing this, these rules and policies could actually become future constraints themselves.

In step 4b, if it is needed, you will elevate the constraint, which is simply the execution of part of the plan you developed in step 4a. If you need to add capacity to your constraint, you do so only according to your plan—and no more. It is possible and even more likely that you have already broken your constraint during the first nine steps of this process. If this is the case, you simply move to step 4c. Remember, even if you might have broken the constraint during the first nine steps, you must still review any rules and policies that you might have implemented during this process so as to avoid system inertia. In the final step, step 4c, you will implement protective controls to make certain that you maintain the gains you have made to this point.

Be sure to avoid system inertia; in fact, Dettmer advises you to "remember that the cycle never stops: there's always another constraint waiting behind the one we're working on now. Also, in successive cycles of the five focusing steps you might have to revisit a constraint you thought you'd previously broken."[21] Clearly, Dettmer is correct to say that you always have to remember that the cycle never stops, but the real concern here is that you must always keep your eye on the ball for nonconstraints' becoming constraints. It is why I place so much emphasis on planning the changes rather than making changes blindly. It is also why, in the first step, I stress locating both the current and next constraint. You must be on guard and ready for constraints coming at you from all directions, but if you follow UIC, I am confident you will be successful. In addition, any of the activities that you complete in any of the previous steps may result in the constraint's being broken. If this happens, be prepared to move to it and start the cycle again.

Now that you have completed the first rotation of this improvement cycle, you are ready to start the second cycle of improvement on the next constraint.

Fortunately, in the first step of this initial cycle, you are able to logically think through and predict where this new constraint would be. If you did this step correctly, in the first improvement cycle, you should be able to begin with step 1b of the second cycle of improvement relatively quickly, except for preparing for the third cycle of improvement. You should always identify where you believe the next constraint operation could be before starting any improvement in the current constraint. It should come as no surprise that this cyclic process is a continuous improvement cycle that never really ends. Remember, because TH theoretically has no upper limit, you should be continually improving your TH and profits, now and in the future.

Chapter 3

The Value Stream, a Scheduling System, and Performance Metrics

In their ground-breaking book, *Learning to See*, Mike Rother and John Shook introduced the world to a new value-identifying and value-creating tool called the VSM. Actually, Toyota had been using a variation of Rother and Shook's technique long before, but it was Rother and Shook who launched American businesses and the rest of the world on their journey to first identify and then eliminate all forms of waste through the eyes of this tool. Toyota refers to it as "material and information flow mapping,"[22] and it clearly serves a vital function. It allows you to view and depict the total process as it exists today and then imagine the future, or ideal state, as you would like it to be. If used as intended, this tool will tell you how your own flow of material, information, and people is and might be. To quote Rother and Shook, "Whenever there is a product for a customer, there is a value stream. The challenge lies in seeing it."[23]

Scheduling in a UIC environment is completely different from a mass production environment. In a UIC environment, production is based on actual orders, while in a mass production environment, you forecast what should be produced and develop a build schedule. UIC scheduling is based upon real-time information; mass production is not. As is demonstrated in this chapter, knowing the real-time floor status and activating resources according to this status will always result in a much more profitable organization.

Finally, identifying the appropriate performance metrics to track in both the constraints and nonconstraints is critical to the success of any improvement initiative. Performance metrics will impact how an operation will perform, so it is important to select metrics that will motivate desirable behaviors.

Identifying the Value Stream

It is assumed, by now, that most of you understand the concept of value and what a value stream is, but in case you have missed it along the way or have not been exposed to it, in simplistic terms, the value stream is all those things you do to convert raw materials into a finished product that creates value. Value is simply all of those things that a customer is willing to pay for. Rother and Shook tell us, "Taking a value stream perspective means working on the big picture, not just individual processes, and improving the whole, not just optimizing the parts."[24] I categorically agree with Rother and Shook and further emphasize that improving the whole, not just optimizing the parts, is paramount to the success of any for-profit business or organization.

As a tool or technique, the VSM uses a variety of symbols, or a sort of shorthand notation, if you will, to depict various elements within the process. For example, a triangle with a capital *I* inside it represents inventory, with the amount of inventory entered directly beneath the triangle. There are various material flow icons, general icons, and information flow icons used to represent all the specific elements within the process. I highly recommend Rother and Shook's *Learning to See* for details on the specifics of their methods and styles for producing a VSM and the various icons they use. From my perspective, it is not as important to get the VSM perfect as it is to get it functional.

Why Value Stream Mapping Works

Why is value stream mapping such an essential tool? Rother and Shook have answered that question with a list of eight reasons:

- It helps you visualize more than just the single-process level (i.e., assembly, welding) in production. You can see the flow of the process and the information.
- Mapping helps you see the sources of waste in your value stream that may not be obvious to you without visualizing it.
- It provides a common language for talking about manufacturing processes.
- It makes decisions about the flow apparent, so you can discuss them. Otherwise, many details and decisions on your shop floor just happen by default.

- It ties together Lean concepts and techniques, which help you avoid cherry-picking.
- It forms the basis of an implementation plan. By helping you design how the whole door-to-door flow should operate—a missing piece in so many Lean efforts—VSMs become a blueprint for Lean implementation. Imagine trying to build a house without a blueprint.
- It shows linkage between the information flow and the material flow. No other tool does this.
- It is much more useful than quantitative tools and layout diagrams that produce a tally of non-value-added steps, lead time, distance traveled, the amount of inventory, and so on. In other words, value stream mapping is a qualitative tool by which you describe in detail how your facility should operate in order to create flow. Numbers are good for creating a sense of urgency or as before and after measures. Value stream mapping is good for describing what you are actually going to do to affect those numbers.

Although I agree with most of these eight reasons, I have added a ninth reason to this list: identifying the current and next constraint. This, I might add, is actually *first* on my list because it trumps the first eight. The reason I consider this step the most important is because it is the quintessential starting point in any improvement process.

Another point on which I absolutely agree with Rother and Shook is that value stream mapping is a pencil-and-paper tool that helps you see your way through your own value stream. VSMs are not intended to be pretty or even artsy; they are meant to be functional. You cannot create a value stream from your office, and you cannot do it effectively in a vacuum, because it will not be accurate or even complete. For this reason, please do not create a VSM by yourself. Instead, other resources, like hourly operators and material handlers, should assist you to make sure you have included all facets of the flow of information and product.

Knowing What to Map

The next question to be answered is: Which products should I map? All of them? Some of them? If you are producing only a single product, it is a simple selection as to what you should map. But if your company produces multiple products, it is always best to select a product family to map. My recommendation is that you spend some time practicing VSMs until you have learned to capture everything that you need, but again, it is not about making your VSM pretty.

So just what should be included in your VSM? Well, think about what you are trying to accomplish. If your goal is to make money now and in the future, one thing you want to be able to identify is the operation that is limiting your TH. Additionally, you want to be able to identify any opportunities that will reduce both inventory and OE. With this in mind, what are the things that are important to answer these three profit essentials? Obviously, inventory stacked up is an excellent indicator of where your constraint operation might be, so inventory must be listed. What about processing and cycle times? Cycle times certainly can have an impact on the rate of generation of TH, can't they? How about delays—don't they negatively impact TH? How about equipment downtime? And let us not forget inspection sites as well as defect rates and rework locations. I have created my own list of things that I include in my version of a VSM. Just remember what you are attempting to determine. You want to identify the operation that is constraining your TH and all the other opportunities that could be used to reduce inventory and OE. My list of entries that you might use (and a brief explanation of each) is as follows, for each process step:

1. Identifying the product or product family being studied.
2. Identifying each individual process step listed by the name of the function (e.g., assembly, drilling).
3. Identifying, step by step, value-added time, wait times, P/T, cycle times, and lead times.
   a. *Value-added time*: The average total time taken to transform the product into value. (Note: This does not include wait times.)
   b. *Wait time*: The average time that a part waits within a process step before being able to move to the next process step. This might include any drying or curing times, waiting for an inspection to occur, and so on.
   c. *P/T*: The average length of time it takes for a single part to be completed by a single process step, which should equal a. plus b.
   d. *Cycle time*: The average length of time it takes from release of raw materials into the process to completion of finished goods ready to ship.
   e. *Lead time*: The average total elapsed time from receipt of the order from the customer to the receipt of the order by the customer.
4. Identifying inventory levels: The number of individual pieces or parts waiting to be processed in each step.
5. Determining capacity: The average number of pieces or parts that a process step is able to produce in a given unit of time.
6. Determining actual demonstrated capacity: The average total pieces or parts produced/unit of time minus total average scrapped during the same time. This can be any unit of time depending upon the overall speed of the process.

7. Determining percent repaired: The average number repaired compared to the average total produced for any unit of time.
8. Determining customer demand or order rate.
9. Determining the actual rate to be produced compared to order rate (i.e., takt time).
10. Determining average defect rates and the actual defects based upon inspection data for a given period of time (Pareto chart).
11. Determining inspection points and average inspection time required.
12. Determining the average downtime rates and a description of actual downtime based upon maintenance history (Pareto chart).
13. Identifying the number and location of operators (i.e., how many and where they are).
14. Determining the average travel time and distance traversed per any unit of time (use a spaghetti diagram).
15. Determining the average percent order on-time completion.

As you can see, I have included items that should help you answer first where the constraint operation is and then where and how you might be able to improve the TH, OE, and inventory within the constraint. Remember, unless you improve the TH of the constraint operation, you will not be improving the overall system.

One final point is the boundaries I establish when preparing VSMs. Because I am looking for ways to increase TH within the factory, I do not always include suppliers. The obvious exception to this is if I *know* that a particular supplier is the constraint. That is, if I am frequently waiting for raw materials to begin production or the quality of the incoming raw materials is poor, and I am confident that this supplier is constraining my TH, it is easy to determine my focus. Typically, I am concerned with what goes on inside the walls of the facility that limits TH. It does not mean that I ignore suppliers; it only means that most of the time the problems I see with limited TH and less than optimal margins are related to internal issues, not external ones.

Identifying the Current Constraint

Step 1a also involves identifying the current and next constraint. The first consideration when attempting to identify the current constraint is deciding if the constraint is internal or external to the facility. Simply put, if your current capacity is greater than the market demand, the constraint is external. If, on the other hand, your current capacity is less than market demand, the constraint is internal. Knowing where your constraint is located is important for several reasons. First, if your constraint is market demand, your actions must be focused upon gaining additional market share. These actions involve improving your company's competitive position and would include reducing lead times, improving the quality of your products, and improving customer service—basically, any action that would result in increased sales. Conversely, if your constraint were internal, meaning your capacity were less than the market demand, your actions would be centered around increasing the TH of your processes. With this in mind, let us now focus our attention on internal constraints.

One of the first symptoms of an internal constraint operation is inventory stacked in front of an operation. Consider the simple five-step process in Figure 3.1. You are attempting to identify the constraint operation, or the operation that is limiting the output of the entire process. If you consider only inventory stacking in front of each step to locate your constraint, step C, with eight parts in front of it, would have been your choice. But is this correct? If you consider the current capacity of each process step, you might conclude that step B is the constraint because its output is only 5 parts/hour. Is this the step that is limiting this process? Which one is it? Step B or step C?

If you only considered the capacity, you would be correct in saying that step B is the constraint, but what about demonstrated capacity? Demonstrated capacity takes into account the number of parts produced minus the number you lose to scrap (or sometimes rework). In step C, you see that the scrap rate is 30 percent, meaning that, on average, for every ten parts you produce, you lose three. The demonstrated capacity then, for step C, is only 70 percent of the capacity (6/hour – [100% – 30%], or 6 × 70%), or 4.2 parts/hour. Because no other process step's demonstrated capacity is as low as step C's, step C is your capacity constraint. This means that the output of this entire process is limited to 4.2 parts/hour, and that any attempt to improve any other process step would not improve the overall TH of this process. This simple process gives you your area of focus, your current capacity constraining resource, step C.

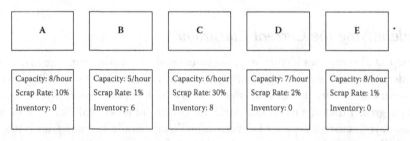

Figure 3.1   Simple Five-Step Operation.

Identifying the Next Constraint

The first step in UIC tells you to identify the value stream, the current, and the next constraint, so let us return to your example and look again at Figure 3.1. You have decided that step C of your operation is your current constraint because the excessive scrap rate drives down the demonstrated capacity from 6 to approximately 4 parts/hour. The question you must ask is: What would be the effect of reducing the scrap rate from its current 30 percent to, say, 1 or 2 percent? If that were to happen, the most obvious effect would be an increase in the demonstrated capacity on step C from 4.2 parts/hour to 6 parts/hour. In so doing, the next constraint would have to be step B because its demonstrated capacity is 5 parts/hour. Thus, in this simple example, you have easily identified the current constraint and the next constraint.

By knowing where your next constraint will be when you break your current constraint, you can begin planning your resource requirements in advance. In addition to planning resources, it is equally important to identify the next constraint, because in the process of breaking the current constraint, you must consider the impact on future constraints. This is how UIC works: identify the current and next constraint, apply the tools of Lean and Six Sigma to break the constraint, implement protective controls to make sure the gains are sustained, and then move through the next cycle. It is my belief that this process not only results in the maximum return on your investment dollars, but it is self-sustaining as well.

If this process were really as simple as the example I just presented, I would probably have many immediate converts to this method and book sales would go through the roof. But the reality is that many times there is much more to selecting the constraint operation than just demonstrated capacity and inventory. On the other hand, sometimes just knowing the level of inventory in front of a process step will answer the question. I do not want to make this process sound too effortless or too demanding, but I do want you to know that it works. Keep in mind that in the next two steps of the improvement cycle, you will be identifying sources of waste and variation, so as you construct your VSM, any up-front data gathering you can do now that helps focus your resources later will be rewarded. Let us continue with our discussion on identifying the value stream and identifying the constraint operation.

An Example Identifying the Constraint(s)

The actual VSM can take many different forms, so you should not get hung up on creating the perfect VSM. Just keep your objectives in mind and create your own version of this tool to guide you. Figure 3.2, for example, is a sample

Tank Type	Schedule	Oper 10	Oper 9	Oper 8	Oper 7 Mold 1	Oper 7 Mold 2	Ready Inventory	Oper 6	Oper 5	Oper 4	Oper 3	Oper 2	Oper 1
A	1-Delq 4-March 4-April 2-May 4-June 4-July 4-Aug	1 Tank		4 Tanks	1 Tank	1 Tank	3 Tops 3 Bottoms	3 Tops 3 Bottoms		1 Top 2 Bottoms	2 Tops	2 Bottoms 1 Top	1 Top
B	3-Delq 4-March 6-April 0-May 6-Jun 4-Jul 4-Aug	1 Tank		1 Tank	Empty	1 Tank	2 Bottoms 1 Top	4 Tops	2 Tops	5 Bottoms 1 Top	3 Bottoms 1 Top	1 Bottom	1 Bottom
C	3-Delq 3-March 7-April 4-May 8-June 8-July 8-August			1 Tank	Empty	1 Tank	5 Bottoms 1 Top		1 Top	1 Top	3 Tops	EMPTY	1 Bottom
Yield Cycle Time Lead Time		Y= 100% C/T 2 Days LT 3 Days	Y= 99% C/T 1 Day LT 4 Days	Y= 99% C/T 2 Days LT 3 Days	Y= 85% C/T 6 Days LT 9 Days	Y= 83% C/T 8 Days LT 9 Days		Y= 95% C/T 3 Days LT 4 Days	Y= 99% C/T 1 Days LT 2 Days	Y= 99% C/T 1 Day LT 3 Days	Y= 99% C/T 2 Days LT 2 Days	Y= 100% C/T 2 Days LT 2 Days	Y= 100% C/T 1 Day LT 1 Day

FULL PERSON ASSIGNED   ✂ 1/2 PERSON ASSIGNED   ✂ # PERSON ASSIGNED

Figure 3.2 Hybrid Value Stream Constraint Analysis.

of a very simple VSM that I created for a company that produces flexible tanks used to hold volatile organic fluids. The typical lead time to build one of these tanks from start to finish is measured in weeks (i.e., six to ten weeks, depending upon the size and complexity of the tank). The process consists of operations 1 through 6 that are used to manually construct a top and a bottom for each tank in a stationary mold. The top and bottom halves of the tank are then joined in operation 7 in one of two joining molds.

In operation 8 the tanks are repaired, and in operation 9 the tanks go through a final inspection and are prepared for shipping, which takes place in operation 10. I listed the number of tanks or half-tanks within each operation, and the number of operators assigned to each operation are designated as little stick people. You will notice that some of the stick figures are only half the size of the others. This was intended to reflect partial use of operators. To the far left, I listed the schedule of expected shipments for each of the three tank types along with the number of delinquent tanks. On the bottom of the VSM, I listed the important metrics that relate to quality and output of each operation. The three metrics are:

- **Yield:** The percentage of good tanks or half-tanks for each operation.
- **Cycle time (C/T):** The amount of time spent completing work on the tank by operation (i.e., individual P/T).
- **Lead time (L/T):** The total amount of elapsed time, from start to finish, required for the tank or half-tank to pass through each operation. (*Note:* This company's definition of lead time included only time within the process. So as to avoid confusion, I modified my definition to match theirs in this example.)

All three of these metrics represent the previous twelve-month average for each tank by operation. I tried to keep this hybrid VSM as visual as possible and in line with terms commonly used by this company, so it was easy to interpret and understand for the operation's people who would use it.

Just looking at this layout, where would you have concluded that the constraint operation was located? Keep in mind that in operation 6 the tanks are essentially complete, and ready to be joined in operation 7. If your conclusion from the available information was that operation 7 was the constraint—because of the excessive amount of inventory sitting in front of this operation, the lengthy cycle time (P/T) relative to the other process steps, and the percent yield for each of these tanks within operation 7—you would be correct. If you look closely at the schedule column, you will see that shipments of all three tank types are behind schedule (i.e., delinquent), and even though there are plenty of tanks within the system, they are stalled and piling up in front of the constraint operation. The key point here is that the most quickly the company might move tanks through this process is one tank every nine days (i.e., based upon lead time through the joining operation with an average rate of nine days), so by breaking this constraint, the TH should improve dramatically.

In addition to helping you identify the constraint operation, Figure 3.2 gives you a hint as to the production mentality existing within this company. In all three tanks types depicted in this hybrid VSM, the constraint operation was operation 7. You know that the cycle time (P/T) was the longest as well as the yield being the lowest. If you were to speculate as to why the inventory was so high in front of operation 7, what would you guess?

This company has historically tracked operator efficiency as its primary performance metric, and as such, each department is rated on its overall efficiency. It was not out of the ordinary for a manager to be taken to task if his or her efficiency went below the target value, which was different for each department. In other words, "Show me how you measure me and I'll show you how I'll behave." Well, in this department, the behavior was quite predictable.

The manager had figured out that his best chance to increase efficiency was directly proportional to how many half-tanks (i.e., tops and bottoms) he could produce in operations 1 through 6. He reasoned that if he overproduced in these operations, his efficiency would increase, and he was correct. As a result of his actions, the inventory stack-up in front of operation 7 was pretty dramatic. It was especially evident in tank type A, where the combined total of operation 6 and inventory ready to be joined was an astounding six tops and six bottoms. Why is this astounding, you may ask? Because each half-tank requires an average of 14 working days to progress from operation 1 to operation 7. Thus, if there were six tops and bottoms waiting to be joined, the first tank in the joining queue had been produced at least 84 workdays in the past (i.e., 14 days/half-tank × 6 tanks). If you consider that this operation only works five days per week, the first tank in the joining queue would have started in operation 1 almost seventeen weeks in the past, or a little more than four months. In addition, the remaining operations require, on average, sixteen additional workdays, so if a quality problem had been found in operation 9, final quality inspection, there was a possibility that all the tanks waiting to be joined and waiting for final inspection could also be defective. Fortunately for this company, the tanks had no major quality problems, so it dodged a bullet.

I had concluded that the primary reason for the excessive amounts of inventory within the process was the operation manager's requirement to keep his efficiencies at the target level. In effect, this department manager, through no real fault of his own, was sacrificing profit to satisfy a performance metric simply because this metric was used to judge his and his department's performance. I recommended that the company temporarily abandon this metric on these three tank types for the nonconstraint operations because it was obviously motivating the wrong behaviors. But because of pressure from the corporate office and the vice president of operations' own beliefs, this was not done immediately.

In February 2006, the company initiated a waste reduction program (sort of a quasi-Lean initiative) on these three lines, and although the profit margins on these three tanks improved slightly, the rate of improvement was not substantial. Eventually, after many conversations, I was able to convince the vice president of operations that if he wanted to drive margins through the roof, he had to focus on the constraint operation and allow the efficiencies to be temporarily ignored in the nonconstraint operations. I explained that instead of trying to optimize the individual process efficiencies (local optima) by building parts that were not needed (and losing money) or building parts ahead of schedule (and building inventory), if he would concentrate on improving the TH of the constraint, revenue would improve, inventory would decrease, and OEs would be reduced. He reluctantly agreed, and the results of this change were not only substantial— they were also prompt.

The first thing we did was shut down the front end of the process (i.e., operations 1 through 6) and redirected the nonconstraint operators to cross-train and assist the operation 7 operators to help work off the excess inventory. At the same time, I taught members of the team basic problem solving and basic Six Sigma so that we could reduce defects and variation. Simultaneous to these actions, we redesigned the process and developed simple work cells, established a work-in-process (WIP) cap in front of the constraint, and implemented a pull system. In doing so, we were able to improve the line balancing and implement one-piece flow to the point that product moved through the constraint operation in 5 days, or 44 percent faster than before. The net effect of all this activity was a very significant increase in TH for these three tank types as well as savings due to less inventory and OE.

Figure 3.3 is the monthly plot of profit dollars (coded numbers and not actual numbers) by month (not the real profit dollars) for the three tank types, and as you can see, by focusing on the constraint operation while simultaneously implementing Lean and Six Sigma tools and techniques, the company moved from losing money on these three tanks (i.e., approximately $50,000/month on average) to making money (i.e., approximately $200,000) in about three months. The vast majority of increased profit dollars came from increased revenue dollars, which was directly proportional to the increased output rate of the constraint. You might be wondering what happened to the efficiencies on these three tanks. Remember, I had convinced the vice president of operations to forego using operator efficiency on nonconstraint operations and focus only on the efficiency of the constraint operation, at least temporarily. In addition,

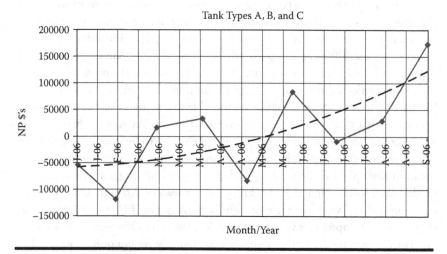

Figure 3.3 Coded NP by Month.

the support functions like the cutting center, quality assurance (QA), and maintenance were subordinated to the constraint.

Figure 3.4 is a plot of the monthly efficiencies for the total process on these three tank types, and as you can see, the efficiencies predictably declined from an average of about 80 percent to approximately 70 percent. The efficiency in

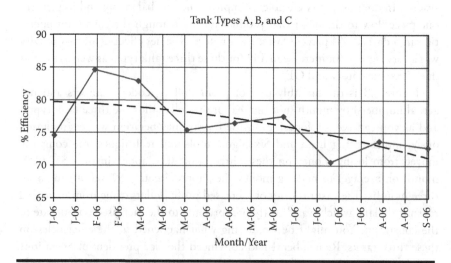

Figure 3.4 Coded Percent Efficiency by Month.

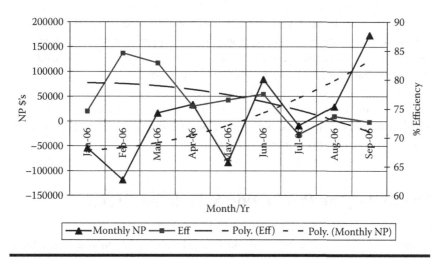

Figure 3.5   Coded Net Profit versus Efficiency.

the constraint operation, however, increased dramatically as the rate of tanks passing through the constraint increased.

Figure 3.5 is a plot of both metrics (i.e., NP and percent efficiency), and if you key on the trend lines for each metric, an interesting nuance occurs in the June–July timeframe. The two lines intersect, and even though the overall efficiency of these three tank types decreased, the NP improved substantially. This increased rate of tanks through the constraint translated directly into increased revenue dollars that hit the bottom line. Think about it: with no increase in labor, the margins on these three tanks improved by a quarter million dollars per month just by focusing the department's efforts on the right operation, the constraint. In addition, the number of delinquencies dropped to zero.

What do you suppose happened as a result of this obviously successful experiment? You might imagine that the next step would be to take what was learned here and expand it to the other areas of the operation and plant, right? Unfortunately, this was not the case. Because of pressure from cost accounting and the corporate office, our experiment was terminated. Once again, efficiency was used to measure the performance in the area and things returned to normal. It was a classic case of "Show me how you're going to measure me, and I'll show you how I'll behave!"

This simple example was an illustration of how simple yet imaginative you can be in your search for the constraint operation and what can happen by focusing your resources correctly. In this case, there was a physical constraint, for certain, but the real culprit was a policy constraint, the erroneous policy decision to use the performance metric efficiency to judge the performance of an operation. The lesson learned here is one I have repeated over and over again: using efficiency to drive performance works if you apply it only to the constraint operation. That is, do not sacrifice the performance of the system by focusing on local optimization of nonconstraints. But there is one more lesson. Unless you have the passion to change and the authority to influence the change, and the moral fiber and courage to implement a change that flies in the face of conventional thinking, do not make the change. But if you do have both the influence and daring, the rewards can be mind-boggling.

Identifying the Production Scheduling System

Scheduling is an important tool for manufacturing because it tells a production operation what to make, when to make it, what materials to use, and which equipment to use. Production scheduling aims to maximize the efficiency of the operation while minimizing costs. Companies typically use backward and forward scheduling in order to correctly plan and allocate equipment and human resources, plan production processes, and purchase materials. Forward scheduling is planning the tasks from the date resources become available to determine the shipping date or the due date, while backward scheduling is planning the tasks from the customer due date to determine the start date or any changes in capacity required.

If done correctly, some of the benefits derived from effectively scheduling a production unit include inventory reduction, production leveling, less scheduling effort, maximum TH, and improved on-time delivery. The most effective production scheduling method I have utilized in conjunction with the UIC is referred to as *drum-buffer-rope* (DBR), so named for its three components. The *drum* is the constraint operation that you have already identified as limiting the plant's TH. The drum sets the pace of production for the rest of the plant in that the rest of the plant (i.e., the nonconstraint operations) follows the beat of the drum. The nonconstraints make sure the drum (constraint) is never starved and that anything the drum (constraint) has processed does not get wasted.

The *buffer's* purpose is to protect the drum from starvation, so that it always has work flowing to it. The buffer in a DBR system uses time as its unit of measure, rather than quantity of material, even though you utilize a physical buffer to protect the constraint. In a typical DBR system there are three strategically placed buffers. The first buffer is in front of the constraint to, again, protect the constraint from starvation. The second buffer is in front of an assembly operation to ensure that all nonconstrained resource parts arrive and are waiting in front of the assembly until the constraint parts arrive. A third buffer of finished goods is placed in front of shipping to ensure the on-time delivery to protect against any disruptions in the upstream operations.

The rope is essentially a work release mechanism for the plant's raw materials to the first operation to ensure that they will reach the buffer before the constraint (drum) is scheduled to work on them. The rope ties the first operation to the pace of the constraining operation. The length of the rope is simply the length of time required to keep the constraint buffer full. Although it is not my intention to provide the finite details of how to implement DBR, I will discuss both the basics of doing so and the potential benefits of such an implementation. Debra Smith explains that there are predictable and proven effects of implementing DBR, which include:[25]

- Machine utilization and labor efficiencies at nonconstraints will decrease.
- Raw material, WIP, and finished goods inventories will contract.
- Lead and cycle times will shrink.
- Scheduling will be much easier.
- Batch sizes can be reduced.
- Cash flow will spiral upward.
- There will be a one-time negative net income hit as the excess work-in-process and finished goods inventories are reduced and overhead stored in inventory is expensed through cost of goods sold.
- Excess capacity will become visible.
- Because the constraint will eventually move to the marketplace, resources will eventually need to be refocused to the marketplace.
- Competitive advantage for the company is improved because of shorter lead and cycle times, which can be used by sales and marketing to improve market share.

One of the key points to remember regarding the implementation of a DBR system is that it will not be sustainable unless traditional performance measurements like machine utilization, operator efficiency, and incentive systems throughout the company are either abandoned or radically changed to be compatible with the TOC concepts and actions. Another key point to keep in mind is that one of the rules of DBR is that there will be no fixed batch sizes or setups at the nonconstraint operations. In order for DBR to be successful, nonconstraints must be flexible enough to stop for setup when they are required to and not according to a predetermined schedule. The same thing applies to fixed batch sizes. When the DBR schedule calls for more parts to be at the constraint, it is imperative that whatever is on hand should be transferred immediately rather than waiting for a fixed amount.

Identifying Performance Metrics

Now that we have identified the current and next constraint and the value stream, the question becomes how to tell whether you are making progress toward your goal of making more money now and in the future. You need some type of feedback mechanism. When I talk about feedback, I am really implying that there should be one or more measurements that tell you how you are doing. Measuring performance is important because you need a way to be able to know that the direction you are traveling is on course in the event that you need to make any midcourse corrections. These performance metrics should be system related in that they tell you how the system is doing versus how an individual process is functioning. Remember, your focus is on system performance and not individual performance.

The Purpose of Performance Metrics

Performance measures are intended to serve three very important functions or roles:

- First and foremost, the measures should stimulate the right behaviors.
- The performance measures should reinforce and support the overall goals and objectives of the company.
- The measures should be able to assess, evaluate, and provide feedback as to the status of the people, departments, products, and the total company.

The right behaviors of people and departments are critical to achievement of the overall goals of the company, but many times the performance metrics chosen encourage the opposite behaviors.

According to Standard and Davis, in order to be effective, performance measures must have the following three criteria:[26]

- They must be objective, precisely defined, and quantifiable.
- They must be well within the control of the people or department being measured.
- They must encourage the right behaviors.

Although these three criteria for performance metrics are clear and absolutely necessary, there is one additional criterion that I believe is necessary for the metrics to be understood and utilized by the organization as a whole. The performance measure must be translatable to everyone within the organization. That is, each operator, manager, and engineer must understand how his or her actions impact the metric. As such, the metric should be presented as a hierarchy.

For example, if the higher-level metric is something like on-time delivery to the customer, the lower-level metric should tie directly into it. Maybe the lower-level metric involves average cycle time or schedule compliance at individual workstations. Or if the higher-level metric is parts per million (ppm) defective to the customer, the lower-level metric might be defect rate at the individual workstation. Performance metrics are intended to inform everyone, not just the managers.

The performance metrics chosen should also lend themselves to trend and statistical analysis, and as such, they should not be yes or no in terms of compliance. The metric should also be challenging but at the same time be attainable. There should be a stretch involved. If it is too easy to reach the target, you probably will not gain much in the way of profitability. If it is too difficult, people will be frustrated and disenchanted.

So let us look at the performance metric *efficiency* (or utilization) that was used by the fuel tank company. Was the metric objective, precisely defined, and quantifiable? Yes, clearly, it demonstrated these three qualities. Was the metric within the control of the people or department being measured? The answer to this question is yes, as demonstrated by the manager's continuing to produce tanks in the nonconstraint operations when he clearly should not have. But did it encourage the right behaviors? Clearly, the answer is a resounding no. Instead of focusing on improving the overall TH of the process, this manager was forced to maximize efficiencies of all process steps because he was evaluated on the basis of his overall efficiencies rather than what it cost the company.

What if this manager had only focused on the constraint operation? What if he attempted to maximize the efficiency of only the constraint operation at the expense of the nonconstraint operations? The overall system efficiency decreased, but the overall TH and revenue generated by the system increased dramatically. Wouldn't this have made more sense than building excess inventory? By focusing efforts on the constraint operation at the expense of individual operational efficiencies, profitability of the production line responded quite well. The lesson that should have been learned by this manager was that using efficiency as a performance metric works well as long as it is focused on the constraint operation. In fairness to the production manager, however, he was bound by the performance metric chosen, in this case, by the corporate office (i.e., a policy constraint). As you can probably conclude, I am not a fan of performance metrics such as labor efficiency, standard labor variance, overhead absorption, and capacity utilization, all of which motivate the wrong behaviors at the shop floor level.

With regard to the other questions about the efficacy and hierarchy of this metric (i.e., efficiency) relative to the operators, the nonconstraint operators clearly understood their role but questioned why they were being asked to build so much inventory. Although the metric was understood by the operators, they failed to see its usefulness. Finally, trend and statistical analysis were able to be performed, so it did satisfy this requirement.

Financial Metrics

When using TOC financial metrics (TH, inventory, and OE), TH (T) is the rate at which the system generates money through sales or all the money entering the company from outside sources minus truly variable costs like sales commissions, consumable supplies, and so on. Basically, if it is an expense that is incurred while producing a unit of product (or delivering a service), it is a variable cost. If the cost would have been incurred if you were not producing a product, it is a fixed cost. Inventory (I) is all the money invested in things we intend to sell, like raw materials or purchased parts, WIP, and finished goods. This does not include the added value of labor or overhead. OE includes all fixed expenses, including direct labor and overhead, office supplies, utility costs, interest expense, and so on.

So which of these three is the most important to an organization? We all agree that reducing OE and inventory are two of the things everyone needs to do in order to be profitable. In fact, most companies *incorrectly* believe that the path to profitability is through these two metrics. We see downsizing, layoffs, and generally cutting OEs to the bone every day, but is this the right approach? It must be, because everyone does it, right?

These three metrics are tied together to calculate NP and ROI by using the following two equations:

$$NP = T - OE$$

$$ROI = (T - OE) \div I$$

The key to using these metrics is simple. If TH is increasing while OE and inventory are decreasing, you are doing well. These three metrics (T, I, and OE) and the two derivatives (NP and ROI), if used correctly, will tell you all you need to know regarding how well your business is running and whether or not your decisions are the right ones. My advice on using these metrics is simple. At the shop floor level track TH, inventory, and OE (with appropriate lower-level metrics), and at the organizational level track NP and ROI, but do not use the traditional definitions of both. Instead, use the definitions I just presented. And make sure they are visible for everyone to see.

I mentioned "appropriate" lower-level metrics. Just what might these be? Think about what you are trying to accomplish. You know that each minute a constraint sits idle is a minute of lost TH, so monitoring constraint availability is a good metric to track. You also know that if a constraint operation misses its release date to downstream operations, that too will cause a missed TH opportunity, so on-time delivery is also a good metric. My advice is this: think hard about what you are trying to accomplish and design your performance metrics around this.

Knowing Which Metrics to Track

With this in mind, allow me to offer suggestions on several constraint metrics that you might consider tracking. Obviously, you want to make certain that the constraint operation is occupied as much as possible. Think about the reasons why a constraint operation might not be producing. If equipment malfunctions and causes downtime, you lose TH. If quality problems occur and the equipment is forced to shut down, you lose TH. If repairs to equipment take an excessive amount of time, you lose TH. If materials are not available at the right time and the equipment shuts down, you lose TH. The reality is there are many reasons why equipment might be forced to stop producing, and they all cause you to lose TH. One metric, overall equipment effectiveness (OEE), takes all these sources of downtime into account and provides you with a single number that you can track and improve. The good news is there is a very positive correlation between OEE and TH. It is for this reason that I believe OEE is an excellent performance metric, and I highly recommend that it be used to track constraint performance. We'll discuss OEE in more detail in Chapter 6.

Metrics for Nonconstraint Operations

Remember, the assumptions regarding how nonconstraint operations run are dramatically different from those for constraint operations. Because you will be subordinating all nonconstraint operations to the constraint operation, it makes little sense to evaluate performance in the nonconstraints in the same way you do for constraint operations. Think about it: in order to maximize total system TH, you must never let a constraint operation sit idle. This is not so in a nonconstraint operation. Because nonconstraints have sprint capacity, there will be idle time, so right away, you see that metrics like operator efficiency or machine utilization are not good metrics for nonconstraints. If these two metrics are not acceptable, what would be good metrics?

Remember, the properties of a good performance metric are:

- They must be objective, precisely defined, and quantifiable.
- They must be well within the control of the people or department being measured.
- They must encourage the right behaviors.

My question to you is this: What behaviors do you want to encourage in nonconstraint operations? Let us think for a minute about the function of a nonconstraint operation. First, a nonconstraint in front of the constraint operation can never starve a constraint. If it did, you would lose valuable TH and could never recover it. By the same token, a nonconstraint downstream from a constraint can never be permitted to produce scraps simply because these scraps are lost TH for the system. Second, you know that too much protective inventory in front of a constraint operation simply adds unnecessary cost to the organization. Thus, maintaining the "right" amount of inventory (or time buffer) in front of the constraint should be another consideration as a metric. Third, you know that the constraint operation sets the pace for all other resources, so schedule compliance in a nonconstraint becomes important.

Based upon these three functions, there are four generic metrics that should be considered, as follows:

- **Workstation availability:** The percentage of time the nonconstraint was available to produce product.
- **Yield:** The percentage of "good" product produced for the constraint operation (or for downstream operations supplying the shipping buffer).
- **On-time delivery to the next operation:** The percentage of compliance to schedule.
- **Protective buffer (parts or time) in front of the constraint, assembly, and shipping:** Percentage of protective buffer (too little, <100%; too much, >100%).

The answer to the question regarding what performance metrics should be used at nonconstraint operations is: it depends. The key decision on performance metrics for nonconstraints is really up to you, but remember the important functions of a nonconstraint:

- You can never starve a constraint operation (or shipping buffer).
- Too much or too little inventory can either drive up costs or drive down TH.
- Run only according to the schedule, which is determined by the constraint operation.

What is a time buffer? Because the nonconstraints have sprint capacity, or the capacity to catch up when they fall behind, it is not always necessary for this buffer to be a physical inventory. Instead, another way to hold down costs is to think of this buffer in terms of time. That is, instead of having parts in front of the constraint, assembly, and shipping operations, you could actually substitute time as the buffer. You know what the release schedule is for the constraint, assembly, and shipping operations, and you know how long it typically takes to produce product at the constraints and nonconstraints, so as long as you can supply the constraint, assembly, and shipping operations with parts that are inside this release schedule, you know that you will not starve either the constraint, assembly, or shipping operation. Thus, instead of a physical inventory, it is perfectly acceptable to use both a time and a physical buffer.

Managing the Interaction of Constraints and Nonconstraints

How should you manage the interaction of constraints and nonconstraints? And what are the implications and consequences of using traditional measures of efficiency and utilization? Umble and Srikanth[27] present five basic resource interactions as follows:

- Product flowing from a constraint resource to a nonconstraint resource
- Product flowing from a nonconstraint resource to a constraint resource
- Product flowing from a nonconstraint resource to another nonconstraint resource
- Product flowing from a constraint resource to another constraint resource
- Product flowing from a constraint and a nonconstraint to an assembly operation

As stated previously, in discussing these interactions I will focus on the consequences and implications of managing these resources using the traditional measures of efficiencies and utilization. In this discussion a constraint or bottleneck resource is any resource that has less capacity than market demand. Incidentally, by using this definition of a constraint, any resource that has capacity less than the market demand could theoretically be considered a constraint. In this context, the resource that has the least capacity for satisfying market demand is referred to as the *critical constrained resource* (CCR).

Product Flowing from a Constraint Resource to a Nonconstraint Resource

In this case materials are first processed by the constraint resource and then passed on to the nonconstraint resource. Because, by definition, the constraint has less capacity than market demand, the constraint must work 100 percent of the time to try to meet the demand placed on it. In other words, the constraint should be managed to maximum efficiency and utilization. Because, by definition, the nonconstraint resource has a capacity greater than market demand, it has the capacity to work faster than the constraint. But because the constraint works slower, the nonconstraint can only process material as fast as it is received. This causes the nonconstraint to be starved part of the time so the calculated efficiencies and utilizations will appear to be unsatisfactory. The traditional measurements of efficiency and utilization ignore this interactive effect of competing resources. The proper management action for this case is for the nonconstraint to operate at exactly the same pace as the constraint at the expense of lower efficiencies and utilization.

Product Flowing from a Nonconstraint Resource to a Constraint Resource

In this case materials are processed first by a nonconstraint operation and then passed on to a constraint operation. If you use the traditional measures of efficiency and utilization to manage this case, the nonconstraint operation will produce at maximum efficiency as long as there is material to process. Because the constraint has less capacity than the nonconstraint operation, the unavoidable consequence will be a stacking of inventory in front of the constraint. Because none of this excess inventory can be utilized by the constraint operation, inventory holding costs and lead times increase while the possibility of undetected quality problems also increases.

Product Flowing from a Nonconstraint Resource to a Nonconstraint Resource

In this case materials are first processed by the first nonconstraint operation and then passed on to the second nonconstraint operation. Because both operations are nonconstraints, you know that both can process materials faster than the market demand rate. If these two nonconstraint operations are in front of the constraint operation and they are permitted to process materials at their maximum efficiency, the net effect will be excess inventory, protracted lead times, and potential hidden quality problems. In reality, both of the nonconstraint operations should process materials at the rate of the market demand or to the pace of the constraint at the expense of lower efficiencies or utilizations. If the two nonconstraints are downstream from the constraint, both will be limited to the output of the constraint operation with the efficiencies or utilizations of each being less than optimal according to traditional measurement advocates.

Product Flowing from a Constraint Resource to Another Constraint Resource

This scenario is unlikely because it implies that both resources are producing at a rate that is below the market demand rate. In this case, you should look at P/T, determine which has the slowest rate, and treat the interaction accordingly. That is, the operation with the slowest P/T will remain the constraint, and the other will be treated as a nonconstraint and then be managed to work at the rate of the slower operation. In this case, efficiencies or utilizations will not be impacted much.

Product Flowing from a Constraint and a Nonconstraint to an Assembly Operation

In this case material simultaneously flows to and out of the constraint and non-constraint operations directly to an assembly operation. Here the constraint operation must produce all the time to satisfy the market demand at the assembly operation, while the nonconstraint does not. It only has to work at the rate of the constraint but can never let an assembly operation be starved. If the nonconstraint operation feeding the assembly operation were permitted to maximize efficiency or utilization, inventory and lead times would increase.

Because of the interdependencies and interactions that exist within a manufacturing operation, the following principle emerges: the level of utilization of a nonbottleneck resource is controlled by other constraints within the system. Because of this basic principle, the traditional performance measures of efficiency and utilization are only effective if applied to a constraint operation. Any attempt to increase nonconstraint efficiencies or utilizations is just counterproductive.

External Market Constraints

The problem with external market constraints is that you have the capacity to satisfy additional market needs, but you do not have sales orders for your products. For this type of constraint, if you are to increase sales, you must improve your competitive edge in the marketplace. So what are the components of competitive edge? Basically, if companies want to achieve a competitive edge in the marketplace, they have to improve in one or all the following:

■ Product quality
■ Customer service
■ Product cost

- Lead time from order to delivery
- Product flexibility

Product quality improvement is directly related to compliance to customer specifications. Compliance is not just producing product that is within the customer specification, but moving closer and closer to the center of the specification. If the specifications are truly functional, logically products that fall just within the limits of the specifications are not nearly as good or functional as products near the center. Your efforts here should be aimed at not just meeting customer expectations but, rather, always exceeding them.

Customer service is many times a deciding factor in the selection of a supplier. It does not matter how good the quality of your product is if it is not available when it is needed. By focusing your efforts on higher and higher levels of on-time delivery and reliability, improvements made will translate into a competitive edge for your company and will typically result in additional sales.

Closely related to on-time delivery is lead time. Lead time is the elapsed time from receipt of the order to fulfillment and delivery of the order, so in order to become more competitive, lead time must be continually reduced. Even if your on-time delivery results are excellent, if your lead time is longer than the competition's, you will not get the orders.

Being the lowest-cost producer is probably the most obvious competitive advantage that could increase your market share. The good news here is, assuming all other competitive factors between you and your competitors are equal, reducing your cost will generally translate into improved market share. And remember, all this new revenue (minus the cost of raw material) will flow directly to the bottom line because your labor and other expenses will be the same as they were before the cost reduction.

Finally, product flexibility can sometimes be the deciding factor in the selection of a supplier. Being able to rapidly and flawlessly execute a change to an existing order to something else, for example, can differentiate your company. In today's manufacturing environment, companies are always trying to reduce the number of suppliers, so if your company portfolio is flexible for the buyer, you have a competitive advantage.

So how is it that a company can achieve all these competitive advantages? Quite frankly, using UIC as your manufacturing strategy will deliver each and every one of these competitive advantages. Because the P/T on the constraint operation will be less, lead times will be reduced. Because TH and revenue will be higher and OE and inventory will be lower, your product cost will be lower and more competitive. Because defect, rework, and scrap problems will be reduced, quality and reliability will improve. And because your changeover and setup times have improved, your flexibility to meet changing orders will be improved.

In reality, it does not matter whether your constraint is internal or external because the actions outlined in UIC will deliver better cycle times, less OE, fewer inventory costs, better ROI, and better cash flow, to the point that your market share will increase and your profits will go through the roof.

Chapter 4

Finding Waste in the Constraint

Lean teaches you that when you find waste, you should immediately remove it, and while this might sound logical to many people, in my opinion the reality is that many times the improvement effort becomes disjointed and lacks continuity. The scope of the improvement effort can actually become overwhelming and all-consuming to many organizations, especially if resources are limited. Think about it for a minute. If you find apparent waste in a nonconstraint operation and remove it, has it really had an impact on profitability? It could have, but my belief is that the real gains come from removing waste in the constraint operation.

Six Sigma, on the other hand, teaches you to relentlessly reduce process variation everywhere, and although I agree with this strategy, the variation reduction effort can also become overwhelming and disjointed, especially for organizations with limited resources. There are even reports that say Six Sigma might not even be the right thing for small companies with inadequate resources. To further emphasize this point, Womack and Jones report, "Sadly, we've watched firms set off full of vision, energy, and high hopes, but make very little progress because they went tearing off after perfection in a thousand directions and never had the resources to get very far along the path. What's needed instead is to form a vision, select the two or three most important steps to get you there, and defer the other steps until later. It's not that these will never be tackled, only that the general principle of doing one thing at a time."[28] I could not agree more with Womack and Jones that companies should not go after perfection immediately, but where I disagree is their contention that you should select the two or three most important steps to get you there. What is really needed is the discipline to follow a cyclical method of continuous improvement that starts in a single focused area, the area of greatest leverage for the organization, the constraint operation.

Steps 1a to 1c of UIC are intended to overcome the irresistible urge to tear off after perfection in a thousand directions, moving hastily and impulsively into the improvement mode. Although you want improvement as quickly as you can have it, it has to be done within the capabilities of your organization, and then done in a controlled and systematic manner. In these three steps of the UIC, you are methodically and systematically identifying where the focus should be and the *possibilities* that exist to reduce waste and variation. That is, you want to identify all non-value-added waste, all sources of excessive variation, and all sources of defects that currently exist only within your *constraint operation* for now. It is one thing to identify waste, variation, and defects, but it is a completely different thing to reduce or eliminate them. Doing so, under control and correctly, necessitates the development of a coherent plan, and steps 1b and 1c form the input for such a plan.

Identifying Waste

So what is waste and how do you identify it? You experience waste in your personal lives every day because it is seemingly everywhere and easy to see. Waiting in long lines at airports and grocery stores, sitting idle in your car waiting for a light to change from red to green, and being put on hold on the telephone are all examples of everyday waste of waiting. Why do you consider them waste? Because you are squandering or idling away your precious time and money without accomplishing anything, and it affects you personally. It is no different for your customers. Customers plainly and simply do not like paying for things that they feel they should not have to pay for. You (and your customers) do not mind paying for value, but when you perceive that something is not of value to you, you actually resent having to shell out your hard-earned cash.

Waste, then, is anything that provides little or no value and causes feelings of resentment if you are asked to pay for it. As you think about your processes, there should be things that just jump right out at you that have little or no value. Is rework considered valuable, or does it tie up resources that could be used to produce product? Is moving your product from one side of your plant to the other or storing it in a warehouse, waiting to process it in the next process step, valuable? Is employees walking around looking for things they need to do their jobs a value-added activity? As you are looking for sources of waste in your processes, look for things that your customers might resent having to pay for. If you think they would, it is non-value-added waste and should be removed.

It may not be obvious to you, but very little time in a typical process actually is spent on value-added work. In fact, value-added time compared to non-value-added time is usually an infinitesimal portion of the total cycle time. Think about it: How much of your process time is actually consumed in transforming material into your finished product? If your process is typical, it is full of activities like staging, waiting, stacking, waiting, counting, waiting, reworking, waiting, moving, waiting, storing, waiting, and so on. It is this non-value-added time reduction, especially the waiting component, that results in the greatest amount of payback. In spite of this, many improvement efforts focus on reducing value-added cycle time. But keep in mind that reducing waiting time in a nonconstraint operation does not do much for your bottom line. It does give you additional sprint capacity, but it does not contribute much to your bottom line. On the other hand, reducing waiting time in a constraint operation provides an immediate improvement in TH, revenue, and margins.

If you were to ask a typical manufacturing manager how his factory can increase the amount of value-added work, he might tell you to do more of everything. Add another shift. Hire more workers. Work more overtime. Run the equipment longer. All these would definitely increase the amount of value-added time, but at the same time, they would increase the amount of wasted effort. The correct answer, of course, is to reduce the amount of waste. Reducing waste of time (waiting time, travel time, rework time, and so on), material waste, waste of space, and so on is where the real payback is as long as it is focused in the constraint operation.

Basic Tools and Techniques for Locating Waste

Because there are many excellent sources of information available on how to use various tools and techniques for locating and eliminating waste, it is only my intention here to provide primarily information of their existence. I do, however, want to briefly discuss two tools that you should become intimately familiar with in your quest to identify waste within your processes.

Time and Motion Study

The first tool, time and motion study, is one of the oldest and most useful tools of all for not only identifying or discovering process waste, but also quantifying it. In doing time studies, you do things like mapping out the process, measuring the time required to accomplish each activity, recording operator trips away from the workstation, and so on. As you are recording data, you should be making notes as to whether or not the tasks are adding value.

You should be imagining how these same process steps might be done more quickly and more efficiently, or perhaps not at all, and make notes on this as well. You can then estimate what percentage of your current process time is non-value-added, which you will use in the development of your action plan. Remember, reducing value-added cycle time is not where the big payback is; it is reducing the non-value-added time that is important.

Part of your study will involve following an operator as he or she moves around looking for tools, raw materials, or supplies; seeking advice on how to perform a task; searching for someone to make a decision; or following a product being transported to the next processing step or, worse yet, put in a storage location. You should give thought to and make notes on how the process might be organized better so as to eliminate these non-value-added activities. You should even begin to envision a new cellular process layout and make sketches of the future layout. You should also think in terms of what the cell might look like after you perform a 5S on it. You will become intimately aware of other things, like wasted motion, defective product, inventory, and waiting, which are all excellent examples of waste. My advice to you is simple: take prolific notes and make appropriate sketches while the observations are fresh in your mind. Keep in mind that what you observe and measure will form the basis for part of your improvement plan.

Spaghetti Diagram

The second tool, used in conjunction with the time study, is the spaghetti diagram. The basic premise of the spaghetti diagram is that operators (or product) waste a lot of time either leaving (operators) their workstations in search of stuff or being transported (product) to some other location. The spaghetti diagram provides a graphical record of the operator's (or product's) movements within and outside the process and can contain things like the number of trips away from the work post, the distance traveled looking for stuff, and an explanation of why the trip was needed.

The time study, of course, captures the elapsed time away from the work area, while the spaghetti diagram depicts the distance traveled and can also be used to capture time away. Figure 4.1 is an example of a spaghetti diagram, and in case it is not obvious to you, the spaghetti diagram, like the VSM, is a paper-and-pencil activity. Notice the number of trips away from the actual work post. Most of these are simply wasted motion that could be eliminated by doing things like relocating the process, producing product within cells, performing a 5S, having needed products and supplies delivered to the operator, and so on. The time made available can then be turned directly into value-added build time with a corresponding increase in TH. With these two tools, you will be able to clarify and quantify much of the waste within the process.

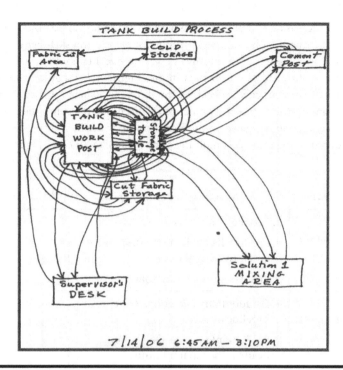

Figure 4.1 Spaghetti Diagram.

But just like a crime scene investigation, you must "go and see" the process to look for evidence of the existence of waste. Prosecutors cannot solve crimes and convict criminals from their desks; they must go to the crime scene to find evidence, and so, too, must you. The evidence comes in the form of observations and measurements, and believe me, you will have no problem finding them.

Reviewing the Common Wastes

In order to help you find waste in your process, I have prepared a simple list of some the various forms of waste and the symptoms to look for (see Figure 4.2). For example, if you notice operators wandering around your facility in search of tools, materials, supplies, or even you, you are experiencing waste of motion and space. If your equipment changeovers take hours instead of minutes, you have found waste of waiting. Just keep your eyes and ears open because waste exists everywhere and is very easy to find. Finding waste is one thing, but eliminating it is another.

Study your constraint operation for signs of waste and record your findings that will be acted upon later in the cycle. During this go-and-see activity, it is also a good idea to make notes about what you see in nonconstraint operations. You will not be acting on them just yet, but your notes and sketches might help you later on as you attempt to improve flow, improve TH, and so on.

What I recommend to my clients is to use Figure 4.2 as a guide and systematically search your process for each of the different forms of waste. Your team members should use Figure 4.2 as a checklist to guide them in their search for waste. Trust me, you will have no problem finding waste in your process. Let us look at several of the more common forms of waste contained in Figure 4.2.

Waste Description	Symptoms to Look For	Notes
Waste of Transportation	1. Too many forklifts 2. Product has to be moved, stacked, and moved again 3. Process steps are far apart	
Waste of Waiting	1. Frequent/chronic equipment breakdowns 2. Equipment changeovers taking hours rather than minutes 3. Operators waiting for inspectors to inspect product	
Waste of Organization and Space	1. Operators looking for tools, materials, supplies, parts, and so on 2. Large distances between process steps 3. Not able to determine process status in 15 seconds 4. Many different work methods for same process 5. Pool lighting or dirty equipment	
Waste of Over-processing	1. Rework levels are high 2. Trying to produce perfect quality that isn't required by customer 3. No documented quality standards	

Figure 4.2   Common Wastes and Symptoms to Look For.

Waste of Motion	1. Process steps located as functional islands with no uniform flow 2. Excessive turning, walking, bending, stooping within the process	
Waste of Inventory	1. Product being made without orders 2. Obsolete inventory 3. Racks full of product	
Waste of Defective Product	1. Problems never seem to get solved and just keep coming back 2. Independent rework areas have become just another step in the process 3. Excessive repairs	
Waste of Over-production	1. Long production runs of the same part to avoid changeovers and setup time 2. Pockets of excess or products earlier or in greater quantities than the customer wants or needs	
Waste of Under-utilization	1. No operator involvement on problem-solving teams 2. No regular stand-up meetings with operators to get new ideas 3. No suggestion system in place to collect improvement ideas 4. Not recording delays and reasons for the delays	
Waste of Storage and Handling	1. Many storage racks full of product 2. Damaged parts in inventory 3. Storing product away from the point of use	

Figure 4.2   (Continued.)

Of all the forms of waste, would it surprise you that waste of waiting is the most prevalent? Think about it for a minute and imagine your process. Are there drying times associated with your products? How about inspections: do you have to wait for them? How long does it take you to change from one product to another? Is it minutes or hours? All these are wasteful forms of waiting.

Another of the more common forms of waste is overprocessing. How high are your rework levels? If they are high, how complete and documented are your quality standards? I consulted for one company that had many cosmetic defects, but when I asked to see the acceptance standards, they were contained in documents that were scattered in many locations. We did three important things to resolve this problem. First, we studied each of the individual standards and consolidated them into a single document. Second, we performed an attribute error of measure study and discovered that there were so many different interpretations of the standards that essentially no two inspectors inspected the product the same way. As a result of this error, many of the defects were misclassified and many others were not defects at all. We then developed visual cosmetic acceptance standards and, wherever possible, developed simple measurements to use to classify the defects, if they existed. The results were rather dramatic in that the defect and rework levels decreased significantly. This was clearly a classic case of overprocessing.

Another common example of waste is motion. If your process is still arranged as a functional island configuration, you have plenty of this form of waste as well as waste of storage and handling. You probably have pockets of inventory located throughout your plant and storage racks probably full of inventory waiting to be processed, become obsolete, or be repaired because of damage. Yes, waste is not at all difficult to locate, so go find it and do something about it. Trust me: the rewards will be plenty.

Chapter 5

Reducing Variation and Defects

In a manufacturing environment there are two completely different categories of variability that have profoundly different impacts on a manufacturing process. The first one, *processing time variability* (PTV), is primarily concerned with the speed that parts progress through an individual process step or the time required to actually process materials to produce the products (or deliver services) or components. The second category is *process and product variability* (PPV), which involves the variation associated with the physical process used to produce the product and variability of the actual product produced. By *process*, in this context, I am referring to the physical process parameters or machine settings used to produce the product. By *product* I am referring to the physical characteristics or critical-to-quality characteristics (CTQs) that you measure on the product being produced.

Because each category of variability presents completely different challenges for a company, I have elected to treat each one separately in this discussion of variability. However, as will become apparent, PPV has a profound influence on PTV. Let us look at PPV first.

Measuring Variation

In order to reduce variation you must be able to accurately and precisely measure it. This means that you must have a measurement system that is capable of measuring your products and processes both accurately and precisely. I am assuming that you understand basic measures of variation like range (R), standard deviation (σ), and variance (σ^2), and basic measures of central tendency like population mean (μ) and sample mean ($\overline{X}$), but in the event that you do not, here are some basic definitions for each measure.

- *Range* is the highest value minus the lowest value.
- *Variance* is a measure of absolute variability.
- *Standard deviation* is the square root of the variance and is a measure of relative variability.
- μ is the average of the population.
- $\overline{X}$ is the average of a sample from the population.

Measurement System Variability

Process and product variation consists of the actual variation of the product's physical characteristics or process parameters plus the variation of the measurement system plus any other error not accounted for. Mathematically, this concept looks as follows:

$$\sigma^2{}_{Total} = \sigma^2{}_{Process} + \sigma^2{}_{Measurement\ System} + \varepsilon^2$$

Solving for σ:

$$\sigma = \sqrt{\sigma^2{}_{Process} + \sigma^2{}_{Measurement\ System} + \varepsilon^2}$$

Measurement system errors can be classified into two distinctly different categories, accuracy and precision:

- **Accuracy (or bias):** A measure of the difference between the average value of the measurements on the parts studied and the *true value* or *master value* of the parts. Having an acceptable accuracy guarantees that the measurements on parts are close to what their true values are. Clearly, you want your measurement device to be as accurate as possible.
- **Precision:** Precision is the variation you see when you measure the same part repeatedly with the same measurement device. Obviously, you want precision to be very low compared to part variation so that you can detect differences between parts.

With any measurement system, you want measurements to be both accurate and precise, but that does not always happen. For example, you may have a measurement device that measures parts precisely, but not accurately. Or you may have a device that is accurate, but not precise (i.e., measurements have a large amount of variation). You can also have a device that is neither accurate nor precise. Precision is further broken down into two components:

- **Repeatability** assesses whether the same tester can measure the same part multiple times with the same measurement device and get the same value. Repeatability is the variability associated with the measurement device.
- **Reproducibility** assesses whether different testers can measure the same part/sample with the same measurement device and get the same value. Reproducibility is the variability associated with the operator of the measuring device.

Mathematically speaking, the formula for these two components of precision is as follows:

$$\sigma^2_{\text{Measurement System}} = \sigma^2_{\text{Gage}} + \sigma^2_{\text{Operator}}$$

Solving for σ:

$$\sigma = \sqrt{\sigma^2_{\text{Gage}} + \sigma^2_{\text{Operator}}}$$

Visually, accuracy and precision are demonstrated in Figure 5.1.

The accuracy of a measurement system can be further reduced into two additional components:

- **Stability:** The capacity of a measurement system to produce the same values over time when measuring the same sample or part. Stability means

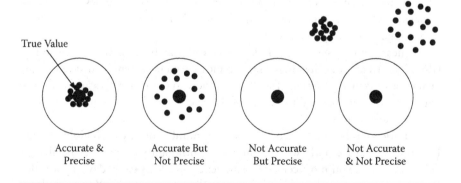

True Value

| Accurate & Precise | Accurate But Not Precise | Not Accurate But Precise | Not Accurate & Not Precise |

Figure 5.1　Accuracy and Precision.

that no special cause variation is present in the measurement process, and that only common cause variation is present.

■ **Linearity:** A measure of the consistency of accuracy (bias) over the expected range of the measurement device. For example, if a bathroom scale is under by 2 pounds when measuring a 150-pound person, but is off by 10 pounds when measuring a 200-pound person, the measurement device (or system) is not linear over the expected range of use.

There are two additional properties that must be considered in order to have an acceptable measurement system:

■ **Resolution:** The ability of a measurement device to discriminate between parts. As a rule of thumb, the measurement system should have a resolution of at least one-tenth the smaller of either the specification tolerance or the process spread. If the resolution is not fine enough, process variability will not be recognized by the measurement system.

■ **Number of distinct categories:** Ratio of the standard deviation of the parts to the standard deviation of the measurement system. The number of distinct categories estimates how many separate groups of parts or samples the measurement system is able to distinguish.

$$\text{Number of distinct categories} = \sigma_{parts} \div \sigma_{measurement\ system}$$

Needless to say, PPV originates from many different sources within the process and includes things like lot-to-lot differences of raw material, differences in operator technique, differences in machines, temperature changes, and so on. Figure 5.2 is a graphical presentation focused primarily at variation associated with the measurement system. Keep in mind that the many sources of variation associated with part-to-part variation are not included here. Is it no wonder why measurement system problems exist?

A measurement system analysis, or gage repeatability and reproducibility (R&R) study, assesses the properties of a measurement system to ensure its adequacy for a given application. The details of how to perform a measurement system evaluation are beyond the scope of this book, but there are many excellent sources available to you.

Variation has been declared public enemy number one by both Goldratt and Deming. But just exactly what is variation? Although you may not be able to define variation, you most certainly experience its effects every day in your life. Variation interferes with and hinders your ability to plan things. You might have planned to go to a baseball game, only to have it canceled by rain or inclement

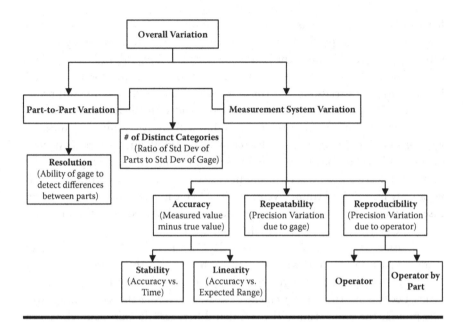

Figure 5.2   Overall Variation Hierarchy.

weather. Sure, you checked the weather forecast ahead of time, but we all know how inaccurate the weather forecasts can be. Or maybe you wanted to renew your passport, but because of new laws regarding travel outside the United States, the time required to complete the process was highly variable and therefore unpredictable. I am sure that you have and will continue to experience the negative effects of variation every day in your personal life.

From a process perspective, you might have planned to produce and ship x number of widgets today, but your equipment unexpectedly went down, or maybe a quality problem sprang to life and forced you to miss your delivery date to a customer. Variation has been defined as an unwanted condition and is the difference between where you are (current state) and where you would like to be (desired end state). My definition is much simpler in that variation is defined by one word: inconsistency. If variation exists, consistency does not. How much variation that exists determines how consistent (or inconsistent) your processes will be.

Effects of Variation

How serious are the effects of variation? Variation creates all sorts of problems for you, both on and off the job. Variation is serious enough for W. Edwards Deming to have said, "If I had to reduce my message to management to just a few words, I'd say it all has to do with reducing variation." These words from Dr. Deming are so profound and insightful, but he had more to say on the subject. "The central problem in management, leadership and production, as my friend Lloyd S. Nelson put it, is failure to understand the nature and interpretation of variation."[29] If you assume that the specifications your products are being judged against are functional and were correctly established, up or down deviations from the target value will always result in changes to your product's performance, for better or worse. How much worse is dependent upon how far your process deviates from its target. In effect, you will be creating defective product, resulting in either rework or scrap, both of which negatively impact lead time, inventory, OE, TH, capacity, and so on. In either case, when the TH of the constraint operation is infected with the variation virus, the system TH and profitability suffer.

Variation has existed since the early days of the industrial revolution, and there are plenty of reasons why. The fact is that no two things are ever exactly alike, and even if they were, you probably could not confirm it with measurements because no two measurement devices, measuring the same thing, will ever provide the same results. The fact that differences do exist compels you to develop a strategy on how to deal with variation effectively. Shewhart, for example, suggested that in order to master variation, you should "minimize variation so that it will be so insignificant that it does not, in any way, affect the performance of your product."[30]

On the other hand, Taguchi suggests that you should "construct (design) the product in such a way that it will be robust to any type of variation."[31] Shewhart's approach is to focus on variation during the production phase, while Taguchi's approach focuses on the design phase. So who's right? Actually, they both are. In order to maximize your variation reduction efforts, both methods work to reduce process variation. Taguchi offers a way to create a more robust process that will mitigate noise effects, while Shewhart teaches you how to systematically reduce all forms of variation present in your process.

Cycle Time (C/T) and Processing Variability

From a TH perspective, variability of P/T hinders your ability to meet production requirements, and that translates directly into delivery performance. This form of variability comes from both internal and external sources, such as equipment downtime (planned and unplanned), inconsistent or nonstandardized work methods, absenteeism, long equipment setup times, late deliveries from suppliers, and a host of other sources.

Standard and Davis explain that there are three ways to handle variability: eliminate it, reduce it, or adapt to it.[32] Because it is impossible to eliminate variability, you must reduce variability as much as possible, and then adapt to the remaining variation.

Reducing overall process cycle time variability and lead time is, in some respects, the single most important manufacturing strategy of all, simply because reducing it typically leads to improvements in TH, revenue, delivery performance, factory congestion, inventory levels, production costs, and repeat orders. Although cycle time variability is important, variation within processes creates all sorts of problems, especially when the variability is located in the constraint operation. PPV has a profound impact on PTV.

Fundamental Points to Remember

Hopp and Spearman, in their breakthrough book, *Factory Physics*, provide valuable insights into variability by providing seven fundamental points to remember.[33] If you do not have a copy of this book, I suggest you purchase one.

Variability Is a Fact of Life

From a management perspective, it is clear that the ability to recognize and deal effectively with variability is perhaps the most critical skill to develop for all managers and engineers. Without this skill your decisions will be full of uncertainty and might even be wrong most of the time.

There Are Many Sources of Variability in Manufacturing Systems

Process variability comes at you in many different forms. It can be as simple as work method variations or as complex as machine setups and changeovers, planned and unplanned downtime, or scrap and rework. Flow variability is created by the way you release work into the system or how it moves between stations. The result of variability present in a system can be catastrophic if its underlying causes are not identified and controlled.

The Coefficient of Variation Is a Key Measure of Item Variability

The coefficient of variation, given by the formula $CV = \sigma/\mu$, is a reasonable way to compare the variability of different elements of a production system. Because it is a unitless ratio, you can make rational comparisons of the level of variability in both process times and flows. In workstations, the CV of *effective* process time is inflated by equipment downtime and setups, rework and scrap, and a host of other factors. Interruptions that cause long but infrequent periods of downtime increase CV more than ones that cause short, frequent periods of downtime as long as the variability remains somewhat constant.

Variability Propagates

If the output of a workstation is highly variable, downstream workstations receiving products will also be highly variable.

Waiting Time Is Frequently the Largest Component of C/T

Two factors contribute to long waiting times: high utilization levels and high levels of variability. It follows then that increasing the effective capacity and decreasing variability will reduce cycle times.

Limiting Buffers Reduces C/T at the Cost of Decreasing Throughput (TP)

Because limiting inventory between workstations is the equivalent of implementing a pull system, it is the primary reason why variability reduction is so critical in JIT systems.

Variability Pooling Reduces the Effects of Variability

Pooling variability will dampen the effects of variability because it is less likely that a single occurrence will dominate performance. The inevitable conclusion is that variability degrades the performance of a manufacturing organization.

The Origin of Variability

Where does this variability come from? Before you attempt to identify and locate sources of variation, it is important to first understand the causes of variability. It is equally important to be able to quantify it, and you can do this by using standard measures from statistics to define variability classes. Hopp and Spearman report that there are three classes of P/T variability, as seen in Table 5.1.

When you think about P/T, you may have a tendency to consider only the actual time that the machine or operator spends on the job actually working (i.e.,

Table 5.1 Classes of Variability

Variability Class	Coefficient of Variation	Typical Situation
Low (LV)	$CV_t < 0.75$	Process times without outages (e.g., downtime)
Moderate (MV)	$0.75 \leq CV_t < 1.33$	Process times with short adjustments (e.g., setups)
High (HV)	$CV_t \geq 1.33$	Process times with long outages (e.g., failures)

not including failures or setups), and these times tend to be normally distributed. If, for example, the average process time were 20 minutes and the standard deviation were 6.3 minutes, $CV_t = 6.3 \div 20 = 0.315$ and would be considered a low variation (LV) process. Most LV processes follow a normal probability distribution. Suppose the mean P/T was 20 minutes, but the standard deviation was 30 minutes. The value for $CV_t = 30 \div 20 = 1.5$. This process would be considered highly variable.

You may be wondering why you care whether a process is LV, moderate variation (MV), or high variation (HV). Suppose, for example, that you have identified a constraint that is classed as an LV process with an average process time of 30 minutes and a standard deviation of 10 minutes. The calculated value of the coefficient of variation $CV_t = 10 \div 30 = 0.33$. Suppose that the nonconstraint operation feeding the constraint has an average P/T of one-half that of the constraint, 15, but its standard deviation was 30 minutes. The calculated value for $CV_t = 30 \div 15 = 2.0$ and is considered a HV process. A value of 2.0 from Table 5.2 suggests that this process probably has long failure outages, which could starve the constraint. When developing your plan of attack for reducing variation, using the coefficient of variation suggests that you include nonconstraint processes that feed the constraint operation if they are classified as HV.

Hopp and Spearman present five of the most prevalent sources of variation in manufacturing environments as they apply to P/T, as follows.

Natural Variability

Natural variability includes minor fluctuations in process time due to differences in operators, machines, and material and, in a sense, is a catch-all category, because it accounts for variability from sources that have not been explicitly called out (e.g., a piece of dust in the operator's eye). Because many of these unidentified sources of variability are operator related, there is typically more natural variability in a manual process than in an automated one. Even in a fully automated machining operation, the composition of the material might differ, causing processing speed to vary slightly. In most systems, natural P/Ts are low variability, so CV_t is less than 0.75.

Random Outages

Unscheduled downtime can greatly inflate both the mean and the coefficient of variation of process times. In fact, in many systems, this represents the single largest cause of variability. Hopp and Spearman refer to breakdowns as *preemptive outages* because they occur whether you want them to or not (e.g., they can occur right in the middle of a job). Power outages, operators being called away on emergencies, and running out of consumables are other possible sources of preemptive outages.

Hopp and Spearman refer to *nonpreemptive outages* as stoppages that occur between, rather than during, jobs and represent downtime that occurs but for which you have some control as to when. For example, when a tool begins to wear and needs to be replaced, you can wait until the current job is finished before you stop production. Other common examples of nonpreemptive outages include changeovers, PM, breaks, meetings, and shift changes. So how can you use this?

Suppose you are considering a decision of whether to replace a relatively fast machine requiring periodic setups with a slower, flexible machine that does not require setups. Suppose the fast machine can produce an average of 1 part/hour but requires a two-hour setup every 4 parts on average. The more flexible machine takes 1.5 hours to produce a part but requires no setup. The *effective capacity* (EC) of the fast machine is

$$EC = 4 \text{ parts} \div 6 \text{ hours} = 2/3 \text{ parts/hour}$$

The effective process time is simply the reciprocal of the effective capacity, or 1.5 hours. Thus, both machines have an effective capacity of 1.5 hours. Traditional capacity analysis would consider only mean capacity and might conclude that both machines are equivalent. Traditional capacity analysis would not recommend one over the other, but if you consider the impact on variability, the flexible machine, requiring no setup, would be my choice (and that of Hopp and Spearman). Replacing the faster machine with the more flexible machine would serve to reduce the process time CV, and therefore make the line more efficient. This, of course, assumes that both machines have equivalent natural variability.

Setups

This is the amount of time a job spends waiting for the station to be set up for production. Setups are like changeovers in that they contain internal and external activities. Internal activities are those that must be done while the equipment is shut down, while external activities can be completed while the equipment is still running. The key to reducing setup time is to turn as many internal activities into external activities, thus reducing waiting time.

Operator Availability

This is the amount of time a job spends waiting for an operator to be available to occupy the workstation and begin to produce product. The best way to reduce this type of time delay is to create a flexible workforce. Having to wait for a specialist operator is no longer acceptable. Companies today must cross-train operators so that if one is called away or is absent, another can step in and perform his or her tasks. This is especially critical in the constraint operation.

Recycle

Just like breakdowns and setups, rework is a major source of variability in manufacturing processes. If you think of the additional P/T spent "getting the job right" as an outage, it is easy to see that rework is completely analogous to setups because both rob the process of capacity and contribute greatly to the variability associated with P/T. Rework implies variability, which in turn causes more congestion, WIP, and cycle time.

Flow Variability

One of the keys to understanding the impact of variability is that variability at one station can affect the behavior of other stations in the process by means of another type of variability referred to as *flow variability*. Hopp and Spearman explain that flow refers to the transfer of jobs or parts from one station to another, and if an upstream workstation has highly variable process times, the flow it feeds to downstream workstations will also be highly variable. In other words, variability propagates.

The concepts of P/T variability and flow variability are important considerations as you attempt to characterize the effects of variability in production lines, but it is important to understand that the actual P/T (including setups, downtime, and so on) typically accounts for only about 5 to 10 percent of the total cycle time in a manufacturing plant (Hopp and Spearman). The vast majority of the extra time is spent waiting for various resources (e.g., workstations, transporting, storage, operators, incoming parts, materials and supplies). Hopp and Spearman refer to the science of waiting as *queuing theory*, or the theory of waiting in lines. Because jobs effectively "stand in lines" waiting to be processed, moved, and so on, it is important to understand and analyze why queuing exists in your process. Doesn't it make sense that if waiting accounts for the vast majority of time a product spends in the system, one of the keys to TH improvement is to identify and understand why waiting exists in your process?

A queuing system combines the impact of the arrival of parts from other processes and received parts from outside suppliers, the production of the parts, and the inventory or queue waiting to be processed. Hopp and Spearman go into depth on this subject, and I suggest you read their work, but the important thing to remember is this: because limiting interstation buffers is logically equivalent to installing a kanban, this property is a key reason that variability reduction via production smoothing, improved layout and flow control, total PM, and enhanced QA is critical to reducing variability.

Variability Pooling

In the previous section, I identified and discussed a number of causes of variability and how they might cause congestion in a manufacturing system. I said that one way to reduce this congestion is to reduce variability by addressing its causes. Hopp and Spearman point out that

> another, and more subtle, way to deal with congestion effects is by combining multiple sources of variability known as *variability pooling*. An every day example of this concept is in financial planning. Virtually all financial advisers recommend investing in a diversified portfolio of financial instruments. The reason, of course, is to hedge against risk. It is highly unlikely that a wide spectrum of investments will perform extremely poorly at the same time. At the same time, it is unlikely that they will perform extremely well at the same time. Hence, we expect less variable returns from a diversified portfolio than from a single asset.[34]

Hopp and Spearman go on to discuss how variability pooling affects batch processing, safety stock aggregation, and queue sharing, but the important point to take away is this: pooling variability tends to reduce the overall variability just like a diversified portfolio reduces the risk of up and down swings in your earnings. The implications are that safety stocks can be reduced (less holding costs), or that cycle times at multiple-machine process centers can be reduced by sharing a single queue.

Laws of Variability

There are two basic but fundamental laws of factory physics relevant to variability provided to us by Hopp and Spearman:

■ **Law of variability:** Increasing variability *always degrades* the performance of a production system. This is an extremely powerful concept, because it implies that variability in any form will harm some measure of performance. Consequently, variability reduction is central to improving performance.

■ **Law of variability buffering:** Variability in a production system will be *buffered* by some combination of inventory, capacity, and time. This law is an important extension of the variability law because it specifies the three ways in which variability impacts a manufacturing process and the choices you have in terms of buffering for it.

Primary Points, Conclusions, and Principles of Variability

The primary focus of these last few sections has been the effect of processing time variability (PTV) on the performance of production lines. The primary points, conclusions, or principles are provided, once again, by Hopp and Spearman:

■ **Variability always degrades performance.** As variability of any kind is increased, either inventory will increase or lead times will increase or TH will decrease, or a combination of the three. Because of the influence of variability, all improvement initiatives must include variability reduction. UIC includes steps that focus on variability reduction.

■ **Variability buffering is a fact of manufacturing life.** If you cannot reduce variability, you must buffer it or you will experience protracted cycle times, increased levels of inventory, wasted capacity, diminished TH, and longer lead times, all of which will result in declining revenues and customer service.

■ **Flexible buffers are more effective than fixed buffers.** Having capacity, inventory, or time available as buffering devices permits the flexible combination of the three to reduce the total amount of buffering needed in a given system. Examples of each type of buffer are included in Table 5.2.

■ **Material is conserved.** Whatever flows into a workstation must flow out as either acceptable product, rework, or scrap.

Table 5.2   Flexible Buffer Types

Flexible Buffer Type	Buffer Example
Flexible capacity	Cross-trained workforce—by floating to operations that need the capacity, flexible workers can cover the same workload with less total capacity than would be required if workers were fixed to specific tasks.
Flexible inventory	Generic WIP held in a system with late product customization.
Flexible time	The practice of quoting variable lead times to customers depending upon the current backlog of work (i.e., the larger the backlog, the longer the quote). A given level of customer service can be achieved with shorter average lead time if variable lead times are quoted individually to customers instead of a uniform fixed lead time quoted in advance.

■ **Releases are always less than capacity in the long run.** Although the intent may be to run a process at 100 percent of capacity, when true capacity, including overtime, outsourcing, and so on, is considered, this really will never occur. It is always better to plan to reduce release rates before the system "blows up" simply because they will have to be reduced as a result of the system's blowing up, anyway.

■ **Variability early in a line is more disruptive than variability late in a line.** Higher front-end process variability of a line using a push system will propagate downstream and cause queuing later on in the process. By contrast, stations with high process variability toward the end of the process will affect only those stations.

■ **Cycle time increases nonlinearity in utilization.** As utilization approaches 100 percent, long-term WIP and cycle time will approach infinity.

■ **Process batch sizes affect capacity.** Increasing batch sizes increases capacity and thereby reduces queuing, while increasing batch size also increases wait-to-batch and wait-in-batch times. Because of this, the first focus in serial batching situations should be on setup time reduction, enabling the use of small, efficient batch sizes. If setup times cannot be reduced, cycle time may well be minimized at a batch size greater than one. In addition, the most efficient batch size in a parallel process may be between one and the maximum number that will fit into the process.

■ **Cycle times increase proportionally with transfer batch size.** Because waiting to batch and unbatch is typically one of the largest sources of cycle time length, reducing transfer batch sizes is one of the simplest and easiest ways to reduce cycle times.

■ **Matching can be an important source of delay in assembly systems.** Lack of synchronization, caused by variability, poor scheduling, or poor shop floor control, will always cause significant buildup of WIP, resulting in component assembly delays.

Defect Identification

At this point, I would like to turn your attention to the subject of identifying defects within your process. My advice to you is to analyze the defect data; develop a Pareto chart of the defects, prioritizing them based upon which is having the most detrimental effect on the output rate of the constraint operation (or downstream operations); and decide how you are going to attack them. Once you have resolved the highest-priority defect, move to the next one, and so forth. You cannot simultaneously attack all defects, and you cannot afford to have your available resources working on problems that are not going to give you payback in the constraint operation. If you want to start a fire with a magnifying glass, you have to be able to *focus* the rays of the sun in one location. So too with improving the output of the constraint operation. It is really all about being able to focus.

Chapter 6

Exploiting the Current Constraint

When Goldratt introduced the world to TOC, he did so by laying out his five focusing steps. His second of five steps was to decide how to exploit the constraint. In other words, develop a plan on how to wring the maximum efficiency out of the constraint, the way it exists now. If the constraint is a piece of equipment, this means to eliminate all forms of downtime. Downtime includes time spent waiting for product to be processed, quality problems, equipment failures, flow problems, and so on. If the constraint is related to a specific work method, this means eliminating or reducing nonproductive or non-value-added time in the constraint work method. Nonproductive time is any activity that impedes TH through the constraint, such as unnecessary travel time or unnecessary steps in the process that, if removed, would translate into more or faster TH.

Because the pace of the constraint determines the pace of the entire manufacturing operation, exploiting the constraint means that every operation produces at the pace of the constraint. This is such an important point to remember as you develop your plan for exploiting the constraint. Thus, one of the first things you need to do is develop a production schedule that is completely tied to and subordinated to the pace of the constraint. Once this schedule is in place, it follows then that the first question you need to ask is: How well are you meeting the constraint schedule? Remember, each time you miss this schedule, you miss an opportunity to "make more money" that can never be recovered. Likewise, when you miss your constraint schedule, you risk missing a shipping schedule. If you are producing and delivering product to your schedule, everything is working as it should. If you are not meeting the constraint's schedule, you must determine the reason(s) why and correct it.

Waste Reduction

In step 1b, you looked for various forms of waste using time studies and spaghetti diagrams to identify how many unnecessary trips the operator has to make away from the process to find things like tools, supplies, parts to process, and so on. You then assigned times and distances that each trip took and calculated what impact eliminating or reducing these trips would have on the TH through the constraint operation. Logically, you concluded that if the parts, tools, and supplies were closer to the operator, or were contained within the constraint operation, a significant amount of this wasted time could be eliminated. Therefore, one of the first steps in your plan should be to perform a rapid 5S event on the constraint operation. The end result of your 5S initiative, which I will discuss in the next section, is to only have what is absolutely necessary for completion of the operation, and to have it organized in such a way that whatever is needed is available where and when it is needed.

Because one of the basic premises of TOC is that you can never let a constraint be idle, you need to be creative in your approach. Although the 5S will certainly provide you with a much more organized work space, you must also plan how you will eliminate unnecessary trips for things like supplies and parts. One of the best ways to do this might be to exploit the nonconstraint operator's "free time" to make those trips for the constraint operator.

A Waste Example

For example, during a study of an operation that produced flexible fuel tanks, one of the steps was to apply a specific type of adhesive to the part being fabricated. The adhesive in question had to be mixed just prior to use because it had a very short shelf life. The distance the constraint operator had to travel away from the constraint operation to retrieve the adhesive was several hundred feet, and the round-trip time was approximately six minutes. Because we did not want to add additional labor just to secure the adhesive, we met with the nonconstraint operators and developed a system that would permit the nonconstraint operators to get the adhesive for the constraint operator during their free time.

The question became: How would the nonconstraint operators know when the constraint operator actually needed the adhesive? The operators met and were able to develop a multicolored flag system, with each of five different colored flags dictating different needs. In this case, a yellow flag was used to signify something in need at the constraint operation. The actual procedure called for the constraint operator to write on the yellow flag his or her need at least thirty minutes in advance of the time it was needed. As one of the five nonconstraint operators saw the flag being posted, he or she would stop what he or she was doing, travel to the adhesive mixing operation, mix it, and then deliver it to the constraint operator before it was needed. Because the constraint operator typically needed this adhesive a minimum of five times per shift, we were able to reduce the non-value-added time in the constraint operation by an average of thirty minutes per day just for adhesive needs without adding any additional labor.

We also noticed during our study of the constraint operation that the constraint operator had been waiting up to several hours for a QA inspector to become available to inspect the completed tank. The operators developed a red-and-white-striped flag that meant that within the next thirty minutes, the tank at the constraint operation would be ready for inspection. We also met with the QA supervisor to develop a priority system whereby QA inspections in the constraint operation took priority over any nonconstraint operation. When the QA inspector (or anyone else) noticed the red-and-white-striped flag, he or she knew that within thirty minutes he or she must be available to inspect the tank within the constraint operation. This seemed to work well, but the system still needed to be refined because the QA inspector was not always in the immediate area to see the flag. To counteract this, the operation's supervisor met with the QA inspector at the beginning of each shift to lay out approximate times that QA inspections would be required in the constraint operations. In addition, the supervisor created an inspection board that indicated approximate times QA inspections would be needed. These two actions reduced the wait time, on average, by about two hours per day, again without adding any additional labor.

The important point here is that when you are developing the waste reduction portion of your exploitation plan, you must use your imagination and, whenever possible, utilize visual systems that automatically notify all parties of impending needs. The other point to keep in mind is to involve everyone in your solutions. The mere fact that we used the operators to develop the visual flag system improved its chances for success, because the nonconstraint operators "owned" the system and would take extreme measures to make it work. In this way, just by involving the constraint and nonconstraint operators, we were able to reduce non-value-added time in the constraint operation by a full two and a half hours at no additional cost to the company.

One final point regarding the involvement of all operators: It is important that you take time to explain the important difference between constraint and nonconstraint operations. That is, the operators must have a clear understanding of why reducing waste in the constraint operation is so critical to the long-term success of their operation. Be open and honest about what happens to revenue and the corresponding profits of the company. In doing so, you will find that the operators will willingly participate and actually make it work.

Implementing 5S Workplace Organization (WPO)

One of the keys to reducing waste in your process is to organize it. 5S is a tool specifically designed to help establish effective organization of tools and equipment so that time is not wasted looking for things needed to produce product and that wasted motion is reduced. The term *5S* is a reference to a list of five Japanese words that start with the letter *S*. Those five Japanese words, plus their translation and meaning, are as follows:

- *Seiri* (sort): Refers to the practice of going through all the tools, equipment, supplies, and materials, and then assigning each one to a specific location close to the point of use.
- *Seiton* (straighten): Refers to the practice of arranging the tools, equipment, and materials according to an order that promotes work flow through unnecessary movement or motion.
- *Seison* (shine): Refers to the practice of keeping the workplace neat and clean on a daily basis.
- *Seiketsu* (standardize): Refers to operating in a consistent and standardized way so that everyone understands what his or her responsibilities are.
- *Shitsuke* (sustain): Refers to maintaining the standards completed in the previous four Ss and to not permit any backsliding.

Davis has developed his own version of 5S, which he refers to as his 6Cs. Davis believes that "there is an important step not included in 5S,"[35] as follows:

- Step 1: Clear (level I)
- Step 2: Confine (level II)
- Step 3: Control (level III)
- Step 4: Clean (level IV)
- Step 5: Communicate (level V)
- Step 6: Continue (level VI)

Davis also tells us, "Whereas 5S tends to be used as a group of things to do, with no special order as to which is prescribed first, second or third other than what might be assumed, the steps and levels noted are an extremely important factor in applying the 6Cs." Davis explains that "unlike 5S, the scoring approach is absolutely critical for determining the effectiveness of each of the of 6Cs steps.... For any plant or operation that has not gone through the process of putting true WPO in place, the initial 6C score will always be zero."[36] Davis says this because he believes that WPO is truly the foundation for continuously improving an operation, and that it is a step-by-step effort, rather than a one-time event. In other words, you do not start level II (confine) until you have completed level I (clear). I absolutely agree with Davis in that I have seen many 5S initiatives fall short of achieving WPO simply because the effort was seen as a one-time event, and clearly it is not.

Davis further explains why he is so adamant that WPO is the foundation for continuous improvement:

- Without WPO, you can exert wasted efforts in dealing with things that are not absolutely needed, thus expending time and energy that could be applied elsewhere.
- Until an area is rid of things not absolutely required, it is impossible to see the real workplace.
- Time wasted trying to find things on the shop floor distracts from productivity.
- A tidy and orderly work area provides the appearance of efficiency, which can have a positive influence on the perception of the organization by customers who visit the plant and on the attitude of employees.
- Applying WPO in an area of the factory where it has not existed before provides a stark contrast to the way things are run in the rest of the factory, thus visualizing the level of change under way.

Whether you are applying 5S or 6C, you will be doing so in the constraint operation, and you will see improvements in both constraint efficiency and TH just by organizing your workplace.

Drum-Buffer-Rope (DBR) Scheduling

In a TOC environment production planning and scheduling is done with a tool known as the DBR. The DBR is designed to regulate the flow of WIP through a production line based upon the pace of the slowest resource, the constraint operation. In order to optimize the flow of product through the factory, material is released according to the capacity of the constraining operation, or capacity constrained resource (CCR). The production rate of the CCR is equated to the rhythm of a *drum*. The *rope* is the communication mechanism that connects the CCR to the material release for the first operation in order to make certain that raw material is released in time to guarantee that the constraint always has material to work on. Thus, the first purpose of the rope is to ensure that the CCR is never starved and not inundated with excess WIP inventory. Because of the existence of statistical fluctuations and disruptions in the upstream operations, a *buffer* is established to protect the CCR from being starved. By the same token, the rope ensures that material is not introduced into the production process more quickly than the CCR can consume it. Thus, DBR has three purposes: protect the CCR from starvation, ensure that excess material is not released into the system, and protect the delivery due dates to the customer.

The Three Elements of DBR

There are three main elements of DBR:

- A shipping schedule, which is based upon the rate that the constraint can produce parts. That is, use the TH of the constraint for promised due dates.
- A constraint schedule, which is tied to the shipping schedule.
- A material release schedule, which is tied to the constraint schedule.

Visually, these three elements might look like Figure 6.1. Here, we see the three elements of the DBR system and the interconnectedness of each. The drum sets the pace of the production line, and its capacity is hopefully greater than the number of orders in the system. In order to satisfy the shipping schedule, you must first fulfill the constraint schedule. In order to meet the constraint schedule, you must satisfy the material release schedule. Failure to release materials per the schedule will jeopardize the constraint schedule, which will in turn jeopardize your shipping schedule. Because of this linkage of schedules, managing the buffers becomes critical.

In Figure 6.1, I have displayed three buffers, the *constraint buffer, assembly buffer*, and *shipping buffer*. These buffers are composed of two different dimensions, space and time. Now what do I mean by that? Because you do not want to have excess inventory in your process, the buffers contain some physical inventory (i.e., space) and a liberal estimation of lead time (i.e., time) from various points within your total process. In the case of the constraint buffer, you place an amount of physical inventory in front of the constraint and establish a time buffer based upon the lead time from raw material release to the constraint operation. Likewise, the assembly buffer contains some amount of material and a time buffer based upon the lead time from the constraint operation to the assembly operation. The shipping buffer contains some amount of WIP and a time buffer based upon the lead time from either the constraint operation or assembly operation (if assembly is required) to completion into finished product. So how much is "some amount of material?"

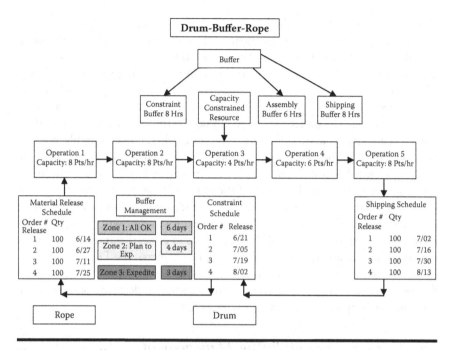

Figure 6.1 Buffer Management System.

To size the buffer correctly, the arrival of parts to the buffer must be monitored and compared to the scheduled arrival time. By monitoring the buffer, you are essentially sending a signal to the plant as to when you need to expedite parts. You will notice a section of Figure 6.1 labeled "Buffer Management." When parts do not arrive into the buffer per the schedule, it in essence creates what is referred to as a hole in the buffer. If you divide the buffer into three zones, you will be able to successfully manage the buffer. The first zone (the medium grayscale zone) means that everything is going according to the scheduled arrival date, so holes in the green zone are no cause for concern. The second zone (the light grayscale zone) tells you that the parts are not arriving to schedule and that it is time to locate the missing parts and create an expediting plan in the event the parts need to be expedited. The third zone (the darkest grayscale zone) means that the parts will not be arriving into the buffer on schedule and that the jobs need to be expedited. Managing the constraint buffer focuses attention on late arrivals to the constraint and tells you when you need to expedite and when not to expedite.

How much physical inventory is a function of how stable or consistent your process is in producing product. That is, if you are never creating holes in your green zone, your buffer is probably too high. By contrast, if you are constantly penetrating your red zone, the buffer is clearly too low. If you have oversized your buffer, you are needlessly increasing OEs and cycle time while at the same time decreasing inventory turns and cash flow. If you have undersized your buffer, you run the risk of starving your constraint and losing valuable TH. My advice to you is to err on the side of conservatism because losing valuable TH is much more damaging to your plant than increasing OEs or reducing cash flow.

How much of the buffer should be physical parts and how much should be time depends upon the variability of your process. If you have a highly variable operation feeding the constraint, or one that has many disruptions, most of your buffer will be in the form of physical materials. If your feeder operation contains very little variability, most of the buffer will be in the form of time. As you improve your process (i.e., reduce waste and variation) and render it more consistent and stable, the ratio of physical inventory to time will change accordingly. Remember, the purpose of these buffers is to protect your constraint from starvation and ensure delivery of product to customers. The DBR system is a finite scheduling method that attempts to balance and control the optimum flow of materials through a plant in accordance with the demands of the market while minimizing lead time, inventory, and OEs.

Improvement through Buffer Management

In addition to protecting the constraint from starvation and inundating the process with excess inventory, buffer management accomplishes another critical aspect of the UIC. Buffer management provides you with a vehicle to systematically identify and quantify potential improvement opportunities in key nonconstraint operations. Focusing improvements on the sources or causes of buffer holes provides you with the opportunity to improve TH and reduce both cycle times and inventory. If you are continuously finding holes in zone 3 (red zone), you know that there are problems in one or more of the upstream processes. If you know this, your improvement actions need to be focused on the operation creating the holes. As you continue to improve your process, the holes in your buffer will eventually disappear and provide you with the opportunity to safely reduce the size of your buffers and consistently improve TH, reduce cycle times, and reduce inventory.

As you analyze and prioritize the causes of the holes in your buffer, another important nuance occurs. You are able to form a picture of protective capacity throughout your process. This is important for several reasons:

■ The nonconstraint that has the least protective capacity will have the highest probability of becoming the next constraint when you break the current constraint. This will allow you to compare the "next constraint" that you identified in step 1a of the UIC to what the latest information is telling you. If they match, you continue with your current plan. If they do not match, you might have to make changes to your plan.

■ This picture provides you with a way of estimating how much of the nonconstraint capacity can be sold in a targeted market of the nonconstraint products, if they are in a form that can be sold. However, you are able to exploit this market only if doing so will not jeopardize the constraint buffer and the constraint TH.

■ You are able to focus in on and prioritize improvement efforts in the right nonconstraints.

Implementing Visual Controls

A *visual control* is any communication method or device that is used to tell you at a glance how work should be done and what its status is. In everyday life a common example of a visual control is a traffic light. You know intuitively that green means it is safe to proceed, yellow means that you can continue with caution, and red means it is not safe to proceed. Effective visual controls help employees see immediately things like the status of WIP, the location and quantity of different items, and what the standard procedure for performing a job is. The primary reason for using visual controls is to define the desired state (i.e., the standard), and then to quickly recognize any deviation from that standard.

One common example of a visual control in manufacturing is andon lights that are used to visualize the status of WIP. Like traffic lights, andon lights typically utilize the color green to indicate no problems, yellow to indicate potential problems, and red to indicate a serious problem that is preventing the operation from producing product. Andon lights permit the easy identification of the status of an operation even from an area not close to the operation. The flag system I discussed in a previous section is basically a manual version of the andon light concept.

Other common examples of visual controls are the use of shadow boards to show the location of each tool required in a particular operation, having clearly visible indicators of minimum and maximum levels for inventory, process control boards with well-designed performance charts and graphs located within a work cell, kanban cards or bins to control the flow of materials in a pull system, and even outlines on the floor to designate where items should be placed.

Toyota uses visual control so that no problems are hidden. Even in a world that is dominated by electronic data, if you walk into a Toyota facility, you will see things like paper kanban cards circulating through the factory, paper flip charts being used for ad hoc problem solving, and manual paper charts and graphs that are updated manually by the operators in the work cell. Toyota believes that people are visual creatures who need to be able to look at their work, their parts, and their product flow, just to make sure they are performing to Toyota's standards. The key to creating effective visual controls is to use your imagination and consider the visual needs of the people who will be using them.

Designing and Implementing Work Cells

In many companies that I have visited over the years, it is not uncommon for products to travel great distances from machine to machine because of the equipment layout scheme. In one particular company located in France that produced pinions for things like turn-signal levers, the distance traveled was actually measured in miles. And this did not include the distance traveled to send parts outside the company for heat treatment. Why so much travel distance?

The distance problem was manifested in the individual pieces of equipment used to produce the pinions (that is, all the turning, drilling, hobbing, grinding, reaming, washing, and crack detection machines) being set up as functional islands located throughout three different factories. (Functional islands are like machines that are used for the same function that are all placed near each other in the same area of the plant.) Because of the location of the equipment, it was not uncommon for the parts to travel back and forth between the factories as they made their way through the process sequence. This company also produced their parts in relatively large batches and did not transfer the parts to the next operation until the containers used to transport them were full.

The deleterious effects of this protracted distance traveled and large batch sizes were prolonged cycle times that were proportional to both the distance traveled and the size of the transfer batch. These long-drawn-out distances and inflated times translated directly into routine delays throughout the process, with the ultimate consequence being late deliveries and missed shipment to customers. To make matters worse, when quality problems were eventually detected, it was not uncommon for very large numbers of defective pinions to be found, requiring massive sorting and reinspection of the parts.

The functional island concept for locating equipment was developed as part of the mass production mindset that still plagues many companies today. The idea behind large batch sizes was the incorrect assumption that it was economically better to build as many parts as possible so as to avoid perceived costly setups. But thanks to Little's law and Ford's EOQ model (both to be discussed later in this chapter), you will see that large batch production can be a recipe for failure, and you know that there are better ways to run a business, namely, one-piece flow or at least optimized batch sizes.

Cellular Manufacturing 101

Cellular manufacturing and work cells lie at the heart of Lean manufacturing, with the general benefits being things like simplified flow, cycle time reductions, improved quality, improved intraprocess communication, and so on. In cellular manufacturing, equipment and workstations are arranged near each other in the normal process sequence. Once processing begins, products move directly from workstation to workstation, with the result typically being significant improvements in overall cycle times and vastly improved teamwork and quality. This arrangement of workstations supports a smooth flow of products and components through the process with minimal transport and delays. In addition, arranging the equipment into manufacturing cells makes it much easier to reduce the transfer batch size.

A manufacturing cell is composed of the people, equipment, and workstations, arranged in the logical sequence required to produce the end product. The positive effects of cellular manufacturing, if done correctly, include smaller batch sizes, one-piece flow, flexible production, reduced travel time for parts, less equivalent manpower, improved quality, less damaged product, less required space, less obsolescence, immediate identification of problems, reduced walking time, and less lead time, all of which can translate to decreased cycle time, increased TH, and reduced inventory and OE.

Achieving One-Piece Flow

One-piece flow is one of the positive benefits of cellular manufacturing. In a one-piece flow production environment, parts are moved immediately to the next operation for processing, making it arguably the most efficient way to process material through a factory. When done in conjunction with the establishment of work cells, one-piece flow works very well. Imagine what happens to the lead time of products being produced in work cells with one-piece flow, providing you have calculated the correct critical WIP.

I recognize that some equipment is simply too large and bulky to be moved into and included in a cell, but even with this scenario there is a solution. If the equipment is too large and difficult to move, build the work cell around this limiting piece of equipment. Large screw machines or stamping presses, for example, might not be possible to move, but do not let that stop you. Either arrange the equipment around these machines or arrange the equipment that can be moved into a cellular arrangement. In the French company I mentioned earlier, we faced the situation just described. We simply left the large screw machines where they were and arranged the remainder of the equipment (drilling, hobbing, grinding, reaming, washing, and crack detection machines) into functional cells, and the result was significantly reduced space, less cycle time, increased TH, improved quality, reduced inventory, and much improved on-time delivery. In fact, the on-time delivery improved from approximately 70 percent to more than 90 percent, while PPMs decreased from more than 20,000 to about 200 in a little more than three months.

The Effect on Variation

There is one other positive effect that typically results from cellular manufacturing that theoretically has a positive impact on variation. When multiple machines performing the same function are used to produce identical products, there are potentially multiple paths that parts can take from beginning to end. There are therefore multiple paths of variation. These multiple paths of variation can significantly increase the overall variability of the process.

Even with reductions in variation, real improvement might not be realized because of the number of paths of variation that exist within a process. Paths of variation are simply the number of opportunities for variation to occur within a process. The paths of variation of a process are increased by the number of individual process steps or the complexity of the steps (i.e., number of subprocesses within a process).

The answer to reducing the effects of paths of variation lies in the process and product design stage of manufacturing processes. That is, processes must be designed with reduced complexity, and products should be designed that are more robust. The payback for reducing the number of paths of variation is an overall reduction in the amount of process variation and, ultimately, more consistent and robust products.

The French pinion company that I mentioned earlier is a classic example of multiple paths of variation. You will recall that this company was being run according to a mass production mindset. Figure 6.2 shows the initial layout of the process from beginning to end after receiving metal blanks from the supplier. The first step is referred to as exterior turning, with two turning machines available to perform this function (labeled A1 and A2 in Figure 6.2). The next step in the process is referred to as interior turning, and again, there are two interior turning machines, labeled B1 and B2. In the third step there were two possible choices for drilling, C1 and C2. After the pinion was automatically inspected for cracks, it then progressed to one of two hobbing machines, D1 and D2. The parts were then collected in bins and sent as large batches to an outside vendor for heat treatment. Upon return from heat treatment, the pinions then proceeded to hard hobbing, E1 and E2, and then on through the remainder of the process, as indicated in Figure 6.2.

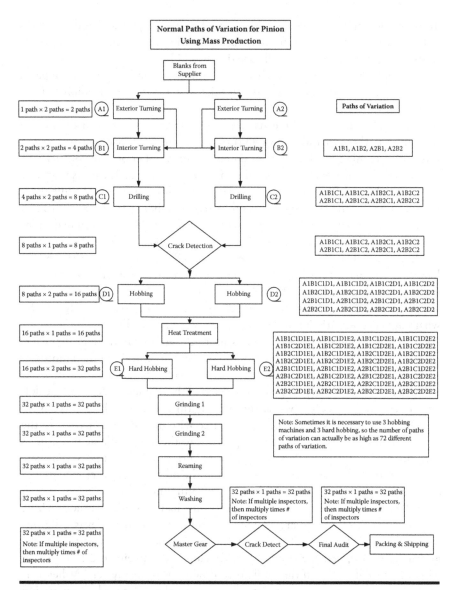

Figure 6.2   Initial Paths of Variations.

The arrows in Figure 6.2 represent the possible paths that the pinion could take as it makes its way through the process. For example, for the first two process steps, there are four possible paths: A1B1, A1B2, A2B1, and A2B2. In Figure 6.2 the possible paths of variation are listed to the right, and as you can see, as the part continues on, the possible paths continue on until all thirty-two are seen. Do you think that the pinions produced through these multiple paths will be the same? If we were able to reduce the paths of variation from thirty-two to two, do you believe the overall variation would be less?

In Figure 6.3, we created a virtual cell, meaning that we limited the paths of travel that an individual pinion can take by removing the possibility for a part to traverse multiple paths. In Figure 6.3, you can see that pinions that pass through turning machine A1 are only permitted to proceed to turning machine B1. Those that pass through turning machine A2 are only permitted to proceed to turning machine B2. In doing so, the number of paths of variation for the first two process steps was reduced from four to two. The parts that were turned on A1 and B1 can only pass through hobbing machine E1, while those produced on A2 and B2 can only be processed on hobbing machine E2. To this point, the total paths of variation remain at two instead of the original number of paths, sixteen. The part continues to hard hobbing, where there are two machines available. The parts produced on A1B1E1 can only proceed to the G1 hard hobbing machine, while those produced on A2B2E2 can only be processed on hard hobbing machine G2. At this point, because of specifying and limiting the paths, the total paths of variation decreased from thirty-two to only two. So what happened to variation when we created our virtual cell?

The key response variables for this process were five individual diameters measured along the surface of the pinion. As a result of limiting the number of potential paths of variation, the standard deviation for the various diameters was reduced by approximately 50 percent on each of the diameters. Not a single dollar—or should I say euro—was spent in doing this, yet the payback was huge.

Of course, there were problems associated with making this change. In the original configuration pinions could proceed to the next available machine as they proceeded along the flow of the process. Prior to this change, when there was downtime, the operator simply diverted the pinion to another machine so as to keep the parts moving. With the new configuration, when a machine in the cell went down unexpectedly, the parts now had to wait until the machine was repaired. The immediate short-term result of this change was a significant reduction in output of pinions because of unplanned downtime. In the longer term, it forced the company to develop and implement a PM system, which eventually reduced the unplanned downtime to nearly zero. When this happened, the new output surpassed the original output and the variation was reduced by 50 percent. In addition, the scrap levels for this process were reduced by 40 percent.

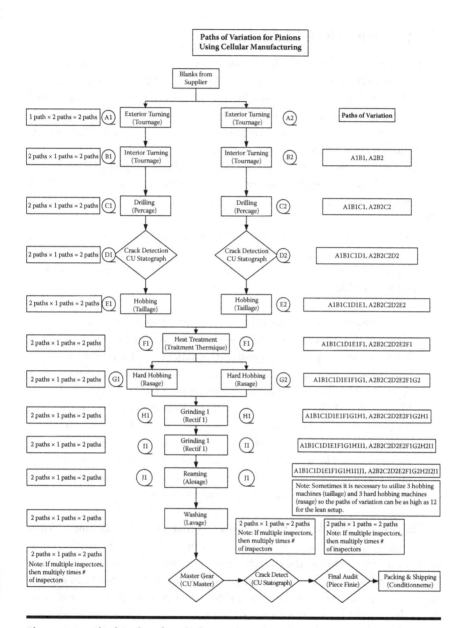

Figure 6.3   Final Paths of Variation.

Changeover Time Reduction

Many companies still produce their products in large lots simply to avoid changing over equipment from one product to another. The belief of these companies is that by running large runs of products or batches, the total costs associated with frequent changeovers will be minimized. Because of this mistaken notion, these companies are saddled with large amounts of inventory with high storage and handling costs, delays in filling customer orders due to long lead times, and even unidentified quality problems that result in either scrapping or reworking the parts. All these problems exist just to avoid changeovers. There is an optimal batch size, but what about changeovers and setups? How do you reduce the time of these?

Many companies have attempted changeover and setup time reduction, but the premise on which setup time reduction is based is often misunderstood or not accepted. As Charles Standard once explained to me (and subsequently included in a book):

> The primary reason for reducing set-up time is to reduce the variability in P/T. Once set-up time has been shortened, reducing lot size is an excellent way to further reduce this variability. It is no surprise that reducing lot size requires a reduction in set-up time to maintain the same TH. This is especially true when production resources are highly utilized. So we can all agree that quick set-up enables small lot production.... Short set-up times make today's factories more competitive, both in terms of cost and responsiveness to customer requirements. However, the most significant advantage of quick set-up is that it enables small lot production, which leads to a significant improvement in total production system efficiency.[37]

The perceived problem with changeovers is that while the machine is down for changeover, no product is being produced. In typical mass production companies, the length of time the equipment remains down is more often than not measured in hours, so production losses could be substantial. In a Lean organization, changeovers are characteristically measured in minutes. So why is there such a disparity? I believe it is a mindset issue.

The actual work involved with a changeover can be divided into two distinct categories of work activities: internal and external. Internal setup work includes all the work that must be done while the machine is shut down, while external work includes all the work that can be done while the machine is still running. In a typical mass production company, the mindset is one of shutting the machine down and then beginning the changeover. In a Lean production company, this simply is not the case.

Performing a Setup Analysis

In a Lean manufacturing company, the most important element of changeovers and setup time reduction is a setup analysis. In this analysis, changeover work is first separated into external and internal in advance of the changeover. The external work includes things like staging of all materials, components, and tools needed to perform the changeover in advance. By completing these obvious things in advance of the changeover, it is not uncommon to see changeover reductions on the order of 50 percent. Notice that no money is expended; only the timing of the events has changed and nothing more.

Converting Internal Setup to External Activities

The next step in the setup analysis involves further reducing setup times by converting some of the current internal setup activities to external activities. So how do you do this? First, look at the true function or purpose of each step in your current setup procedure and imagine that you are seeing it for the first time. In other words, look at it with an open mind and ask yourself how it might be done while the equipment is still running. After you have scrutinized your current method with an open mind, try different ways to convert internal activities to external activities. One example from a stamping press might be coming up with ways to center the stamping die before you install it. Maybe you will be able to develop a centering jig or something along these lines. If the die must be heated, try ways to bring it to temperature prior to installing it, thus reducing wait times for heating the die. Just use your imagination and try different things. I always recommend performing this exercise with a team of people, just because one new idea might stimulate another new idea from another member of the team.

Creating a Standardized Work Method

The next step of the changeover reduction process is to create a standardized work method that summarizes the step-by-step procedure of how to changeover your equipment. Document everything you do and, where appropriate, include pictures to reinforce the method.

One problem often associated with changeovers is the time it takes to produce an acceptable part once the changeover is completed and the process is restarted. Often this problem can be overcome by simply recording a history of process settings and parameters when the equipment is running, and then preset the equipment with these same settings. I have witnessed many changeovers where the time it takes to produce acceptable parts has been significantly reduced just by knowing what settings to start with instead of reacting to the process when it makes a bad part, making adjustments, making another bad part, and making more adjustments. This overadjustment process usually takes you farther away from where you need to be and results in needless defective product. As I said, many times this can be avoided by keeping historical records of key process parameters like temperatures, pressures, and so on. In a typical mass production changeover it is not uncommon to have this step in the process (i.e., trial runs and adjustments) consume as much as 50 percent of the total setup time.

Improving Continuously

The final step in improving setup or changeover times is one of continuous improvement. That is, never stop looking for better ways to streamline your changeover process. In Japan there are actually nationwide changeover competitions where companies compete against each other, and the results have been amazing. In large stamping presses, for example, what used to take hours to complete now takes less than five minutes. I read somewhere that one team actually converted a stamping press in fifty-two seconds.

Practice Makes Perfect

One of the keys to reducing changeover and setup time is to practice. Just like perfecting a great golf swing, it is all about executing flawlessly, and the only way to do this is by defining and documenting what must be done and then practicing over and over. As improvements are made to your changeover procedure, make certain that your visual changeover procedure is updated, and then take the time to train your employees on this new method.

Variation Reduction

In step 1c of UIC, I told you that you must identify all sources of variation that impact the constraint. Please keep in mind when I speak about variation that I am referring to both PPV and PTV. One of the key points is the negative impact of statistical fluctuations and interruptions on the flow of products. Variation takes away your ability to effectively plan and execute. Just imagine how things might work if there were zero variation in your process. Imagine how much simpler life would be if every product you produced were identical and every machine ran 100 percent of the time. But reality tells us that no two things are ever identical and that you will experience PTV due to a host of sources. Knowing this, how do you address or measure variation and limit its effects on the process? In other words, how do you get control of your process, and then keep it in control?

The most effective tool available for accomplishing this is the process control chart. The control chart provides you with a summary of past and present process status and then allows you to project into and predict the future of your process if it is in control. PPV reduction starts first with the identification of the CTQs of products and P/T within the constraint operation. You really cannot afford any more variation in the constraint operation than is absolutely necessary, and by using the control chart effectively, you should be able to systematically identify and eliminate all special cause variation and significantly reduce common cause variation. At the same time, the use of error-proofing devices has a significant impact on eliminating variation. So how do you use control charts to do this?

Effectively Utilizing Control Charts

Control charts serve several extremely valuable purposes as you strive to reduce the variability in your constraint operation. First and foremost, control charts provide you with the current status of your processes in terms of location and variability. Location is the average value of what you are producing relative to what you expect it to be, while variability is how much dispersion you see from part to part. Processes that are in a state of statistical control demonstrate variation that is random and predictable and permit you to plan effectively for the future. For this reason, it is imperative that you make improvements to your constraint process to get to this state. Keep in mind that I am not talking only about measurable product characteristics. I am also talking about PTV.

Control charts also tell you what type of variation is present in your processes. This is extremely important because the actions needed to remove special cause variation are vastly different than if you were attempting to reduce common cause variation. It is this presence of special cause variation that renders your processes unpredictable. Thus, if you want to improve your processes, you must first remove all special cause variation. Once you do so, your processes will be in a state of statistical control and therefore predictable. Once this state has been achieved, you will be able to calculate control limits.

These control limits, which are statistical in nature, are the limits of where your process normally operates and are based upon the variation you see in your process. In fact, the control limits are set at ±3 σ on either side of your process average. It should be apparent to you that your process center should be at or near the center of the specification for products and that your control limits must be less than your specification limits. If either of these is not the case, you have work to do.

As improvements are made to the process, the amount of variation is reduced. As variation is reduced, it permits you to calculate tighter and tighter control limits, which translate directly into a better-quality product with fewer defects and tighter and tighter P/Ts. Both of these improve your ability to effectively plan production. This, then, is the essence of how to utilize control charts. As the variation becomes smaller and smaller, resulting in tighter and tighter control limits, the products produced and the time required to make them demonstrate less and less variation. With smaller amounts of variation, you typically see fewer defects, resulting in less rework and scrap and an increase in TH.

Control charts are built around specific product characteristics and process parameters that require monitoring to ensure the overall quality of the product is achieved. The most effective way of using these tools is to continually drive the sample ranges lower and lower, which in turn reduces the control limits for averages of these samples. Your objective in using control charts is to keep the process average as close to the center of the specifications for products as possible with as little variation as possible. By achieving this objective, the result will always be product that exhibits better and better quality and TH that is more and more predictable. In other words, as you reduce process and product variation, you improve the capability of your processes. For P/Ts, you will use the control chart the same way. That is, you will be constantly trying to tighten the control limits by removing variation in the P/Ts.

Using Designed Experiments to Reduce Variation

Another tool that can be used to identify and reduce variation is DOE. Although control charts are static in nature in that they wait for changes in the process to occur and then measure their effect on variation, DOEs force controlled change and measure the effect. In a DOE, the response variable is measured as a function of ever-changing process factors, with the response variable, in this application, being variation, usually in the form of either the range or the standard deviation.

DOEs use statistically designed matrices (i.e., design arrays) that include the numerous factors, which could affect variation and identify various run conditions to isolate the effects of each factor. As each run condition is implemented under controlled conditions, the variation of the response variable is measured. You then use statistical analysis tools like analysis of variance (ANOVA) to determine which of the many factors tested in our screening test design significantly impact variation. In essence, you separate the vital few from the trivial many as they apply to variation. After you have identified which of the study factors significantly impact variation, you then run a confirmatory study to validate the findings from our screening study. As a final step, you then run an optimization study to determine the optimum process setting for each significant factor that results in the least amount of variation. These few significant factors are the ones on which you focus your attention, through the use of control charts.

Defect Reduction

In addition to reducing variation, you are interested in reducing defects within our constraint operation that limit TH. You have several options available to you, and in both cases, you use the tools and techniques from Six Sigma, including the Pareto chart, the run chart, the cause-and-effect diagram, and the causal chain. These can all be used to identify and eliminate or reduce the defect level in the constraint operation.

Defects in the constraint operation seriously limit the TH, and therefore revenue opportunities, in two ways. First, if the defects result in rework, the cycle time of the constraint operation is lengthened and capacity rate is reduced. Because the constraint operation dictates the rate of revenue generation for the overall system, it is imperative that rework issues be solved as fast as possible. If the defect results in scrap parts, the TH is lost forever. That is, because the constraint limits the system's rate of revenue generation, any part lost to scrap in the constraint (or any of the downstream operations) is a part that is lost to the system forever. It should be clear to you that because of this loss, defect problems cannot be permitted to linger. The longer you have a problem with rework or, worse yet, scrap, the longer you must wait for improvements in TH. By the same token, if you have problems with defects in the operation that feeds the constraint, you will jeopardize your constraint and constraint buffer. The priority order for solving defect problems is important. First, solve any defect problems in the constraint operation; second, solve problems in the feeder operation; and third, solve defect problems in downstream operations that might impact the TH out of the constraint.

One of the most effective tools for reducing or eliminating defect problems is, once again, the designed experiment. Just like it reduces the harmful effects of excessive variation, it is equally effective in reducing and sometimes eliminating defects. In this case, the response variable is the level of the defect. DOEs, if done correctly, will pinpoint the root cause and the factors that create the defects. It is because of this that I strongly recommend that you become intimately familiar with how to run DOEs and make them a routine part of your improvement methodology.

Standardized Work

You may be thinking: What is standardized work? How do you develop it? What is the purpose of standardized work? The purpose of standardized work is to ensure that production operations are performed the same way each and every time a product is made or service is delivered. It serves to minimize the natural variation that inherently exists between one operator and the next. In effect, standardized work creates the opportunity for consistency.

In a typical manufacturing operation, even though there might be documented work methods, there are multiple interpretations of the methods. If, for example, you have a three-shift operation on a given process, I assure you that three distinctly different work methods are present. If there is machine setup, rest assured there are three different methods for it. This is especially true if your organization does not audit work methods for compliance. Thus, if you have three different methods in place, how do you know which one should be used as the standardized method? Or, which parts of each of the three different methods should be used?

Understanding the Data

Here is my recommendation. Look at what the data from the process is trying to tell you.

First, organize the measurement data from the products produced by the operator and perform a simple statistical analysis. For each of the critical quality characteristics, calculate the mean and standard deviation for each of the individual operators. In doing so, you are trying to answer two basic questions:

- Which of the process means (by operator) is the closest to the center of the specification?
- Which of the process standard deviations (by operator) is the smallest?

Obviously, you want to center the process to improve the probability of producing acceptable product, so the method with the mean closest to the center of the tolerance should be selected. For the same reason, you want to select the method that produces the least amount of variation. When this is complete, share the data with the operators and include them in an analysis of the three work methods to determine what about the methods could be giving you the least amount of process variation. One very effective method I have used for facilitating this analysis is videotaping each of the individual work methods and then having the operators critique each one as a group. In my experience, many times the difference in variation has been due to machine setup, and by standardizing the setup, major improvements have been realized.

Two other very effective methods for identifying sources of variation are analysis of means and effects analysis. If you use statistical software like Minitab 15, as I do, there is a tab that will perform both of these analyses for you quite easily. The basis for both of these techniques is to isolate obvious differences in the work methods and test these differences for their effects on mean and variation. Both are similar in nature to a designed experiment, but instead of collecting new data, you will actually be using existing data. There are many books and articles that cover these two techniques, so I will not be discussing them in detail here. The important point is to use observations and data to determine the standardized work method.

Because you are interested in reducing overall process cycle times, it is important that you analyze additional data that impact time. For example, a simple time and motion study of each of the methods would be a simple way to determine which method delivers the best product in the least amount of time. But if you do not want to use this technique, use the same analysis techniques to determine the mean and standard deviation of the P/Ts. An analysis of defect data might tell you which of the methods produces the best quality and has the fewest number of repairs. But remember, faster is not always better! If the fastest method produces the highest percentage of defective parts, it would make little sense to select this method.

Developing Standardized Work Methods

When developing an actual standardized work method, there are six primary points to keep in mind:

- **Always include and involve the normal operators in the development of the work method.** Believe it or not, the operators are the process experts and always know more about the process than anyone else. In addition, if the operators play a major role in the development of the standardized work method, ownership of the method is almost guaranteed and the workers usually follow the method enthusiastically. Including the operators also helps sustain any gains made in the improvement process.
- **Standardized work methods should be dynamic.** When better methods are discovered and tested, update the method.

- **Standardized work methods create more stable processes because the method is performed the same way every time.** Remember, the objective of standardization is consistency. To this point, defects and deviations are more easily recognized, so corrective actions typically happen sooner and more effectively.
- **Stabilizing the process, especially through standardization of the work methods, is a prerequisite for process improvement.** Stabilizing provides you with assurance that the process is being performed consistently.
- **Do not limit the use of standardized work methods only to process operators.** Any repeating method performed on the constraint operation (and all operations for that matter) must be done the same way each time it is performed. PM procedures and inspection procedures that are performed as part of the constraint operation must be carried out consistently, so expand standardized work to include these (and others) as well.
- **Standardized work methods must always be displayed at the workstation and must never be ambiguous.** An untrained operator (or even an engineer) should be able to read the method and perform the task in very short order. I always emphasize creating work methods that are visual and to the point. I recommend the use of photographs and anything else that helps reduce any ambiguity. In addition, because the standardized work methods are displayed at the workstation, use them to perform process audits to ensure compliance to them.

Figure 6.4 is an example of a section of a standardized visual work method from a company that produced gaming tables. This method was developed completely by a team of hourly operators that produced pool tables. It is simple and visual, and because it was developed by the operators performing the work, the method stands a much better chance of being followed by all the operators. When this happens, P/T and product variation are automatically and immediately reduced. You will notice that the work method includes basic instructions, the necessary process tools, any quality checks, and any key safety items to be aware of. My advice is to keep the work method simple, yet informative.

Reducing C/T

Before I discuss this phase of UIC, you need to understand four very important concepts and terms: *cycle time*, *processing time* (P/T), *throughput* (TH), and *work-in-process* (WIP) *inventory*. Cycle time (C/T) in this context will be defined as the total amount of time material spends in a production system being converted from raw material to finished product. Cycle time is measured in units of seconds,

Pool Table Station 9		OPERATOR PROCESS CONTROL	
No.	Step 1 Step 2 Step 3 Step 4	INSTRUCTIONS	PROCESS TOOL(S)
1		1. Wipe/Scrape all exterior sidewalls free of glue and dust with Mineral Spirits rag. 2. Insert small door. 3. Attach Serial # 4. Wipe table top free of dust and debris with Lacquer Thinner soaked rag.	Mineral Spirits Soaked rag. Lacquer Thinner Soaked rag Putty knife.
		QUALITY CHECKPOINT	SAFETY CHECKPOINT
		Exterior and top must be free of glue and dust.	Rubber gloves are suggested.
		DATE:	REV:

Table Station 9		OPERATOR PROCESS CONTROL	
No.	Step 1 Step 2 Step 3 Step 4	INSTRUCTIONS	PROCESS TOOL(S)
2		1. Prep View Door. 2. Insert View Door. 3. Clean and insert Coin Slot. 4. Attach door keys to Coin Slot.	Mineral Spirits soaked rag Masking tape
		QUALITY CHECKPOINT	SAFETY CHECKPOINT
		Exterior must be free of glue and dust. Verify all keys are correct to door locks.	Rubber gloves are suggested.
		DATE:	REV:

Figure 6.4   Visual Work Method.

minutes, hours, days, and even weeks, depending upon the product being produced. P/T is the time required to process product through a single workstation, and, like cycle time, it is measured in seconds, minutes, hours, days, and even weeks, depending upon the product being produced. TH is the rate at which material is processed through a production line and is measured in units of product per unit time (e.g., pieces per hour, units per week). WIP inventory is the amount of WIP product not yet complete, waiting for additional work to be done on it.

C/T Example

You may be wondering why I inject these four terms into the text. I want to perform a simple mental exercise to demonstrate how P/T, C/T, TH, and WIP inventory are interrelated. Let us consider a simple four-step production line where the P/T is exactly one minute for each workstation. Figure 6.5 is an example of such a production process where raw material enters the process at step A and then progresses to steps B, C, and finally D. This process is set up to produce parts in batches of ten pieces at a time. The question is: How long will it take to complete all ten pieces?

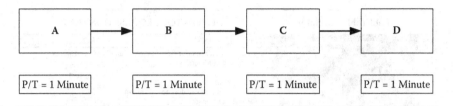

Figure 6.5 Simple Four-Step Process.

Because each piece takes one minute of P/T at the first station, a total of ten minutes will be needed to process the entire batch through workstation A. The batch of ten is then transferred to workstation B, and ten minutes are also required at workstation B and so on, until all ten parts are completed in workstation D. Therefore, ignoring transport time between steps, it would take exactly forty minutes to process the entire batch of ten parts. Each part spends forty minutes in the system, so the cycle time (C/T) is forty minutes. The TH (TH) is 10 parts every 40 minutes, or 0.25 parts/minute, or 15 parts/hour (i.e., 60 minutes/hour × 0.25 parts/minute = 15 parts/hour).

Suppose the factory decides to change its batch size from ten to four. What is the impact on cycle time and TH? Each part still requires one minute of P/T at workstation A, so all four parts would take four minutes total to pass through station A. Likewise, four minutes would be required to process the batch of four parts through stations B, C, and D. Again, ignoring transport time, it would require a total of sixteen minutes of cycle time to process the batch of four parts. The TH is 4 parts every 16 minutes, or 0.25 parts/minute, or 15 parts/hour, so the TH has not changed, but the cycle time is significantly less.

This same exercise can be repeated for any batch size, as seen in Table 6.1, and the results remain the same. No matter what the batch size (WIP), the TH always remains the same, but look what happens to cycle time. Because the parts are transferred from station to station in batches, rather than one piece at a time, the cycle time for the batches grows as a function of batch size. This style of production and production control is characteristic of the mass production mindset and is referred to as *batch-and-queue* or *batch-and-push* production and represents the worst possible way to process material through a factory. In this type of production, the level of WIP (batch size) has a pronounced effect on cycle time but absolutely no effect on TH. For all of you production managers who believe in or insist that it is faster and more efficient to process material in large batches, I hope you have seen the light with this simple exercise.

Table 6.1 Batch Performance versus WIP, C/T, and TP

Batch Size (WIP)	Cycle Time (minutes)	Throughput (parts/minute)	Throughput (parts/hour)
1	4	0.25	15
2	8	0.25	15
3	12	0.25	15
4	16	0.25	15
5	20	0.25	15
6	24	0.25	15
7	28	0.25	15
8	32	0.25	15
9	36	0.25	15
10	40	0.25	15
15	60	0.25	15
20	80	0.25	15
100	400	0.25	15
500	2000	0.25	15

Little's Law and C/T

In 1961 John Little published a mathematical proof known as Little's law, which states that TH is always equal to WIP divided by cycle time, or stated mathematically,

$$TH = WIP \div \text{cycle time}$$

or

$$TH = WIP \div C/T$$

Graphically, the relationship between batch size (WIP) and cycle time can be seen in Figure 6.6. For any batch size (WIP level) the curve clearly behaves in a linear fashion. In fact, for this example the equation for this curve is $y = 4x$.

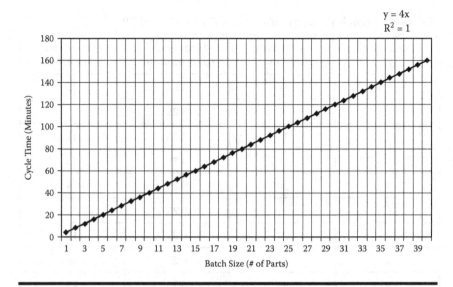

Figure 6.6   Cycle Time versus Batch Size.

Little's law (TH = WIP ÷ C/T) implies that reducing cycle time and reducing WIP are essentially equivalent activities as long as TH remains constant. But you know that reducing WIP without reducing variability will cause TH to decrease (variability buffering law). The real message here is that variability reduction is an extremely important component of WIP and cycle time reduction initiatives.

Keeping C/Ts Short

Before leaving this subject, I want to discuss the importance of keeping cycle times as short as possible, especially in the constraint operation. Hopp and Spearman provide five reasons why this should be your objective:[38]

- **Better responsiveness to the customer:** If it takes less time to produce product, the lead time to the customer can be shortened. Shorter lead times can result in increased sales.
- **Maintaining flexibility:** Changing the list (backlog) of parts that are planned to start next is less disruptive than trying to change the set of jobs already in the process. Because shorter cycle times allow for later releases, they enhance this type of flexibility.

- **Improving quality:** Long cycle times typically imply long queues in the system, which in turn imply long delays between defect *creation* and defect *detection*. For this reason, short cycle times support good quality.
- **Relying less on forecasts:** If cycle times are longer than customers are willing to wait, production must be done in anticipation of demand rather than in response to it. Given the lack of accuracy of most demand forecasts, it is extremely important to keep cycle times shorter than quoted lead times, whenever possible.
- **Making better forecasts:** The more cycle times exceed customer lead times, the farther out the forecast must extend. Hence, even if cycle times cannot be reduced to the point where dependence on forecasting is eliminated, cycle time reduction can shorten the forecasting time horizon. This can greatly reduce forecasting errors.

The batch-and-queue production system is not the worst possible scenario for a company. If a company practices *batch-and-store* production, whereby instead of processing the material to the next process, it moves the material to a storage location, the cycle time becomes even more protracted.

Suppose that, instead of producing material in batches, when a part is completed in one station, it moves immediately to the next station and then on to the next station until it is completed (remember the four-station process in Figure 6.5). This type of production is referred to as *single-piece flow* or *one-piece flow*. One-piece flow refers to the concept of moving one work piece at a time between individual workstations. One-piece flow has several distinct benefits, like keeping WIP to low levels and encouraging work balance and improved quality, but in a system like this, what happens to cycle time? Let us take a look.

Again, let us look at the process in Figure 6.5 and assume that the P/T is one minute. The first part is processed through workstation A and takes one minute. The first part continues immediately to station B, and simultaneously the next part enters station A. After one minute the first part continues to station C, the second part moves to station B, and a new part enters station A. After another minute the first part moves to station D, the second part moves to station C, the third part moves to station B, and a new part enters station A. After another minute, the first part has been completed in station D so that the total time the first part remained in the process was exactly four minutes. The TH is 1 part every four minutes, or 0.25 parts/minute (15 parts/hour).

The question is: What would happen if you increased WIP to two instead of one? Once again, you begin measuring as soon as the first part enters workstation A. You know that this first part will take one minute before it is passed to station B. At the same time, the second part is introduced to station A. These

Table 6.2 One-Piece Flow versus WIP, C/T, and TP

Batch Size (WIP)	Cycle Time (minutes)	Throughput (parts/minute)	Throughput (parts/hour)
1	4	0.25	15
2	4	0.5	30
3	4	0.75	45
4	4	1	60
5	5	1	60
6	6	1	60
7	7	1	60
8	8	1	60
9	9	1	60
10	10	1	60

two parts follow each other through the four-station line, so both remain in the process for four minutes total.

Therefore, this system produces 2 parts every 4 minutes, or 0.50 parts/minute (30 parts/hour). But what happens when you increase the WIP even more? Table 6.2 contains all WIP values from 1 to 10, and as you can see, there is an interesting phenomenon or nuance that takes place in this process when the level of WIP reaches five parts. If you make the assumption that the process is full (one at each station), and each part is ready to be processed, when the fifth part is introduced to workstation A, it must wait until the station has finished processing the fourth part and it moves to station B. Therefore, the fifth part remains in the system for five minutes. Each time a part is completed, the next part is introduced at station A and waits one minute before it can proceed. Look at the column for cycle time. As long as the system has no more than four parts in it, the cycle time remains constant at four minutes. But as soon as the fifth part becomes part of the system, the cycle time begins to increase by one minute for each increase of one part as WIP.

This demonstrates that increasing WIP levels does not result in a corresponding increase in cycle time until the process is full or until its *critical WIP* level has been reached. For this example, the critical WIP level is four parts. If WIP is increased beyond this critical WIP, parts simply stack up and wait to be processed, causing the cycle time to increase. Equally interesting, however, is that reducing WIP levels below the critical WIP (i.e., in this example one, two, or three parts) results in a corresponding decrease in TH. As you can see in Table 6.2, when WIP is at its critical WIP level of 4 (i.e., the system is full), the TH is at its maximum value of 1 part/minute, or 60 parts/hour. But when the WIP level is reduced to 3, TH drops from 1 part/minute (60 parts/hour) to 0.75 parts/minute (45 parts/hour).

Figures 6.7 and 6.8 demonstrate the relationship between WIP and TH, and WIP and cycle time. In this example, there is one WIP value that results in minimum cycle time and maximum TH, which is what you always want. If there is any less WIP, you lose TH with no decrease in cycle time. If there is any more WIP, you increase cycle time with no increase in TH. It is interesting to note that for a balanced line (i.e., all individual P/Ts are equal), the critical WIP level will always equal the number of process steps. For unbalanced lines, this is not the case.

What we have learned here is that too much WIP results in longer cycle time and increased holding costs, while too little WIP results in decreased TH and lost revenue. This means that there is an optimum amount of WIP (i.e., critical WIP) that should be in a system. Even though there are many "experts" who believe in the concept of "zero inventory," we now know that WIP should never realistically be zero.

You know what happens in a balanced line, but what about an unbalanced line? What happens with C/T, TH, and WIP? Consider the four-step process in Figure 6.9.

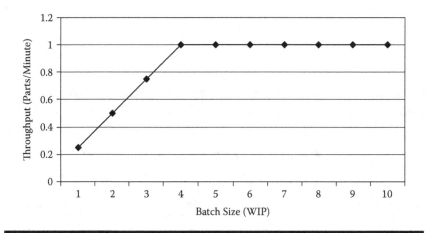

Figure 6.7 Throughput versus Batch Size.

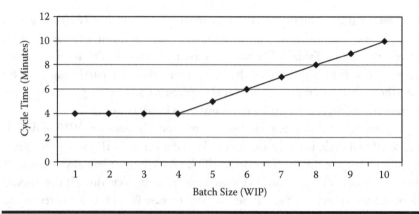

Figure 6.8   Cycle Time versus Batch Size.

In this process, you see that step A has a P/T of one minute, step B's P/T equals two minutes, step C's P/T equals three minutes, and step D's P/T equals one minute. Clearly, this is an unbalanced line because the P/Ts are not all equal. The assumptions you make here are that no variation exists and only one machine exists at each process step. Here, you see that the capacity of each process step is obtained by dividing the P/T in minutes per part into 60 minutes/hour. The capacity of the line is dictated by the bottleneck step, which in this process is step C at 20 parts/hour. Applying Little's law to this process results in a critical WIP level needed to maximize TH while minimizing cycle time, as follows:

$$\text{Critical WIP} = \text{TH} \times \text{C/T}$$

or

$$W_0 = r_b T_0$$

where W_0 is the critical WIP, r_b is maximum TH, and T_0 is minimum cycle time.

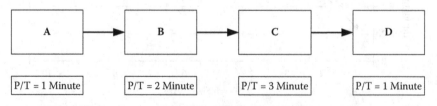

Figure 6.9   C/T, TH, and WIP in an Unbalance Line.

W_0 = 20 parts/hour × 7/60 hour = 20 parts/hour × 0.116667 hour
        = 2.3333 parts

This extension of Little's law tells you that if you want to achieve maximum TH at minimum cycle time, your critical WIP is 2.3333 parts, or 3 parts. Any number of parts above three will lengthen the cycle time, and any number of parts below three will negatively impact TH. Because you are interested in maximizing revenue and on-time delivery, Little's law will help you achieve this. Table 6.3 is a summary of what we have just discussed.

Effectively Utilizing Small Batch Operations

The most efficient form of manufacturing from a flow perspective is single-piece flow. But having said this, there are times when one-piece flow is not appropriate or even possible, so common sense must play a role in the decision to use it. For example, suppose the next step in a process is bead blasting or heat treatment of parts. Would it make sense to run the bead blaster or a heat treat oven with a single part or with a small batch? From a manufacturing efficiency perspective, a small batch probably makes more sense.

You always want to minimize the non-value-added activities in a manufacturing process, which includes travel time. If one-piece flow is not possible and transfer batches are needed, one way to keep the transfer batch size small is through the use of cellular manufacturing. Cellular manufacturing positions all workstations needed to produce a family of parts physically near each other. Because material handling is minimized, it is much easier to move parts between stations in small batches.

Because some processes do not lend themselves to one-piece flow and are better served by producing in batches or lots, how do you know what that batch size should be? Once again, we turn to Hopp and Spearman. In 1913, Ford Harris developed a mathematical model to compute the optimal manufacturing batch

Table 6.3 Key Stats for Figure 6.9

Step Number	Number of Machines	P/T (minutes)	Step Capacity (parts/hour)
A	1	1	60
B	1	2	30
C	1	3	20
D	1	1	60

size. His model, the *economic order quantity* (EOQ), is considered the foundation of research on inventory management. In order to develop this model Harris made six assumptions:

- **Instantaneous production:** There is no capacity constraint, so the entire lot is produced simultaneously.
- **Immediate delivery:** There is no lag time between production and availability to satisfy demand.
- **Deterministic demand:** There is no uncertainty about the quantity or timing of demand.
- **Constant demand:** Demand is linear, meaning that if annual demand were 365 units, this would translate into a daily demand of one unit per day.
- **Fixed setup costs:** Regardless of the size of the lot or status of the factory, the setup cost is the same.
- **Individual product analysis:** Either there is a single product or there are no interactions (e.g., shared equipment) between products.

As Harris developed his model he assumed constant, deterministic demand, ordering Q units whenever the inventory reached zero, with an average inventory of $Q \div 2$ (i.e., maximum + minimum divided by 2). Harris also presented the holding cost of the inventory as $hQ \div 2$ per year, with h being the holding cost in dollars per unit per year. Continuing, Harris next added the setup cost, A, per order to his equation to have $AD \div Q$ per year, with D being equal to demand, because you must place $D \div Q$ orders per year to satisfy the demand. Harris then included the production cost per unit, c, or cD per year to complete the equation for cost. The final equation for cost, then, is as follows:

$$Y(Q) = (hQ \div 2) + (AD \div Q) + cD$$

Without going through "higher mathematics," as Harris put it, you can find the value of Q that minimizes $Y(Q)$, or the EOQ:

$$\text{EOQ} = \sqrt{2AD} \div h$$

The inference you can take away from this formula is that the optimal order quantity increases with the square root of the setup cost or the demand rate and decreases with the square root of the holding costs. What this all boils down to is this: there is a trade-off between lot size and inventory. Increasing the lot size will increase the average amount of inventory in the factory but also reduces the frequency of ordering, and by using a setup cost to penalize frequent replenishment, Harris was able to articulate this trade-off in concise financial terms.

There is another law, the *law of move batching*, presented by Hopp and Spearman that suggests one of the easiest ways to reduce cycle times in some manufacturing systems is to reduce transfer batch sizes.[39] This law states that cycle times over a segment of a routing are roughly proportional to the transfer batch sizes used over that segment, providing there is no waiting for the conveyance device. To simplify, the bottom line is that by holding the transfer batch size to its optimal level, cycle time will also be optimal. Thus, if one-piece flow is not ideal for your process, at least calculate the optimal transfer batch size.

Overall Equipment Effectiveness (OEE)

One of the keys to optimizing TH is that the constraint operation can never be left idle. Every minute lost at the constraint is a minute of TH lost that can never be regained. If your constraint operation involves equipment, this implies that equipment is available 100 percent of the time. But is this realistic? Probably not, but it is realistic to expect that equipment is available most of the time, thus limiting TH losses. What you are really saying is you want to maximize equipment effectiveness in the constraint operation and the equipment directly feeding the constraint.

Equipment effectiveness means that the equipment is available when you need it, performs at the speed that you need, and produces product that is free of defects, rework, and scrap. If you have all three of these components, you can say that your equipment is effective. In other words, having effective equipment means that it is consistent and predictable. But how do you know if your equipment is effective, and how can you measure how effective your equipment really is?

One way to measure the consistency of your equipment is by measuring the amount of downtime you experience. But equipment downtime does not tell you the whole story relative to equipment effectiveness simply because there are reasons unrelated to the equipment that cause downtime. Things like quality issues or material shortages totally unrelated to your equipment can also cause equipment to be stopped. And what about the speed at which your equipment runs? Isn't that a measure of how effective your equipment is? Wouldn't it be nice to have a single performance metric that told you how effective your equipment is performing? It seems as though there is such a metric. OEE is a metric that takes into account the availability, the speed, and the quality of parts being produced. How do you calculate this metric?

Seiichi Nakajima provides the following formula for OEE:[40]

$$OEE = availability \times performance\ rate \times quality\ rate$$

or

$$OEE = A \times P \times Q$$

As you can see, this single metric ties together the impact of the three important components, availability, speed, and quality.

Equipment effectiveness is limited by what Nakajima refers to as the six big losses. These six losses fall under three different categories as follows, each with two types of losses:

- **Downtime:** Breakdown losses; setup and adjustment losses
- **Speed:** Reduced speed (discrepancies between designed and actual speed of equipment); idling and minor stoppage losses
- **Defects:** Quality defect and rework losses; start-up (yield) losses

Let us look at each of these six losses in a bit more detail.

Breakdown Losses

There are two types of losses caused by breakdowns: *time losses*, when productivity is reduced, and *quantity losses*, caused by defective product. When equipment breaks down, the breakdown is either sporadic or frequent (chronic). Sporadic breakdowns are typically sudden, dramatic, or unexpected and are usually obvious and easy to correct through simple problem-solving methods. Typically, sporadic breakdowns are traced back to changes that have occurred, such as a broken part or improper setup. Chronic breakdowns, on the other hand, are typically ignored or even neglected because they still exist even after numerous unsuccessful attempts to correct them, so you tend to give up and ignore them. Chronic breakdowns require a thorough investigation and inventive corrective action. In order to maximize equipment effectiveness, *all* breakdowns must be attacked and reduced to zero. That's right, I said zero! It is entirely possible to eliminate losses due to breakdowns by effectively implementing TPM.

Setup and Adjustment Losses

This type of loss occurs when production of one type of product ends and the equipment is changed over and adjusted to meet the requirements of the new product. One clear example of this type of loss is extended changeover time, such as is seen in changing dies in a stamping press. It is not uncommon to see changeovers lasting hours when, in reality, these should be completed in minutes. In the next section I will go into detail on this subject.

Reduced Speed Losses

When you purchase equipment, one of the key factors in the selection process is the design speed at which the equipment is intended to operate. When the equipment fails to operate at the design speed, you have speed losses. Because speed losses occur gradually over time, they are often overlooked in the day-to-day operation of the plant. In reality they can represent a significant loss and should never be ignored.

There are several reasons why equipment might not operate at the design speed. Maybe running at design speed produces defective product. Or maybe running at design speed causes mechanical problems. Or maybe there is a fear that if you run at design speed you will end up abusing the machine. It is also possible that the reason for not running at design speed is that you do not know what the design speed actually is. Whatever the reason, the goal must be to reconcile the difference between design speed and actual speed.

Idling and Minor Stoppage Losses

Idling and minor stoppages happen as a result of production being interrupted by a temporary malfunction of the equipment. A typical example of this type of loss is a jam occurring somewhere in the operation. The equipment is still functioning, but it may be temporarily blocked and will sit idle until the jam is removed. These types of losses are typically never recorded on a downtime sheet, but can account for a significant amount of lost TH if they are ignored. With an effective TPM initiative, this type of loss can be reduced to near zero.

Quality Defects and Rework Losses

Whenever you have defective product and rework that is being caused by an equipment malfunction, you have this type of loss. If the defects appear suddenly and sporadically, you can typically tie them back to a change in how the equipment is operating and usually can fix the problem in very short order. Unlike sporadic defects, chronic defects are not as easy to solve and, just like chronic breakdowns, will require a thorough investigation and innovative solutions. Of course, the goal here is zero defects.

Start-up (Yield) Losses

These are yield losses that occur during the early phases of production during the stabilization period. How much of a loss is dependent upon several factors, including process stability, how much maintenance is already being performed on the equipment, how experienced the operator is, and so on.

Putting It All Together

So how do these six losses relate to your measure of equipment effectiveness and the components of availability, performance rate, and quality rate? And, then, how do you measure these three components? Figure 6.10 provides the answer to the first question.

OEE is the product of the operating rate (availability), the performance rate, and the quality rate. The formulas for each of these three components are:

$$\text{Availability} = (\text{loading time} - \text{downtime}) \div \text{loading time}$$

where loading time = total time = scheduled time – all planned downtime. (Planned downtime includes time allotted for PM, breaks, lunches, scheduled meetings, and so on.)

$$\text{Performance rate} = \left(\frac{\text{output} \times \text{actual cycle time}}{\text{loading time} - \text{downtime}} \right) \times \frac{\text{ideal cycle time}}{\text{actual cycle time}}$$

where:
- output = total product produced
- actual cycle time = total runtime ÷ total product produced
- ideal cycle time = planned cycle time.

$$\text{Quality rate} = \text{number of good parts} \div \text{total parts produced}$$

OEE Component	Loss Type
Availability	1. Breakdown losses
	2. Setup and adjustment losses
Performance Rate	1. Idling and minor stoppage losses
	2. Reduced speed losses
Quality Rate	1. Quality defect and rework losses
	2. Start-up losses

Figure 6.10   The Six Big Losses.

where the number of good parts = number of parts produced – (start-up defects + process defects + trial products).

Now that you have the formulas, how do you use them and what do they tell you?

Suppose that your plant's working hours are 60 minutes/hour × 8 hours, or 480 minutes. You also have lunches and breaks, but let us assume that you relieve this machine during these times so that you do not lose any TH. You have planned 30 minutes of downtime for scheduled maintenance, so your loading time is 480 minutes – 30 minutes, or 450 minutes. Further suppose that you experience only 30 minutes of unscheduled equipment downtime on this day. Your availability on this day was

$$\text{Availability} = (\text{loading time} - \text{downtime}) \div \text{loading time}$$
$$= (450 \text{ minutes} - 30 \text{ minutes}) \div 450 \text{ minutes}$$
$$= 0.9333 \text{ or } 93.33\%$$

Now let us look at performance rate. Suppose that your output on this day was 360 parts and that your actual cycle time was 0.8 minute/part. Further suppose that your ideal cycle time is 0.7 minute/part. Your performance rate is

$$\text{Performance rate} = (\text{output} \times \text{actual cycle time} \times \text{ideal cycle time}) \div$$
$$(\text{loading time} - \text{downtime actual cycle time})$$

$$= \left(\frac{360 \text{ parts} \times 0.80 \text{ minute/part}}{480 \text{ minutes} - 30 \text{ minutes}} \right) \times \frac{0.7 \text{ minute/part}}{0.8 \text{ minute/part}}$$

$$= 0.640 \times 0.875$$
$$= 0.560 \text{ or } 56\%$$

Now let us look at your quality rate. You know that you produced a total of 360 parts, but suppose your defect rate was 2 percent, so you actually produced 353 parts that were acceptable.

$$\text{Quality rate} = \text{number of good parts} \div \text{total parts produced}$$
$$= 353 \text{ parts} \div 360 \text{ parts}$$
$$= 0.981 \text{ or } 98.1\%$$

So how did you do from an OEE perspective? OEE is the product of these three components, so let us calculate it:

$$OEE = \text{availability} \times \text{performance rate} \times \text{quality rate}$$
$$= 0.9333 \times 0.560 \times 0.981$$
$$= 0.5127 \text{ or } 51.3\%$$

So how did we do? Levels for OEE differ depending upon the industry, equipment features, and production systems involved, but as a general rule, world-class levels for OEE are at 80 to 85 percent or better. Thus, based upon an OEE of 51.5 percent, the process in your example is ripe for improvement, but where should you focus your efforts? If you look at each of the individual components and rank order them from lowest to highest, you can get an idea of where you need to prioritize and focus your efforts. In this example, because your performance rate was only 51.5 percent, this is the area for greatest opportunity as it relates to TH improvement. In fact, in order to raise OEE to 0.80 (80 percent) you would need to raise your performance rate to 0.87, or 87 percent. And how might you do that?

You know from Figure 6.10 that the factors or losses affecting the performance rate are idling and minor stoppage losses and reduced speed losses, so your improvement focus would first be on reducing both of these losses. Likewise, if availability had been the component of OEE that needed to be improved, break-down losses and setup and adjustment losses would be addressed. Similarly, if quality rate were the problem, quality defect and rework losses and start-up losses would be addressed. The key point is to use OEE and its component parts to establish the priority and focus to improve equipment effectiveness.

Although OEE is a great performance metric, in a TOC environment it does not tell you all you need to know in terms of maximizing TH. OEE is the product of availability (actual runtime minus scheduled downtime), the speed rate (actual speed versus ideal speed), and the quality rate (good product versus total product produced). OEE is a measure of how well your equipment is functioning, but it subtracts all scheduled downtime. Even though you know you need to perform scheduled downtime, it represents a loss of TH just the same.

The Human Component

In addition to the equipment downtime causing TH losses, there is a human component associated with how well your equipment functions. That is, there are other reasons why equipment may not be producing product other than the machine itself failing. Perhaps materials are late arriving to the machine, so you are forced to wait. Or maybe a quality inspector is not available when you need an inspection, so again you wait. These are both examples of downtime that are totally unrelated to how well your equipment is performing yet represent TH losses. In many cases this human side of downtime analysis is overlooked.

How quickly you restore equipment so that TH is not lost is a function of how efficient you as humans are. Thus, if in your calculation of OEE you include this human downtime factor, your OEE calculation becomes a measure of your total effort, linking manpower performance with equipment performance. In essence, OEE relates how well your employees are making product. Let us return to our previous OEE example and see what the impact of the human element is on OEE.

Remember from our previous example that the plant's working hours were 60 minutes/hour × 8 hours/day, or 480 minutes/day. We have lunches and breaks, but we assumed that we relieved this machine during these times so that we would maximize TH. We did have 30 minutes of scheduled downtime, so we subtracted that amount from our available time, making our loading time equal to 450 minutes. You recall that we experienced only 30 minutes of equipment downtime on this day, so our availability on this day was

$$
\begin{aligned}
\text{Availability} &= (\text{loading time} - \text{downtime}) \div \text{loading time} \\
&= (450 \text{ minutes} - 30 \text{ minutes}) \div 450 \text{ minutes} \\
&= 0.9333 \text{ or } 93.33\%
\end{aligned}
$$

But now suppose that in addition to the thirty minutes of constraint equipment downtime, we also had another forty-five minutes of constraint downtime that was not related to the equipment. Suppose, for example, that we had fifteen minutes of downtime due to late-arriving materials, twenty minutes waiting for a quality inspection, and ten minutes waiting for a relief operator to arrive. What happens to our availability?

$$
\begin{aligned}
\text{Availability}_{\text{overall}} &= (\text{loading time} - \text{total downtime}) \div \text{loading time} \\
\text{Availability}_{\text{overall}} &= (450 \text{ minutes} - 75 \text{ minutes}) \div 480 \text{ minutes} \\
A_o &= 0.8333 \text{ or } 83.33\%
\end{aligned}
$$

As you can see, our availability factor decreases from 93.33 percent to 83.33 percent. What happens to our OEE?

$$
\text{OEE}_{\text{overall}} = A_o \times P \times Q
$$

Our original values for P and Q were 56 percent and 98.1 percent, respectively, so our new overall OEE (OEE_O) is

$$
\begin{aligned}
&= 0.833 \times 0.560 \times 0.981 \\
&= 0.4576 \text{ or } 45.76\%
\end{aligned}
$$

Because our original OEE was 51.3 percent, this represents a difference of 5.5 percent, and although this difference may appear to be subtle, the implications to the improvement effort can be quite profound. It is the difference between considering only equipment issues and considering all the factors that limit TH within your process. In fact, if you are to make meaningful gains in TH, you need to consider and focus on all the interruptions and subsequent downtime caused by the equipment, the people operating the equipment, the people maintaining the equipment, and the people supplying the equipment, because these factors all have an impact on downtime and TH losses. This consists of all forms of downtime, including planned and unplanned maintenance, material and component shortages, quality inspections, or anything that prevents us from achieving maximum TH. As a constraint performance metric, OEE_O is much better than OEE, and my recommendation is to use it.

There is an interesting phenomenon that takes place in many companies. Although most people recognize that breakdowns cause major losses in manufacturing, for a variety of reasons very few companies do much to reduce the scope of that loss. According to Nakajima, "To take this loss seriously and begin reducing it requires, first of all, new thinking about breakdowns." What is this "new thinking" that Nakajima talks about? Nakajima further explains that equipment breakdowns are often caused by human assumptions and actions. Nakajima clarifies, "Many people assume that (1) it is not the operator's responsibility to perform inspection; (2) all equipment eventually breaks down; and (3) all breakdowns can be fixed." Nakajima further tells us, "First, people concerned with equipment must replace their assumption that all equipment eventually breaks down"[41] with the belief that equipment should *never* break down. Nakajima believes that if this change in thinking happens, everyone else, including operators, is more likely to accept the idea that equipment can be used in a way that actually prevents breakdowns. When people accept the view that everyone is responsible for equipment, operators will want to learn how to use their own machines, so they will not break down. What he is saying is akin to the concept of the self-fulfilling prophecy. That is, if I believe something can happen, it has a better chance of happening. Likewise, if I believe something cannot happen, it probably won't.

Reducing Equipment Breakdown

There are basically two types of equipment breakdowns: *function loss* breakdowns, where all functioning equipment stops, and *function reduction* breakdowns, where the equipment function deteriorates. In many companies maintenance efforts focus on sporadic, unexpected breakdowns and significant, highly visible equipment defects. TPM addresses both function loss and function reduction breakdowns caused by hidden defects. Although a single, significant defect can trigger a breakdown, a combination of small, hidden defects, which may be completely unrelated to the breakdown (e.g., dust, abrasion, vibration, loose bolts), is often the major cause. Eliminating breakdowns caused by these hidden defects requires a different approach from conventional maintenance thinking.

Nakajima tells us that there are five types of actions needed to uncover these hidden defects and treat them properly:

- Maintain basic equipment conditions by properly cleaning, lubricating, and bolting.
- Maintain operating conditions, which are those conditions that must be met for equipment to operate at its full potential.
- Restore deterioration because equipment slowly deteriorates over time and breakdowns occur as fatigues develop.
- Correct design weaknesses, which requires changes in equipment design.
- Improve operating and maintenance skills because many breakdowns are caused by a lack of skill.

"Breakdowns cannot be eliminated until basic assumptions and beliefs are changed, particularly those regarding the division of labor between the production and maintenance departments."[42] To this end, there must be a sharing of responsibilities between maintenance and production if you are to be successful at reducing breakdowns and losses. That is, there are functions that must be performed by operators and there are functions that must be performed by maintenance. Let us review each of these functions.

Responsibilities of Operators

- Maintain the basic condition of equipment (i.e., cleaning, lubricating, and bolting).
- Maintain the basic operating condition of the equipment (i.e., proper operation and visual inspection of equipment).
- Discover deterioration of equipment through visual inspection and early detection of problems.
- Enhance skills for things like equipment operation, setup, and adjustment as well as cleaning, lubrication, bolting, and visual inspection.

These responsibilities come under the general heading of *autonomous maintenance*, which I will discuss shortly. Although I agree with Nakajima's needed functions, I also believe that operators must be trained in and given responsibility for basic problem solving.

Responsibilities of Maintenance Personnel

- Provide technical support for the department's autonomous maintenance activities.
- Restore deterioration thoroughly through preventive and predictive maintenance and overhauls when needed.
- Improve equipment maintainability to reduce the time required to restore equipment to normal operational level.
- Develop operating standards by defining and correcting design weaknesses.
- Enhance skills for things like preventive and predictive maintenance, condition monitoring, inspections, and overhauls.

Like operators, maintenance personnel must be trained in basic problem-solving techniques.

One important but often overlooked function of the maintenance department is improving the maintainability of the production equipment. Because production is aggressively trying to slash minutes and seconds from its processing and cycle times, any way that you can do this will result in a net gain in TH, especially through the constraint. One way you can do this is to reduce the time required to make equipment repairs, adjustments, and changeovers.

Maintainability

Maintainability is a measure of the ease and speed with which equipment can be restored to operational status after a failure or downtime occurs. Unfortunately, this aspect of maintenance is many times disregarded, resulting in precious production time being lost. Thus, an important function of maintenance is to look for ways to reduce the time required to restore equipment after a period of downtime. This is especially important when PM is being performed. In this case maintenance should be using the same mindset during PM that you use when you are making a changeover. That is, plan the PM, complete all external work offline while the equipment is running, and work to reduce internal maintenance time.

How do you measure how effective your efforts are at improving maintainability? First, the definition of maintainability is a measure of the ease and speed with which equipment can be *restored* to operational status. The time required to restore the equipment is much different from the time required to *repair* the equipment. The repair time is the time required to correct the equipment fault, but it does not automatically result in the equipment's being production ready. The equipment has to be checked out by maintenance, and the operator and acceptable parts have to be produced before it is said to be restored. Many companies measure their maintenance effectiveness or maintainability by the time required to make the repair, with the time usually beginning when maintenance arrives at the machine and ending with when they leave. Do not fall into this trap! Downtime begins when the equipment is forced to stop and does not end until acceptable product is being made.

The total downtime includes stopping production, the initial diagnosis by the operator, deciding what repair should be made, contacting maintenance, waiting for maintenance to arrive, a second diagnosis of the problem by maintenance, retrieving required parts and tools, physically making the repair, checking out and testing the repair, restarting the equipment, making and checking production parts, and cleanup. All these activities must be completed before restoration is complete, and all the while the equipment has been down and losing valuable TH. If you want to measure maintainability accurately, measure the total elapsed time that TH was lost. Efforts to improve maintainability should focus on ways to reduce all the time required to perform all the restoration activities.

Deterioration Prevention through Autonomous Maintenance

The key to improving equipment effectiveness is the involvement of everyone who touches or has responsibility for the equipment and, in particular, the involvement of the equipment operators. *Autonomous maintenance* or maintenance performed by equipment operators will contribute significantly to equipment effectiveness. At the heart of autonomous maintenance is the concept of *deterioration prevention*. If you want to maximize the runtime of the constraint, you must place a maximum effort into preventing breakdowns rather than fixing them. If you want to reduce the number of breakdowns, you need to focus on reducing deterioration.

All equipment changes slowly over time, but the timing and extent of these changes can be impacted by the daily functions of operators and maintenance. *Natural deterioration* is the normal wear-out that occurs in spite of proper use and maintenance. *Accelerated deterioration* is caused by neglect. When equipment is not properly used or maintained, deterioration will increase over time and can spread to other parts of the machine through a chain reaction. A single loose bolt can cause vibration that loosens other bolts, and so on.

It is clear that equipment effectiveness must be improved if the TH of the constraint is to be improved. The two types of activities that are required to do this are effective maintenance that prevents equipment deterioration and breakdowns and improvement activities that extend the life of equipment, reduce the time required to perform maintenance, and essentially eliminate breakdowns. Improving equipment effectiveness is possible, but it involves changing basic assumptions and the total cooperative efforts of production and maintenance. Thus, let us summarize the activities required by both production and maintenance in order to improve the OEE. Figure 6.11 is an adaptation of a similar figure developed by Nakajima that lists the three primary activities (preventing deterioration, measuring deterioration, and equipment restoration) as well as defining which group, operators or maintenance, is responsible for each.

As you can see in Figure 6.11, there are two primary activities: maintenance and improvement. If I had to choose a single set of activities from Figure 6.11 that would help you the most, it would be the daily maintenance activities assigned to the operators. Operators effectively performing the daily activities of cleaning, lubricating, and bolting set the stage for slowing the deterioration process and ultimately reducing unplanned equipment downtime. Everything is important, but these three actions are nonnegotiable.

Before we leave the subject of PM, I want to point out an important application of the coefficient of variation as it applies to deciding when to shut down for maintenance. That is, is it a better maintenance policy to make short, frequent stops for PM, or is it better to stop after longer, protracted runs of product? Recall that the calculations for coefficient of variation and squared coefficient of variation are as follows:

$$cv = \sigma \div t$$

$$scv = (\sigma \div t)^2$$

The *scv* of P/Ts always conveys much more information about production systems than simply using the mean (μ) or standard deviation (σ) by itself. That is, by using *svc* you are able to make comparisons regarding the variability of two systems simply because *svc* is a unitless number.

In trying to answer the question regarding when to shut down for PM, you also need to consider the computation of *availability*, because that is the parameter you will be impacting. One way to calculate availability is by using the following equation:

$$A = m_f \div (m_f + m_r)$$

where A = availability, m_f = mean time to failure, and m_r = mean time to repair.

Let us assume that the current maintenance policy calls for equipment to be shut down for a total PM after one hundred hours of machine time and your PM takes, on average, ten hours to perform. Suppose that there is a proposal to reduce your machine time from one hundred hours before PM to ten hours. Along with this proposal, through the use of SMED techniques

| General Area | Method | Prevent Deterioration | Activity | | Responsibility |
			Measure Deterioration	Restore Equipment	
Maintenance Activities	Normal Operation	Proper operation of equipment			X
		Basic setup and adjustment			
	Daily Maintenance	Cleaning and detecting hidden faults			X
		Lubrication and oiling			X
		Tightening nuts and bolts			X
		Conditions of use, daily deterioration checks			X
	Periodic and Predictive Maintenance		Periodic inspection		X	X
			Periodic testing (oil, IR, vibration, leak, crack, noise, thermal, corrosion)		X

Figure 6.11 Deterioration and Restoration Actions.

General Area	Method	Prevent Deterioration	Activity			Responsibility	
			Measure Deterioration	Restore Equipment			
Improvement Activities	PM		Trend and Pareto analysis			X	X
				Non-routine service			X
	Breakdown Maintenance		Rapid discovery of abnormalities, prompt and accurate reporting to maintenance			X	
				Repair breakdowns			X
	Improving Reliability	Strengthen				X	X
		Reduce Load				X	X
		Increase precision				X	X
	Improve Maintainability		Develop condition monitoring				X
			Improve testing procedures				X
			Improve servicing procedures				X
			Improve servicing quality				X

Figure 6.11   (Continued.)

and the fact that you perform only parts of the PM (i.e., different parts of the PM are performed at each stop), you are able to reduce the PM time from ten hours to thirty minutes. On the surface, it would seem that this new proposal would be a worse condition because, intuitively, you believe that the more frequent stops would increase the variability of the equipment. Let us find out if this is true.

First, calculate the impact on availability for the current policy and the new policy you are considering, as follows:

$$A_{current} = 100 \text{ hours} \div (100 \text{ hours} + 10 \text{ hours}) = 0.909$$

and

$$A_{proposed} = 10 \text{ hours} \div (10 \text{ hours} + 0.5 \text{ hours}) = 0.952$$

Interestingly, the actual machine availability has increased from approximately 91 percent to 95 percent, but what happens to variability?

Assume that the average P/T for this machine was ten minutes and the standard deviation of the P/T was two minutes. The current *scv* for this equipment is

$$scv = (\sigma_{current}/t_{current})^2 = (2 \div 10) = 0.20$$

There is another important production parameter known as the *effective P/T,* which takes into account the effects of availability and is calculated as follows:

$$t_e = (t_o \div A)$$

In our example, we said that the average P/T was ten minutes, and because we have already calculated the availability of 0.909, the value for t_e can now be computed as follows:

$$t_e = (t_o \div A) = (10 \div 0.909) = 11.01$$

What this tells us is that although the average P/T is ten minutes, the long-range, or effective, P/T, is eleven minutes.

Now let us return to the question of which maintenance policy—the current or proposed—introduces the least amount of variability into the system. You can determine this by calculating the *effective scv* for this equipment considering both alternatives. Because the equipment does not run constantly and must be repaired periodically (that is, PM'd), the *effective scv* takes this fact into account. Hopp and Spearman present us with the following formula for effective *scv*:[43]

$$svc_{effective} = svc_0 + (2_{mr}A\ [1 - A]) \div t_0$$

For our current maintenance policy,

$$svc_{current} = 0.20 + (2)(10)(0.909)\ (1 - 0.909) \div 11 = 0.334$$

The effective *scv* for the current policy is 0.334, which is fairly low for equipment variability. But what about the proposed maintenance policy change? For the proposed change to the maintenance policy, assume the same $svc_{current} = 0.20$, and for the proposed maintenance policy,

$$svc_{effective} = svc_0 + (2_{mr}A\ [1 - A]) \div t_0$$

$$= 0.20 + (2)(0.5)(0.95)(1 - 0.95) \div 11 = 0.204$$

The variability associated with shutting down the equipment more frequently for short maintenance activities (i.e., PM) is much lower, which is obviously a better condition than the variability associated with the current maintenance policy. This leads us to the inescapable conclusion that, generally speaking, shorter, more frequent maintenance interventions result in lower levels of variability. Because in our assumptions we assume a known average repair time (based on historical data), and we do not assume PM time (or repair time) is constant, this conclusion is valid for both planned and unplanned downtime and supports the need for regular periodic maintenance as a way of reducing equipment variability.

Predictive Maintenance and Equipment Reliability

Two subjects not yet discussed are predictive maintenance and equipment reliability. Predictive maintenance is another form of PM that utilizes measurements to accurately diagnose the condition of equipment during operation to help determine when maintenance is needed.

Predictive Maintenance

Predictive maintenance is especially important for equipment that is expensive to repair or that can cause significant losses if it breaks down. For example, many companies have compressors that produce compressed air for several pieces of equipment. If the compressor were to break down, imagine the devastating effect on the TH of the company. Every piece of equipment that utilizes compressed air would become inoperative.

There are five main objectives of predictive maintenance:

■ To *predict*, in advance, if and when equipment might break down
■ To *reduce* breakdowns of equipment that can cause significant losses to a manufacturing organization
■ To *increase* the uptime of equipment and therefore the TH
■ To *reduce* maintenance times and costs
■ To *improve* the quality of products

In reality, predictive maintenance is a condition monitoring technique, which can and should be used to monitor things like temperatures, vibration, noise, and corrosion, all of which could result in a catastrophic breakdown. The techniques or testing used in predictive maintenance are intended to be diagnostic and include:

■ Vibration monitoring used on equipment with moving parts to prevent or limit abrasion and damage
■ Ultrasonic and acoustic noise monitoring to detect leaks, bearings failing, and so on
■ Infrared temperature monitoring to determine abnormal temperature rises caused by things like abrasion and wearing of parts or hotspots in electronic parts
■ Oil and lubricant monitoring analysis to determine the presence of metal chips and foreign particles that could be caused by abrasion, misalignment, and so on
■ Crack detection to prevent any propagation that could result in major downtime
■ Corrosion monitoring to prevent structural weakening of parts

Predictive maintenance permits the prediction and prevention of deterioration and breakdowns and is a critical element of equipment effectiveness.

Equipment Reliability

Reliability, on the other hand, is the probability that a piece of equipment will perform its intended function over its intended operation time. This means that equipment has a finite life, so making equipment more reliable is all about extending the length of time between failures or preventing failures of key components. So how do you do this? One simple way to do this is to track the history of component failures as a function of time. In reliability terms this is known as mean time between failures (MTBF). By tracking the life of parts and calculating MTBF, you can predict in advance when components will likely wear out and change them before they do. This automatically reduces unplanned downtime by scheduling, in advance, when to make the change and ultimately improve OEE. It is always better to plan downtime than it is to have to react to it.

The Plan for Exploiting the Constraint

Throughout this chapter, I have discussed how to reduce waste, variation, downtime, and defects and the idea of doing so only after formulating a coherent plan. Plans are like road maps and are intended to lead you to your ultimate destination. So what should your plan for exploiting the constraint look like? Like any plan, it must include the actions you intend to take, your expected outcomes or deliverables, the timing of the actions, who is responsible for executing each particular step in the plan, the current status of the plan, and any results obtained as a result of the action taken.

Although you probably already use project management software, my advice to you is to keep your plan simple. Develop a plan that is uncomplicated without overextending your valuable resources. You could go to great lengths to develop a full-blown project management plan complete with all the bells and whistles, but in the interest of simplicity, do not do it. If you want the plan to get done, keep it simple! Do not misunderstand me: project management is a wonderful tool, but I have seen many teams get bogged down in the details of the plan and end up with a *failure to launch*. One other important point is to make certain that you keep your plan visible in or near the constraint operation.

Figure 6.12 is an example of a simple plan that provides all the necessary elements and is simple to maintain. It includes the actions, expected outcomes, estimated start and completion dates, the person responsible for making the action happen, the current status, and any results obtained to date. The key point in any plan is that in order to make the plan happen, it must be reviewed on a regular basis and the people responsible must be held accountable for making things happen per the dates in the plan. Unless there are frequent/regular reviews of the plan's status, it will just be another document gathering dust on someone's desk.

Some of the key points in this plan include reducing P/T and downtime in the constraint operation; designing and implementing a drum-buffer-rope scheduling system; creating pull systems in the nonconstraints; and implementing visual controls, performance metrics, and waste and variation reduction plans. Your plan will not look exactly like this simply because your plant's needs will be different. The key to remember when developing your plan is what you are trying to achieve. You want your product to flow through your constraint more quickly than before, so you must take actions to that end. Your own version of the DBR and your buffer management plan will help you achieve that end.

As you can see in Figure 6.12, the plan is simple, uncomplicated, straightforward, and it follows the actions prescribed in UIC. Also notice that there are not details on how things like the DOE will be performed or what will happen during the 5S. This plan is simply intended to be a document that will be used to define the required activities, expected outcomes, and who is responsible for making things happen, and for reviewing progress against each of the action items. Each one of the teams will develop its own detailed plan, so again, do not make your constraint improvement plan overly complicated, and be sure to use it for its intended purpose. I have seen many examples where teams spent an inordinate amount of time on developing the plan at the expense of its execution.

Three final points regarding the improvement plan: You will notice that the final step in the plan is the development of *standardized work instructions* within the constraint. This is the final step for a very good reason. Many of the other steps in the plan will have a profound impact on how the operators perform their tasks and how the material flows through the process, so it is important to develop the work method after all improvements have been identified and implemented, and not before. Having said that, it is perfectly correct to prepare the standardized work method earlier in the process, but if you do, make certain that it gets updated after all improvements have been made. Remember, the standardized work method is a *living and dynamic document*, and as changes are made, they must be reflected in this method.

The second point is that the order in which you execute your plan is strictly a function of the *current status* of your operation. For example, if you have a major problem with equipment downtime, activities aimed at reducing downtime should be included in the early stages of your plan. If you have problems related to defective product, your early efforts should be focused here. The point is that there is no cookie-cutter approach or step-by-step recipe for the order in which activities are planned and executed. It is all dependent upon your own situation and status.

The final point to remember is that you must involve the *right players* as you develop the improvement plan. Perhaps the most important members of the team are the hourly operators who will be responsible for operating the new process and making product when the new process is ready. Operators are so often left out of planning activities when in fact they are the people with the most information—the true process experts. My advice is very clear-cut: if you want your plan to work, you had better involve the operators. In addition, the operators must be provided assurance that they are not planning themselves

Action Items	Expected Outcome	Start Date	Complete Date	Responsible	Status	Results
Implement 5S on the constraint operation to reduce NVA time	Reduce NVA time by 25%	6/3/06	6/5/06	B. Kilmer	Complete	NVA time reduced by 31%
Develop and implement DBR scheduling system	Improve throughput by 30% and ontime delivery to >95%	6/08/06	6/12/06	B. Kilmer	Complete and functioning	Throughput improved by 23% and ontime delivery improved to 91%
Develop and implement visual controls and performance metrics in the constraint operation	Improve operation's awareness of process status and progress	6/15/06	6/23/06	B. Kilmer	Complete	Process status is now highly visible
Perform a gage R&R on measurement system in the constraint	Total GR&R <10%	6/3/06	6/6/06	T. Jones	Complete	GR&R = 9.75%
Run a DOE on constraint operation to reduce product variation	50% reduction in std deviation	6/6/06	6/13/06	T. Jones	In process	Team formed, study factors and levels identified
Design and implement manufacturing work cell	Reduce total cycle time by 40%	6/25/06	6/28/06	B. Kilmer	In process	Kaizen event under way
Reduce changeover time in the constant operation	Reduce changeover time from 58 minutes to 25 minutes	6/29/06	7/03/08	B. Kilmer	Planning complete	Kaizen event participants selected

Figure 6.12   Constraint Exploitment Plan.

Solve number one defect problem in the constraint operation	Reduce defect level by 50%	6/10/06	6/17/06	T. Jones	Team formed			
Resolve number one cause of machine downtime	Reduce D/T by 50% and increase OEE by 20%	6/15/06	6/21/06	T. Jones	Team formed			
Improve equipment maintainability	Reduce time to repair by 20% and OEE by 10%	6/22/06	7/01/06	T. Jones	Team formed			
Implement pull system in non-constraint operations	Improve constraint schedule compliance to >95%	7/07/06	7/11/06	B. Kilmer	Team selection complete			
Develop and implement process controls and error proofing in the constraint operation	Reduce product variation by 10%	6/23/06	6/29/06	T. Jones	Team selected			
Rebalance the process and establish one-piece flow	Improve throughput by 10%	7/15/06	7/22/06	B. Kilmer	Team selected			
Develop standardized work instructions in the constraint operation	Reduce processisng time by 10%	6/30/06	7/07/06	T. Jones B. Kilmer	Team selected			

Figure 6.12 (Continued.)

out of a job. The worst possible thing that can happen is that as cycle times are reduced, or defects and downtime are eliminated, people get moved out of their jobs or, worse yet, laid off. If this is your strategy, I suggest that you stop right now because it is a strategy for disaster. If this were to happen even one time, you would lose your sense of team and the motivation to improve, so do not lay people off. I realize that business conditions can change or the economy can take a downturn and that there are times when you simply cannot avoid layoffs, but if people sense that the reason their fellow workers are losing their jobs is because of improvements to the process, improvements will stop immediately.

Chapter 7

Reducing Waste and Variation in the Current Constraint

In this chapter, I discuss why you do not want to consider rapid improvement events an improvement strategy, why involvement of the workforce is so important, why your team members need to learn to work as a team, and why throughout accounting is the way to go. This is a mixed bag, to be sure, but it all relates to reducing waste and variation.

Constraint Improvement Plan Execution

Now that your improvement plan has been developed, it is time to make things happen. All the planning that you did in step 2a of UIC will finally begin to pay off in the form of improved TH and reduced OE and inventory in the constraint operation and its feeders. Ultimately, you will see a substantial increase in your profits. In steps 2b and 2c, you will execute the plan you just developed and will do so swiftly.

You will notice that in the plan in Figure 6.12, the action items occur in very short increments so as to avoid a protracted or long-drawn-out execution scenario. In some of these steps, you might be using a kaizen or rapid improvement event to complete each of the individual steps. What you do not want is for the improvement plan to become stalled or take months to complete, so by applying kaizen techniques to *some* of the key action items, you should be able to complete these items in relatively short order. The key action items will be dependent upon your actual situation. But having said this, I offer the following caution. Although kaizen events usually speed up the completion of specific activities, do not let them become your manufacturing strategy. Remember, you are trying to do three things here: eliminate waste, reduce P/T and product variability, and improve the flow of materials through the overall process.

I once worked with a company whose entire approach to improvement was based on kaizen events—so much so that they actually rated the performance of their managers based upon the number of kaizen events, rather than on the results they achieved. This is not a manufacturing strategy. Companies need a manufacturing strategy that:

- Reduces variability in products and processing times throughout the value stream
- Improves the flow of materials from the supplier to the customer
- Focuses activities on the area constraining TH

This strategy will result in meeting or exceeding customer requirements and significant bottom-line improvement. UIC is such a strategy.

Standard and Davis tell us, "Surprisingly, 90% of American companies have no manufacturing strategy. It is the fortunate factory that has the benefit of well-aligned, clearly communicated, and widely understood long-term direction."[44] So if you are one of those companies, you had better consider developing a manufacturing strategy sooner rather than later. My belief is the UIC offers a coherent, long-term strategy that maximizes TH and bottom-line improvement. The UIC is self-perpetuating, and as one constraint is broken, new ones will appear and they too will be broken. As this cycle keeps repeating itself, TH and profits will continue to improve in a methodical fashion.

The Power of Involvement

Successful improvement initiatives rarely happen as the result of a single person, and the UIC is no exception. Rarely does a single person have enough knowledge, skills, experience, or abilities to understand the complete inner workings of a process. The synergistic effects of team involvement will be needed to develop and execute the plan that has hopefully been developed by all members of the team. One of the reasons Toyota has been so successful in the "respect-for-human system" they employ, which gives employees responsibility with corresponding authority—one of Toyota's most important operating principles.

I have been in many factories where they claim to have employee involvement, only to discover that it is just meaningless rhetoric. There are photos of teams posted everywhere, supposedly serving as "proof of involvement" of the workforce, but when you talk to the workers in the photo, you get an entirely different story. I have heard comments like "My opinion really doesn't count" or "I've got ideas, but nobody listens to me." People need to feel that their opinion counts and they are partners in the organization's success. Most shop floor workers possess a wealth of experience and expertise, are eager to share what they know, and should be considered a company's true assets. Equipment and materials can be replaced, but workers offer a unique blend of knowledge, skills, loyalty, and abilities that companies must harvest. Those companies that truly recognize and capitalize on the power of involvement are the companies that will have a significant strategic advantage going forward. My advice to companies is clear: involve your people, listen to their ideas, and by all means, if you are giving them responsibility, give them the corresponding authority. In other words, give them the respect they deserve and they will reward you many times over.

Involvement includes the organization's leadership as well. I say this emphatically because in a typical company it is not uncommon for the leadership to become disengaged from the improvement process. Becoming disengaged simply will not cut it in today's economy. Leaders must not just be involved; they must lead and keep the organization focused.

Learning to Work as a Team

Almost twenty years ago, Peter Scholtes published *The Team Handbook*. In his book he discussed his now infamous four stages of team growth: forming, storming, norming, and performing.[45] I can honestly tell you that Scholtes had it exactly right. In all my years of experience with teams, I have yet to work with a team that does not go through these four stages exactly as Scholtes described. Let us review these four stages and the implications of each as you pursue implementation of UIC.

Stage 1: Forming

When employees come together as a single unit, the members may or may not know everyone involved in the team, so they cautiously explore the boundaries of acceptable group behavior. Each member comes to the team with a blend of different feelings ranging from excitement and pride to fear and anxiety about the task ahead of them. They are wondering about expectations the team leader has of them and whether or not they will be able to contribute. If the team has been formed correctly, it will consist of a diversity of functions, ranging from purchasing to engineering, and the members may or may not know each other, so there is an automatic hesitation about working with these strangers.

Stage 2: Storming

Of the four stages Scholtes tells us about, storming is by far the most difficult to get through for a team. The euphoria that the team experienced during the first stage is replaced with impatience. Members are impatient about the lack of progress but at the same time are still not experienced enough to know what to do to make things happen. Members of the team only have their experience to rely on, so after trying all they know to do, they resist the need to collaborate with other members of the team. The behaviors that you will see are arguments, bickering, criticism, defensiveness, competition, and choosing sides. The good news is that the team is finally beginning to understand each other.

Stage 3: Norming

In this stage members begin to reconcile differences and begin to accept the team members, their roles, and the individuality of their fellow members. Emotional conflict is replaced with one of cooperation. The team members realize that they have a job to do and that they each play an important role in the success of the team. A sense of team pervades the group and sets the tone for the final stage.

Stage 4: Performing

The team has finally become a cohesive unit and progress becomes the norm. The team members now recognize the strengths and weaknesses of each other and have finally accepted their roles. It is very clear when the team has reached this stage because they start getting things done and the performance metrics chosen begin to move in a positive direction.

Educating Your Team

Because the approach outlined in the UIC is, in most cases, a drastic change from the way you are now operating, my advice to you is to use the first meeting with your team as an educational session.

Teaching about Constraints

First, all members of your team need to understand the basic premise of TOC, that there is usually only one operation that is limiting the TH of the process (the constraint), and unless and until this constraint is identified and broken, TH will not improve. How might you do this? I have found that if you point out the most common symptom associated with a constraint (i.e., inventory stacked in front of an operation) and then have your team go on a "hunt" for the constraint, it will not take them long to find it.

Once your team has found the apparent constraint, discuss how every process is plagued by both waste and variation and how damaging to TH both of these are. One easy way to reinforce the concept of value-added versus non-value-added activities is to split your group into pairs and have each group go on a *waste and variation scavenger hunt* in the constraint, looking for examples of both. The team members readily see that waste is everywhere and will no doubt see defective product as well. Have the team discuss the examples they have found and why they believe their findings are waste.

Introducing Drum and Subordination

The next step in the educational process is the presentation of the concepts of the drum and subordination. This will be the most difficult concept for your team to grasp and accept simply because of the inherent barriers that exist within the organization. If you are like many organizations that are using utilization or efficiency to measure performance, having nonconstraint processes slow down to match the pace of the drum will be absolutely foreign to everyone. For years the operators in the nonconstraint operations and supervisors have been told to speed up, and now you are asking them to ignore the past. Change is difficult for many people, so there must be assurances that the leadership of the organization will support this new way of operating. For this reason, it is a good idea for the leadership to be a part of this first meeting and to demonstrate that they are solidly behind this new way of running the business.

Explaining Throughput Accounting (TA)

You can also use this meeting as an opportunity to explain the basics of TA and why maximizing TH in the constraint is much better than optimizing every operation. Demonstrate to the team how maximizing TH is the best approach to improving the company's bottom line. Make no mistake about it: this will be a difficult phase for the team, so take your time and get it right.

Taking a Scientific Approach

Another important concept for the team to understand is that they will be using the scientific approach to learn about and make decisions on how their new processes will be run. The two most important messages for your team will be that all decisions will be made based on data rather than opinions and that problems will be solved rather than relying on quick fixes. Scholtes talks about the concept of complexity, which is his term for unnecessary work that complicates a process without adding value. Scholtes explains that complexity arises when people repeatedly attempt to improve a process without any systematic plan. He goes on to explain that there are four types of complexity: mistakes and defects, breakdowns and delays, inefficiencies, and variation.[46] Odds are high that your process or system will have at least one or all of these problems.

Talking about Teamwork and Urgency

The next point to make with the team is one of teamwork and urgency. The thing standing between your current profit level and where you will be in the future is TH, so you must make the point that everyone must have a sense of urgency and complete the improvement plan in as short a timeframe as possible. Small improvements in TH could possibly result in substantial improvements in revenue and profits, so the faster the constraint improvement plan is executed, the sooner the company will realize financial gains. Teamwork is absolutely imperative, so early on in your improvement initiative it is a good idea to introduce and complete a kaizen event. If people experience the impact of teamwork and a rapid improvement event, it will set the stage for future improvements. Having said this, I want to reemphasize that multiple, back-to-back kaizen events is not a business strategy. These rapid improvement events should be carefully planned and interjected in a controlled manner.

Learning to Communicate

The final point I want to discuss is communications. It is absolutely imperative that communication lines are established and maintained. One of the most effective ways of doing this, besides in a meeting format, is the creation of a communications board. This board should contain graphs and charts of key performance metrics that clearly display progress against each one. I have always advocated having a quick, daily meeting of the team in front of the communications board for a quick review of progress. Also included should be the constraint improvement plan with the status of each activity clearly annotated. People will rally around success, and being able to see it on paper is necessary.

Chapter 8

Subordinating Nonconstraints to the Current Constraint

Step 3a of UIC tells you that you need to subordinate nonconstraints to the constraint operation. In this chapter, I further define what subordination really means. I also discuss how to identify a nonconstraint, why this step of the UIC is so important, what you gain by doing so, and how to develop a plan for subordinating the constraint.

Identifying a Nonconstraint Operation

So far we have spent most of our time identifying and characterizing the constraint operation, but now it is time to talk about nonconstraints. Just what is a nonconstraint? Basically any operation that does not limit the TH of the organization or does not stand in the way of the organization's moving closer to its goal of making more money now and in the future can be considered a nonconstraint. For example, suppose you come across an operation that has piles of inventory in front of it. The process steps upstream and downstream from this operation are normally the nonconstraints. But hold on: just because there is no inventory in front of an operation does not mean it is not the constraint operation. What if the operation is utilizing a pull system that limits the amount of WIP inventory? Will there be loads of inventory then?

I have found that a comparison of individual operation P/Ts is a reasonable way to find both constraint and nonconstraint operations. For example, I once consulted for a company that produced flexible bladders used to hold organic liquids. The process was completely manual and consisted of a series of process steps required to produce both the top and bottom of the tank. The top and bottom were then joined together to form a whole tank. The joining process took approximately six to seven days to complete, while the longest individual process step, upstream or downstream from the joining process, took only four days. Because of this disparity in P/Ts, it was very easy to find the constraint and nonconstraint operations. Because this company had no pull systems in place, there were at least four weeks worth of individual tops and bottoms sitting idle ahead of the joining operation. There was no inventory upstream from the joining process, so, clearly, it was an even easier task to identify both the constraining operation (i.e., joining) and the nonconstraint operations (i.e., all other process steps). Why was there so much inventory in front of the constraint operation? One reason was because of the disparity in P/Ts and no WIP cap in place. But the real reason was that this company used operator efficiency as its primary performance metric. Because of this metric and the mandate to optimize efficiency in each of the individual process steps, the nonconstraint operations continued to build the tops and bottoms even though they were not needed. This, of course, increased the total process efficiency but served to build excessive inventory in front of the constraining operation.

Again, the search for nonconstraint and constraint operations comes down to a single statement. If the operation is not impeding TH or is not preventing an organization from moving closer to its goal, it is a nonconstraint operation; if it is, it is a constraint operation. In the case of the flexible bladders, the joining operation was the constraint, but because of the presence of a policy constraint (i.e., using efficiency as a performance metric), the situation was much worse than it should have been.

Subordinating Nonconstraints to Constraints

Step 3a of UIC tells you to plan how to subordinate nonconstraints to the constraint operation. So what does that mean? The best way to understand what this means is to look at the definition of the word *subordinate* itself. Definitions of *subordinate* are as follows:

■ Belonging to a lower or inferior class or rank; secondary

■ Subject to the authority or control of another

The fact that a subordinate is secondary and subject to the authority or control of another really says it all. Literally, the constraint operation should dictate everything that goes on in a process. Of course, you want the constraint working at the rate required to satisfy customer orders, but the nonconstraint operations should work only at the pace that the constraint does, neither faster nor slower. Upstream nonconstraints have the responsibility of never letting the constraint operation run out of material because the TH of the system would stop, and so would new revenue. But by the same token, the nonconstraint operations should not work faster than the constraint simply because running faster would not result in more system TH. In fact, running faster would end up costing the operation more because of the added carrying costs of excess inventory.

In reality, subordinating nonconstraint operations to the constraint operation involves taking a back seat to the constraint. If the constraint operation is experiencing equipment downtime, maintenance must drop everything else, move to the constraint, and get the equipment back on line. If there is a quality problem on the constraint operation, the focus must be on correcting the problem, even at the expense of a nonconstraint quality problem. Because the nonconstraint operations have "sprint capacity," in the event of downtime, they should be able to shut down and wait for resources without negatively impacting TH at the constraint.

Subordination is not limited to typical manufacturing functions, either. For example, engineering must always be available to move to a constraint-based problem at the expense of nonconstraints. Sales must be constantly aware of and pursuing new orders that will keep the constraint operation busy, but not beyond its capacity. In effect, all resources, which include all functional groups and nonconstraint operations, must be available to actively support the needs of the constraint operations without exception. Remember, a constraint operation should never be left idle because lost production can never be recovered.

Knowing What You Gain by Subordinating Nonconstraints to the Constraint

The question is: Why is it so important to subordinate the nonconstraint resources to the constraints? At the risk of being redundant and belaboring the point, because the system constraint determines the overall system TH and the ultimate profitability of the organization, the nonconstraint operations play a subordinate role to the constraint. To quote Debra Smith, "The ability to subordinate will define a company's ability to succeed with the Theory of Constraints.

Exploitation of the constraint is dependent on effective subordination." She further states, "Disruptions cause waste and accumulation of delays. Delays and waste cause costs to go up and TH to go down."[47] Any improvement initiative that utilizes all or parts of TOC, like the one I have presented in this book, must be locked into and committed to the concept of subordination. Without embracing subordination, at some point in time the constraint operation will be starved, TH will decrease, and profits will be less than optimal. And remember, lost TH is lost forever and can never be regained.

Improvement efforts that focus on areas other than the constraint operations are, for the most part, generally fruitless. That is, improving the output of a nonconstraint operation not only increases carrying cost of inventory, but also lengthens the product cycle time. Although the other parts of the system could produce more, there simply is no point in doing so. Subordination changes the way an organization carries out its business and redefines the objectives in every part of the global system. Material should be released according to the needs of the constraint only and according to firm orders. Maintenance priorities will be set according to the needs of the system constraint. Manufacturing engineering will be at the beck and call of the constraint. Every group and employee in the organization must recognize that the key to short- and long-term profitability, and hence realization of the organization's goal, is the recognition and belief that the system constraint is the first priority.

Going about the Business of Subordinating Nonconstraints to the Constraint

Now that you have an idea of what subordination is and why you should subordinate the nonconstraints to the constraint, the question becomes one of how you do it. But before I answer this question, there are some basic guidelines—or maybe a better word is *truths*—to discuss. For your typical American company, these guidelines may be a difficult pill to swallow, because the leadership and management of many companies have been taught, rewarded, and disciplined using the following basic beliefs for many years.

■ If your company is currently using manpower efficiency or equipment utilization as its primary performance metric, be prepared to abandon or at least scale back its relative importance significantly in your nonconstraint operations. Measuring the efficiency of a nonconstraint may result in local improvements, but it will not ensure that the overall performance of the organization will improve. In fact, focusing on improvements in nonconstraint efficiencies will actually cause the performance of the total organization to become worse, not better. Just remember that global or system improvement is not the sum of local improvements.

■ Because you will now be optimizing and making decisions about the organization from a global perspective rather than optimizing locally like so many companies do, be prepared to have some of your nonconstraint operators and machines sitting idle at different periods of time for the good of the total organization. The important point to remember here is that, contrary to some beliefs, an idle resource is not a significant source of waste. I realize this is contrary to what Lean teaches, but the fact is that 100 percent utilization of nonconstraints is not a good thing.

■ The reality is that constraints do exist, and if you do not manage them, they will manage you. If you do not manage them, your organization will be in a constant firefighting mode. Managing constraints is one of the keys to organizational and operational success.

■ Focusing resources on a nonconstraint process will not result in a maximization of a company's ROI. Focusing resources on the system constraint to improve performance will improve the performance of the total system and will maximize the ROI.

■ Be prepared to find many nonphysical constraints. In fact, many of the constraints you will identify are based on outdated policies and beliefs that probably were effective at one point in time, but have outlived their usefulness and are now hurting the organization. These policies are usually traced to things like staffing decisions; how products and materials are scheduled, purchased, and supplied; product pricing policies; how performance is measured; and how people in the organization should be managed. All these types of constraints usually are based upon flawed and outdated assumptions, and many times they are observed as unwritten rules that have been passed down from previous leadership. But beware, nonphysical constraints are not necessarily easy to correct. In fact, most times they are much more difficult to correct simply because they have become part of the DNA of the organization.

Asking Basic Questions

Subordinating nonconstraints to constraints is not as difficult as you might think or as difficult as some writers have suggested. Dettmer, in his book *Breaking the Constraints to World Class Performance*, presents what he calls a TOC decision matrix. In this matrix, Dettmer converts three traditional global measures (i.e., NP, ROI, and cash flow) into TOC terms and local measures of optimization. He then lists a series of questions, which require a yes or no answer. Dettmer concludes that if the answer to the question is yes, do it. If the answer is no, do not do it. These questions can be used to evaluate local decisions and answer the question of how to subordinate nonconstraints to the constraint operation.[48]

- Will it increase sales?
- Will it speed up deliveries to clients?
- Will it reduce backlogs?
- Will it reduce your need for production materials?
- Will it shorten production time?
- Will it reduce fixed expenses?
- Will it shorten the time between product or service delivery and time of payment?
- Will it increase the volume of revenue received in the same time period?
- Will it shorten the time between receipt of order and delivery to the customer?
- Will it free excess capacity?
- Will it make better use of the constraint?
- Will you need fewer materials on hand?
- Will you need less equipment?

When considering any kind of improvement or, in this case, considering an action aimed at subordinating a nonconstraint to a constraint operation, ask these questions.

Taking Action

What kinds of actions am I talking about with respect to subordination? The most obvious action is to never let a nonconstraint operation outrun or outproduce a constraint (i.e., excess inventory). Basically any action that will protect or enhance a constraint's output is a worthwhile action. For example, placing a protective buffer in front of a constraint to protect it from planned and unplanned downtime is a good thing as long as the amount of inventory is not excessive. Any action that reduces flow variability is a worthwhile action. Any time a nonconstraint operation can take on some of the constraint operation's workload, thus reducing the P/T of the constraint, it is a valuable action as long as you do not jeopardize the sprint capacity of the nonconstraint. That is, never attempt to create a balanced production line. Again, any action that enhances or protects a constraint operation is an advisable action.

Creating a Plan

The final subordination step is to create a plan for doing so. Again, keep it simple and it will get done. My advice is rather than creating a new plan, add on to the one you have already created.

Chapter 9

Line Balancing and Flow Optimization

Contrary to what you might have read or been told, having a perfectly balanced line is not the optimal way to run your production operation. In this chapter, I help you develop the concept of an unbalanced line and see how it relates to flow optimization and one-piece flow.

Avoiding a Perfectly Balanced Line

In this step of UIC, you reduce and better balance P/T differences and optimize flow. But before you pursue P/T reduction, I want to make one thing perfectly clear: you are not intending to create a perfectly balanced production line, because it has been proven many times that perfectly balanced processes will always result in a higher incidence of constraint starvation. Why is this true?

First, production should never exceed the rate or pace of customer orders (i.e., takt time) because doing so only serves to increase inventory. Second, Lean manufacturing attempts to create high levels of utilization, but never at 100 percent. In the Lean approach to line balancing, work elements should be distributed so that the amount of time required for each worker to complete his or her tasks is slightly less than the takt time, even if performance metrics like efficiency are reduced in the nonconstraint operations. It is important to understand that if an operator or a machine is underutilized, this is not necessarily a bad thing. In fact, this can be turned into an opportunity.

This approach to imperfect line balancing has some clear advantages. First, if the work cell is out of balance, it is readily apparent that one or more operators have time to assist with other things in the cell, including helping the operator on the constraint operation with things like maintenance activities, paperwork, and so on. Second, if the work cell is significantly out of balance, this sends a signal that other things need to be done to bring it in line. The third advantage is that by producing according to customer orders, there is no overproduction and excess inventory can be avoided. Finally, by avoiding perfectly balanced lines, if there is downtime at a nonconstraint operation, there is sprint capacity to catch up when the machine comes back on line. In doing so, you can avoid starvation at the constraint operation. The primary reason, then, for avoiding a perfectly balanced production line is to avoid starving the constraint operation.

Looking at a New Type of Balance

If you do not want perfect balance, how much of a difference do you want in P/Ts between the constraint and nonconstraint operations? The answer is that it depends. If, for example, your nonconstraints do not have a history of serious downtime and you have an excellent maintenance group that can bring a nonconstraint machine back on line quickly, the difference can be small. If, on the other hand, your process has a history of excessive downtime or quality problems on the nonconstraint operations, the difference must be larger so that there is enough sprint capacity. There is not a law of factory physics or a basic formula that governs this difference, so process variability will dictate it.

Okay, so how do you go about balancing a production line? Let us look at the simple four-step process in Figure 9.1, where operation C is the constraining step.

The capacity of this line is 3 parts/minute or 20 parts/hour. In a perfectly balanced line each operation would take exactly 1.75 minutes (i.e., total cycle time ÷ number of process steps, or 7 minutes ÷ 4 steps = 1.75 minutes/step). But

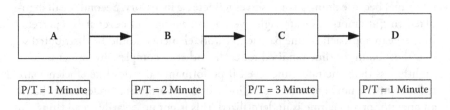

Figure 9.1 Basic Four-Step Process.

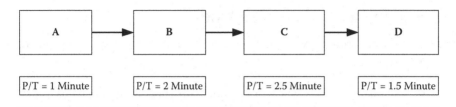

Figure 9.2   Improved Four-Step Process.

as you have seen, you do not want your line to be in perfect balance. But what would happen to your capacity if you could unload some of the work in operation C onto operation D? For example, suppose you studied the line and found that it was possible to move 30 seconds of work from operation C to operation D, as depicted in Figure 9.2. What happens to your line capacity?

By transferring 30 seconds of work from operation C to the nonconstraint operation D, your capacity improves from 20 parts/hour to 24 parts/hour. Notice that you do not have a perfectly balanced the line, but you have changed it to the benefit of an additional 4 parts/hour. Could you have moved this 30 seconds to operation B? Yes, you could have, but would that have been the best move to make? Let us take a look.

Figure 9.3 is the new process after moving the thirty seconds of work from operation C to operation B, and as you can see, you now have dual constraints. Which line, the one in Figure 9.2 or that in Figure 9.3, do you think would be easier to manage?

Remember, one of the key points in managing constraints is to never starve a constraint. In the process in Figure 9.3, what would happen if operation B experienced downtime? Would it eventually starve operation C? Does it now have the necessary sprint capacity to prevent operation C from shutting down? Clearly, it does not, so creating a process configuration of this nature would not be in your best interests. There is not a law of factory physics that dictates how best to balance the line, but you do have common sense, logic, and variation data you can use to make the best decision.

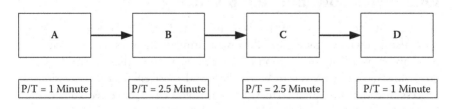

Figure 9.3   New Four-Step Process.

Accepting an Unbalanced Line

Hopp and Spearman give us three reasons why we might want an unbalanced line:[49]

- An unbalanced flow line with a distinct bottleneck is easier to manage and exhibits better logistical behavior than a corresponding balanced line.
- The cost of capacity is typically not the same at each station, so it is cheaper to maintain excess capacity at some stations than at others.
- Capacity is frequently available only in discrete-size increments (e.g., you can buy one or two lathes, but not one and a half), so it may be impossible to match capacity of a given station to a particular target.

According to Hopp and Spearman, "When appropriate consideration is given to these three factors, the optimal configuration of most flow lines will be an unbalanced line.... Despite the arguments in favor of unbalanced lines, sometimes line balancing makes sense.... Balanced lines are applicable only to paced assembly lines, not flow lines."[50] What's the difference? In a flow line all the workstations are independent of each other, such as the hypothetical lines in Figures 9.1, 9.2, and 9.3. Because each station operates at its own speed, the bottleneck is generally the slowest station in the line. In a paced assembly line such as that associated with a conveyor belt or a chain, parts move at a constant speed. Therefore, the bottleneck of a paced assembly line is not the slowest station but, rather, the speed of the transfer device. Unfortunately, many times the idea of a balanced line has become so ingrained in companies, as well as a desire for high utilization and efficiency at every workstation, that many companies actively pursue balanced lines when they clearly should not. In summary, flow lines should generally always be unbalanced, while paced assembly lines should generally always be balanced. In most cases in today's factories, unbalanced lines typically function better.

One-Piece Flow and Line Balancing

What about one-piece flow? What is it and what does it do for you? One-piece flow, also known as single-piece flow or continuous flow, is when product or parts are moved from one station to the next as soon as they are ready. One-piece flow has been proven to be the best and most efficient way possible to process material through a factory. In fact, if you have converted your manufacturing operations from functional islands to cellular manufacturing, one-piece flow becomes almost automatic. The fact is that, if you want to optimize flow and therefore TH, you should be actively pursuing one-piece flow. In addition, there are other benefits associated with one-piece flow. For example, one-piece flow automatically builds in better quality because every operator is an inspector and works to fix any problems in a station before passing them on. In addition, one-piece flow reduces WIP inventory, thus reducing costs.

The concept of one-piece flow can even work for some traditional batch type operations. For example, in a heat treating operation it might seem strange to heat treat a single part. But if the heat treat process is one where a moving conveyor carries parts through the heat treat process, one-piece flow can be realized. Because one-piece flow is the most efficient form of production, sometimes with a little imagination and ingenuity you can make it happen.

Chapter 10

Optimizing the Constraint Buffer and Pulling in the Nonconstraints

Production and inventory control is a management discipline that attempts to ensure that a sufficient and timely amount of material is on hand and ready when and where it is needed to meet both internal and external customers' needs, usually according to a fixed production schedule. It is because of this purpose that production and inventory control can have a huge impact on a company's financials. It has an influence not only on a plant's TH but also on its utilization of capacity, which are both linked to a company's profitability. Because the cost of the inventory can be a major portion of the cost of goods sold, the approach to how materials are managed can significantly impact cash flow, capital spending, and the rate at which orders are filled. In steps 3b and 3c of UIC, your focus will be on how you will implement a new type of scheduling for the constraint operation while simultaneously implementing a pull system in the nonconstraints.

Scheduling Production

One of the first UIC steps was to design and implement a DBR scheduling system to supply the constraint, assembly, and shipping. As part of the DBR system, you established the pace of production (the rate of the constraint, i.e., the *drum*) and inventory and time *buffers* to protect the constraint, any assembly operation that utilizes the output of the constraint, and shipping from starvation. You also said that the DBR was a way to schedule releases of raw materials and purchased components (the *rope*). The question now becomes: How do you schedule the nonconstraints? The quick answer is that you will integrate pull systems into your process. But before we discuss the details of how to design and construct pull systems, let us talk about push and pull systems, forecasting, and scheduling in general.

In today's manufacturing world many companies are utilizing a push-based Material Requirements Planning (MRP) or MRP-like system to plan and deliver the materials required to produce products. In typical fashion, *push* systems *schedule* the release of work based on both actual customer demand and a sales *forecast*. For this reason, push systems are referred to as *make to order*. *Pull* systems, on the other hand, *authorize* the release of work based upon the real-time status of the process and, as such, are referred to as *make to stock*. In push system environments a master production schedule is generated for the plant as well as a purchasing schedule to obtain things from suppliers like raw materials, components, and subassemblies.

MRP calculates a plant's needs per the bill-of-materials, assumed lead times, and customer due dates. Once the master schedule is prepared, though, it becomes nearly impossible to change it simply because of the ripple effect it would cause throughout the entire process, including the supply base. But because of supplier delays, customers changing their order requirements, or even internal issues like downtime and quality problems, if changes are not made, WIP will grow throughout the factory. When WIP levels get too high, management typically reacts by doing things like scheduling overtime, hiring temporary workers, or worse yet, pushing out due dates. In effect, managers *temporarily* stop using a push system until things normalize. The problem is that the cycle generally repeats itself. The damage has already been done because corrective action happens *after the fact*, so the key is to avoid these WIP explosions.

One way to avoid these WIP explosions is the DBR system implemented earlier in the UIC. In this system we do two things. First, the release of raw materials is controlled by the rope that limits the ordering, receiving, and issuing of the raw materials into the process. Second, because you have established WIP caps, you choke off production *before* the system becomes overloaded with excess WIP.

Push Environment

In a push environment, if a key process step experiences downtime, the rest of the process continues to produce product. But you know that no matter how much WIP enters a process, the process is limited by the constraining operation and will therefore not produce more product that turns into TH. By contrast, in a pull environment, if a key process step goes down, the order mechanism and WIP cap prevent this from happening. Likewise, if there is an engineering change order, in a push system the excess inventory could very well become obsolete. In a pull system, the WIP cap limits this loss. Pull systems are self-regulating and self-correcting and are, for the most part, *always superior to push systems.*

If you are working in a push environment, you have no doubt experienced problems associated with building the wrong product at the wrong time or the right product at the wrong time. In a push environment you are attempting to see into the future by means of a forecast and make what you think will be needed. Hopp and Spearman provide you with three fundamental forecasting laws that help explain why you might have built the wrong product:[51]

- **First law of forecasting:** Forecasts are always wrong!
- **Second law of forecasting:** Detailed forecasts are worse than aggregate forecasts!
- **Third law of forecasting:** The further into the future, the less reliable the forecast will be!

With these three laws it is easy to see how one could build the wrong product at the wrong time or the right product at the wrong time.

In a Lean environment the production and inventory control function is vital to the financial health of a company because DBR or JIT requires the close management of all forms of material. The good news is that an effective materials management system always results in shorter cycle times, less inventory, and improved customer service. It is this management of less inventory, including fewer raw materials, fewer purchased components, fewer replacement parts, less WIP, and fewer finished goods, that makes materials management so important.

In pure push systems, material and production orders are released to production and they push their way through each workstation until the job is completed. Therefore, push systems operate with no regard for real-time status of the downstream operations. Push systems are detached from the customer, so it is not uncommon for mountains of inventory to accumulate between process steps, and although inventory accumulations are everywhere, it is not at all uncommon to experience parts shortages and late deliveries to customers.

Pull Systems

Pull systems, on the other hand, operate based on a real-time basis relative to what is actually happening on the production floor. Pull systems see what has been consumed by downstream processes or what has been shipped to the customer and then authorize new materials for new production orders to enter the system. In other words, new production is not permitted until something has exited the system. As I said before, pull systems are both self-adjusting and self-correcting, so if a customer order changes, there is no requirement to update the master production schedule.

The MRP crusade has been with us for more than thirty years now, and for the most part, it has not lived up to its expectation of improved system performance. Although MRP is an excellent tool for determining when and what materials are required, it is simply not a viable tool for controlling production. Two fundamental flaws of MRP are that the time required to produce an item is independent of quantity ordered and the status or loading within the plant is not considered. In fact, the exact opposite is true! The truth is that the time required for production material to be processed through a factory is dependent upon the loading of the plant unless the plant has infinite capacity. In recent years Enterprise Resource Planning (ERP) systems have been developed, but the same MRP logic and algorithms are still embedded in these systems, which you know does not reflect real-time status on the factory floor.

Optimizing the Constraint Buffer

When you first implemented DBR earlier in the UIC, you calculated, or at least estimated, what the size of the buffer needed to be to protect the constraint from starvation. Since then you have made quite a few improvements to not only the constraint operation but also the operation that feeds the constraint. You have probably attacked and solved sources of downtime and defects that have resulted in a much more consistent and reliable operation with fewer stoppages due to these two problems. You also implemented metrics that track constraint schedule compliance, and I am certain that these metrics are trending in a positive direction. Because of your hard work, there is payback. Based upon your improved constraint schedule compliance and the improved reliability of your constraint feeder process, you now have the opportunity to reduce the size of your constraint buffer.

To size the buffer properly, it should be monitored closely against the scheduled arrival time. This monitoring of the buffer sends a signal to the entire plant as to when you need to expedite parts. When a part does not arrive at the buffer according to a schedule, it creates a hole in the buffer. If you are experiencing many occurrences of holes, your buffer is too small and you are at risk of starving the constraint and therefore lose TH. Conversely, if you are never experiencing holes in the buffer, it is too large. Oversizing the buffer needlessly increases OEs and cycle time, which decreases inventory turns and ultimately decreases cash flow. So how do you know what the proper size of the buffer should be? The answer is that proper sizing of the buffer only comes by monitoring it. My advice to you is that if you think you have an opportunity to reduce the size of the buffer, just do it, but keep a close watch on it.

Designing a Pull System

Pull systems are self-regulating and self-correcting and surprisingly simple to design and implement.

Three First Steps

There are three basic steps that must be completed *before* designing a pull system:

1. Diagram the flow of materials and information in a process. Fortunately, back in step 1a of the UIC, you created a VSM, which includes both the flow of materials and information, so you have a starting point. But because you have made changes and improvements to your process, it is time to update your VSM.
2. Identify pull loops. Pull loops are a combination of information being sent upstream and material flowing downstream.
3. Decide which type of pull system to use for each loop.

To this last point, there are two basic types of pull systems (i.e., kanban or CONWIP) that I advocate, but my advice is whichever one you choose, keep it simple! It is important to remember that pull systems manage two things, the flow of information and the flow of material. Because of this, you need a simple method for passing on information (i.e., a pull signal) and a place from which to pull the material. One way is to use containers that convey the material and information. An empty container arrives at the upstream process and sends a signal to refill the container. Another approach is to use kanban cards that, like the containers, send a signal upstream to resupply a specific quantity of material.

Remember that the location from which you pull the material is referred to as a *marketplace*. Just like a supermarket, the marketplace could be just a shelf on a rack, which is stocked with a small amount of raw materials, subassemblies, or components needed to produce the products you are making. When material is pulled from the marketplace, a signal is sent to whomever is responsible for stocking it and it is replenished.

Kanban versus Constant Work-in-Process (CONWIP) Systems

If you are not familiar with kanban, it is a pull scheduling system that passes a replenishment signal directly to the next upstream process. Figure 10.1 is an example of a simple kanban pull system.

There is another type of pull system known as a CONWIP system. By its name, you can probably guess that a CONWIP system maintains a constant amount of WIP at all times. In a CONWIP system, instead of passing information to the next upstream process, the signal is sent to the front of the line. In Figure 10.2, you see the CONWIP-type pull system, where the signal is sent to the first upstream process step. Both CONWIP and kanban are pull systems in the sense that releases into the line are triggered by external demands, and because both systems establish a cap on WIP, both have performance

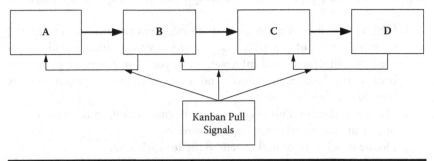

Figure 10.1 Simple Kanban System.

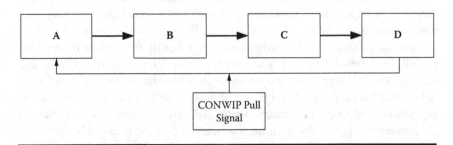

Figure 10.2 CONWIP System.

advantages to push systems using MRP. In particular, both CONWIP and kanban achieve targeted TH levels with much less WIP than push systems while demonstrating significantly less cycle time variability.

In addition to the pull signal destination differences between the two types of pull systems, perhaps the bigger difference is that kanban requires more control parameters than a CONWIP system. In a kanban system, cards (or containers) must be established for every process step and every part number, while in a CONWIP system only one is required. For this reason, CONWIP is easier to control and, in my estimation, is superior to kanban much of the time. Another difference between CONWIP and kanban is that in a kanban system you must identify each part number in the system, and it is therefore part number specific. In a CONWIP system, cards do not identify a specific part number and are therefore line specific.

There are, however, two potential advantages of kanban over CONWIP.

■ Because in a kanban system each station pulls from upstream processes, kanban actually results in better communication between workstations.
■ Because kanban breaks the line at every station, it promotes resource sharing between workstations.

But let us not forget the disadvantages of kanban:

■ Kanban is much more complex than CONWIP and, in general, requires higher WIP levels.
■ Kanban introduces a tighter pacing of the line, meaning that operators have less flexibility for working ahead.
■ When the number of part numbers required in a kanban system is large, kanban becomes impractical from a space requirement because of the number of containers used.
■ Kanban does not accommodate a change in product mix unless additional WIP is loaded into the system because the product-specific card counts rigidly govern the mix of WIP in the system.

Hopp and Spearman tell us that it appears that kanban is best suited to systems with many routings that share resources, especially if products and routings are frequently added or removed. On the other hand, if the various routings have few shared resources and new products tend to follow established routings, the system would probably function more simply and effectively under a CONWIP system, possibly broken into separate loops for span-of-control reasons.

Hopp and Spearman also tell us that there are two problems that could develop with a CONWIP pull system as it applies to UIC in certain environments. First, if there are downstream machine failures, *bottleneck starvation* might occur. Why? Because the signal to produce will not be sent to the beginning of the line soon enough to replenish the constraint buffer. Second, because the WIP level is held constant, *premature releases* might occur even if the part is not needed because WIP in the loop might have fallen below its target level. Although either or both of these could occur, because you are now focused on the constraint (operating in cells with visual management in place), the likelihood of either happening is remote at best, simply because of the improved line communication and visibility.

No matter which type of pull system is used, the key to effectiveness is establishing a cap on the amount of WIP in the system. When you limit the amount of WIP in the process, you have less cost associated with carrying costs, but this is not the only advantage. You know that the key to achieving high levels of on-time deliveries is a predictable flow of product through the production line. You also know that when cycle time variability is low, you are much better equipped to quote and achieve accurate lead times. Pull systems help you achieve less variable cycle times simply because problems are identified and corrected much more quickly without the risk of large amounts of defective inventory (i.e., thanks to your WIP cap).

Establishing Acceptable Levels of Quality

One of the preconditions for implementing effective pull systems is acceptable levels of quality, but there is a rather unique phenomenon that takes place here. Although acceptable quality is a prerequisite, it is also a result of pull systems. Because WIP levels are capped, scrap and rework eruptions are avoided, and the pressure to identify and correct quality issues is greater in a pull environment. The fact is that inspection is much more effective in low-WIP environments. Because communication in a pull system is better defined (i.e., customer–supplier interface is apparent), communication of quality issues happens much more easily.

As you are designing your pull system, remember to consider the drum-buffer-rope system you have already put in place. The DBR system controls the release of raw materials into the system to the first operation and also buffers the constraint, assembly operation, and shipping. Your pull system is needed when you have one nonconstraint operation feeding another nonconstraint operation. The good news is that nonconstraint pull systems and DBR systems work extremely well together to control inventory, prevent starvation, and deliver maximum TH.

Making the Argument: Push or Pull?

There are those that would still argue that push systems are superior to pull systems. So which system—push or pull—is better for manufacturing? Let us consider this question from both a profit and an ease of use perspective. One of the fundamental distinctions between push and pull systems is that push systems control TH and observe WIP, while pull systems control WIP and observe TH.

Using MRP, you create a master production schedule to determine planned order releases, which in turn determine what is released into the system. In so doing, WIP levels may move up and down over a period of time. Conversely, in a pull system the level of WIP is controlled through the kanban cards and caps on the amount of WIP. Depending upon what happens within the process, the TH may vary over time. You ask: Which approach is better? Let us consider what we can observe and what we know to be true regarding push and pull systems.

You know that you can observe WIP directly, but you cannot easily observe TH, so using WIP as the control device is simple. You can simply count the number of parts on the floor and make sure you have not violated your calculated WIP cap. By contrast, in a push system, you set the release rate (TH) based upon capacity. If the rate you select is too high, you choke the system with excess WIP. If the rate selected is too low, TH suffers. You know that because of things like unplanned downtime and quality problems, capacity is difficult to accurately predict. Because of this, push systems are much more difficult to optimize than pull systems.

CONWIP Factory Physics Laws

You also know that pull systems are much more efficient than push systems because the level of WIP required to achieve a given level of TH is lower in a pull system than in a push system. Hopp and Spearman provide us with another factory physics law and corollary:[52]

- **Law (CONWIP) of efficiency:** For a given level of TH, a push system will have more WIP on average than an equivalent CONWIP system.
- **Corollary:** For a given level of TH, a push system will have longer average cycle times than an equivalent CONWIP system.

In addition to having longer average cycle times, push systems characteristically display more variable cycle times than an equivalent CONWIP system.

Hopp and Spearman explain that "the most important advantage of a CONWIP system over a push system is neither the reduction in WIP (and average cycle time) nor the reduction in cycle time variance. Instead the key advantage of pull systems is their robustness,"[53] which can be stated as another factory physics law:

- **Law (CONWIP robustness):** A CONWIP system is more robust to errors in WIP level than a pure push system is to errors in release rate.

In order to understand this important factory physics law more clearly, let us look at an example. Consider a process that contains five individual workstations in series. Assume that the P/Ts for each station are exactly one hour and that they are exponentially distributed. The profit is calculated to be \$100/piece, and the holding costs are \$1/piece/hour. You are interested in deciding whether you want to use a push system or a CONWIP pull system. One of the first things you will calculate to help you with this decision is profit per hour using the following equation:

$$\text{Profit per hour} = (\text{TH} \times \text{profit/piece}) - (\text{WIP} \times \text{holding cost})$$

(Note: In reality there are other factors involved in calculating profit, but for demonstration purposes, this equation will suffice.)

Because pull systems use inventory as the control parameter, TH is a function of inventory in the system. Because of this, TH is considered to be the response variable. For a five-station CONWIP system, TH is calculated as follows:

$$\text{TH} = \text{WIP} \div (\text{WIP} + 4)$$

Selection of the optimal WIP level is the WIP level that generates the highest profit. If you insert different levels of WIP in this system, you can calculate the corresponding TH. For example, for a WIP level of one piece, the TH is

$$\text{TH} = 1 \div (1 + 4) = 0.25$$

For a WIP level of two pieces, the TH is

$$\text{TH} = 3 \div (3 + 4) = 0.43$$

You can insert any value of WIP to generate as many values of TH as you wish.

Unlike pull systems, push systems use TH (or order release rate) as the control parameter, using the following equation for a five-station push system:

$$\text{WIP} = 5 \times (\text{TH} \div [1 - \text{TH}])$$

Selection of the optimal TH is the TH that generates the highest profit. For push systems you can insert a desired TH rate and calculate the level of WIP to achieve it. For example, for a TH level of 0.2, the calculated WIP level is

$$WIP = 5 \times (0.2 \div [1 - 0.2])$$
$$= 1.25, \text{ or } 1$$

For a TH level of 0.33, the calculated WIP level is

$$WIP = 5 \times (0.5 \div [1 - 0.5]$$
$$= 5$$

Table 10.1 contains calculated TH values for a variety of WIP levels in the CONWIP system and calculated WIP values for a variety of chosen TH levels for the push system.

Now that you have the WIP and TH values for both the pull and push systems, let us now calculate the dollar per hour profit for each, using the WIP equation, and determine the optimal level of WIP needed in each system.

Table 10.2 contains the profit values for both types of systems for varying WIP levels. You will notice that for the CONWIP system the optimal profit of $64.00 occurs at a WIP level of seventeen pieces, while for the push system the optimal profit is $60.00 for a WIP level of twenty pieces. Immediately, you see

Table 10.1 Pull (CONWIP) versus Push Profit Comparison

Pull System (CONWIP)			Push System		
WIP	Throughput	$/Hour (CONWIP)	Throughput	WIP	$/Hour (Push)
1	0.2		0.2	1	
3	0.43		0.5	5	
7	0.64		0.6	8	
12	0.75		0.7	12	
14	0.78		0.80	20	
17	0.81		0.85	28	
22	0.85		0.9	45	
27	0.87		0.95	95	

Table 10.2 Pull (CONWIP) versus Push Profit Comparison

Pull System (CONWIP)			Push System		
WIP	Throughput	$/Hour (CONWIP)	Throughput	WIP	$/Hour (Push)
1	0.2	19.0	0.2	1	18.75
3	0.43	39.9	0.5	5	45.00
7	0.64	56.6	0.6	8	52.50
12	0.75	63.0	0.7	12	58.33
14	0.78	63.8	0.80	20	60.00
17	0.81	64.0	0.85	28	56.67
22	0.85	62.6	0.9	45	45.00
27	0.87	60.1	0.95	95	0.00

that the profit per hour for the CONWIP system is $4.00 higher than the push system.

Because in a CONWIP system excessive amount of WIP inventory does not occur, you can see that once the optimal level of profit is achieved by reaching the optimal WIP level, changes to WIP in either direction (up or down) do not have much of an impact on the profitability of the CONWIP system. In other words, the CONWIP system is very robust to changes in levels of WIP.

Because in a push system WIP is permitted to grow without limit, you see that profitability decreases significantly as a function of growing WIP. Figures 10.3 and 10.4 demonstrate this difference graphically. The fact that WIP is controlled in a CONWIP system while TH (order release rate) is pushed into the push system makes a world of difference in terms of profitability.

If you still are not convinced that a push system is typically inferior to a pull system, I am afraid that I cannot help you much! The laws of factory physics are real and applicable to all types of factories.

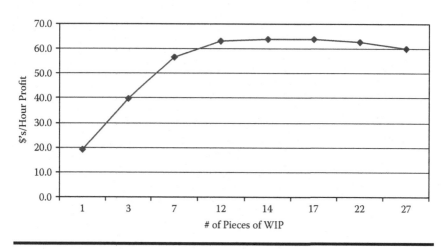

Figure 10.3   **$'s/Hour Profit versus WIP for CONWIP.**

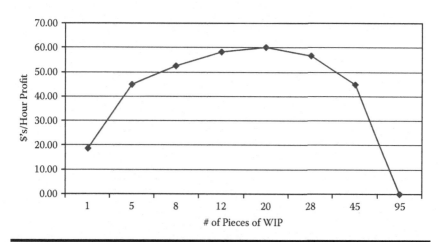

Figure 10.4   **$'s/Hour Profit versus WIP for Push System.**

Chapter 11

Elevating the Constraint and Implementing Protective Controls

With any luck, by using the UIC, you will have increased the capacity of your constraint operation so that it is no longer limiting or constraining your TH and revenue. But suppose that after all the improvements you have made, you still are not producing enough product. In this chapter, you discover what must happen to further increase your capacity.

Elevating the Constraint

Breaking the constraint simply means that the process that was initially limiting the amount of new revenue entering the company—the one that was constraining TH—is no longer doing so. You have significantly reduced process and product variation and processing and cycle time variability by eliminating or significantly reducing things like unplanned downtime, scrap, and rework. You have eliminated much of the waste in your process by eliminating non-value-added activities through things like constraint changeover and setup time reductions, limited line balancing activities, and cellular manufacturing, and you may have even gotten rid of efficiency as your primary performance metric. You have also improved the flow of products through your process through the use of things like DBR scheduling, establishing a WIP cap and protective buffers, pull systems, and establishing one-piece flow or optimizing the batch size.

But what if, after all these improvements, you have not been able to improve the TH of your process enough to satisfy the demands of the marketplace? In other words, you still do not have the needed capacity in your constraint operation to fill the order requirements of your customers. What do you do now? The fact is that you have a decision to make that calls for a management action. If all you have done to this point has not resulted in the constraint's no longer limiting the system's performance, you must elevate the constraint. Quite simply, this means you must take a different kind of action to improve the capacity and TH of the constraint if you are to satisfy market demand. You are most likely going to have to spend money to make more money. You will have alternatives to accomplish this, but how do you know which one is the most attractive?

Although there are several important things you must consider, one is more important than all the rest. Remember that back in step 1 you identified both the current and the next constraint? Before you make any decision that involves spending money to add additional resources you must always consider the impact on the next constraint (or other potential constraints) of your decision. For example, suppose that in order to break the current constraint, you decide to purchase a very expensive piece of equipment. You justify the expenditure on the basis of future TH through the current constraint, and you determine that the ROI is acceptable. You then purchase and install the equipment, and in so doing you are successful in increasing TH at the current constraint. When this happens, predictably a new constraint emerges. But suppose that this new constraint limits TH to the extent that your overall capacity is still less than market demand. The ROI assumptions you made to justify your purchase have been invalidated.

The point is that unless you consider the TH of the next constraint as you are justifying the ROI for this expenditure, it is quite possible that this new constraint will limit your predicted TH and negatively impact the ROI used to justify it. The ROI you assumed with this purchase is limited by this new constraint; therefore, making this investment would be an example of wasteful spending. Once again, before you consider how you are going to break the current constraint, evaluate the limits imposed by other potential constraints.

Increasing Capacity

Increasing the capacity of the constraining operation can be accomplished in several different ways or a combination of each. Capacity is defined as "an upper limit on the TH of a production process."[54] So how could you increase the capacity of the constraint operation without purchasing additional capacity in the form of more equipment? One way is to increase the length of time that the constraint operation runs compared to the nonconstraints. For example, if you are currently not utilizing the constraint process during lunches, breaks, meetings, and training, you could provide operator relief during these periods of time, thus never permitting the constraint operation to sit idle. This would require cross-training to ensure other operators are qualified to run the workstation, but it would be a lower-cost alternative.

Another solution might be to use overtime in the constraint operation to raise its effective capacity. Although other stations continue to operate in the normal eight-hour shift, you might consider running the constraint operation longer. If you do consider this alternative, you must balance this cost against the cost of new equipment so that you make the right decision. Another alternative might be to hire additional operators and add an additional shift in the constraint operation, but again, you must balance this against the cost of purchasing additional equipment.

If using limited overtime or adding additional resources (i.e., adding an additional shift) is too costly, one other alternative might be outsourcing part of the constraint's workload. That is, instead of purchasing additional equipment, contracting with an organization outside the company might be a viable alternative. In general, however, I am not a fan of outsourcing simply because it is easy to lose control of your products. In fact, it is possible that the product being produced outside the company would have worse (or better) quality than that being produced in your own process. What customers are looking for is consistency, so any action that results in inconsistency should be avoided. In reality, however, sometimes it is the best, least-cost option.

The lesson here is that as long as the next constraint's TH is substantially higher than the current constraint's TH, it is probably a good idea to spend the money. Let us look at a few examples.

Suppose after all the improvements you have made to your process, your constraint output is 10 parts/hour. You are considering the purchase of a very expensive piece of equipment that should double the TH to 20 parts/hour. You evaluate the anticipated next constraint and find that its TH rate is 12 parts/hour. Even though the new machine would double your TH rate to 20 parts/hour, you are limited by the rate of the new constraint operation of 12 parts/hour, unless you can easily increase the rate of the next constraint. Your challenge then becomes one of finding a less expensive alternative that raises your TH to some level above 12 parts/hour. Otherwise, you have spent money when you should not have. On the other hand, if the anticipated new constraint's TH is 15 or 16 parts/hour, it is probably a good decision to purchase the new machine.

The point is that before making a purchase to break the current constraint, you should consider its "true" ROI.

Protective Controls

This step in the UIC also calls for you to plan how to implement protective controls. What does this mean? After all the hard work and the improvements you have made to your process, you cannot afford to lose any of the momentum and TH improvement. In effect, you want to protect and preserve all that you have accomplished. So how do you do this?

One of the most effective tools used to protect and preserve your accomplishments is a simple *process audit*. A typical process audit is a series of questions asked to the line leader or supervisor to demonstrate the status of the process. Let us look at a simple example of such an audit in Figure 11.1. (Actually, Figure 11.1 is only one part of a much more comprehensive audit, but for demonstration purposes it will suffice.)

Ref #	Flag System Implementation Audit	Yes	No	Leader or Supervisor	Corrective Action	Due Date
	The function of the flag system is to continuously drive down the amount of downtime or time consumed by delays such as material shortages, quality issues and non-production-oriented activities. Flag presence should match the recorded downtime issues on pacing sheets or standard work sheets.					
1	Is there a status flag present at each step of the manufacturing process?					
2	Is there evidence of corrective action activity for any red or yellow flags?					

Figure 11.1   Flag Audit.

3	Is the Quality organization aware of and responding to any quality flags raised? When was Quality flag raised? _____:____ resolved____:__? Quality rep contacted:_____ by production rep:_____						
4	Do day 1,2,3 flags indicate complete time? Are operators falling behind? Do flags match pacing sheet? Do flags match pacing sheet?						
5	Is cure time complete indicated on white flag? Does it match spec?						
6	For blue flag (material transfer) is there evidence of transfer in a timely manner? Next destination identified? Time in transfer tracked?						
7	For each red or yellow flag present, is there an entry on pacing sheet and Pareto chart for the delay?						
8	Is supervisor aware of flag status at each station and has assembled a reaction plan?						
9	Is area ME aware of flag status and was time delay initiated for any yellow, red flags present? Reaction plan?						
10	Is leader aware of any pace delays in area? Action plan assembled for staffing to correct/ prevent cycle time delay?						

Figure 11.1   (Continued.)

In one company for which I consulted, we had implemented a simple visual flag system to alert the leader or supervisor of the status of each process step. The flag system was simple in that it used different-colored flags to correspond to the status of the process step. For example, if a red flag was in place, everyone knew that this process step was shut down and unable to produce product, so red automatically translated into the highest-priority status and immediate action was necessary. In contrast, a green flag indicated that there were no problems and that everything was running smoothly. Yellow flags were used to indicate a potential problem or impending need, such as running out of materials within thirty minutes or possible quality issues that needed addressing. This flag system was intended to facilitate the supervisor's job by allowing him or her to walk through the various product lines and know at a glance what the real-time status was. The impact of this simple visual system on TH was quite profound. Because we did not want the system to backslide, part of our process audit was a weekly review of this flag system.

The shop manager used the process audit by randomly selecting a process and observing how the flag system was functioning. If the answer to any of the ten questions was yes, a value of 1 was assigned. Conversely, if the answer was no, a value of 0 was assigned. Any negative observation required immediate, short-term corrective action as well as a longer-term plan to avoid a repeat of the noncompliance.

Another example of a protective control is the use of statistical process control (SPC) charts. If, for example, you determine that a process setting is directly correlated to a defect, using a simple control chart could protect the process from backsliding. Another example might be a control chart used to monitor the rate of holes in the DBR system. Because the point of this step is to protect the gains you have made, my advice is to be creative in your choice of protective controls. In Chapter 12, I go into more detail on this step of the UIC.

Chapter 12

Breaking the Current Constraint

Chapter 11 discusses how to break your current constraint. There, I give you some basic insights as to how you might accomplish this. In this chapter, I expand on the basics from Chapter 11 and present a more detailed look at activities aimed specifically at breaking the current constraint, correlating with steps 4a and 4b of the UIC.

Finding Alternatives

Breaking the current constraint is really the same as increasing the capacity of the operation that is limiting the TH of a given process. If the constraint is an internal resource, this simply means developing ways to squeeze more time out of that resource for productive work so that you can meet the demands of the market. As I explain in Chapter 11, this might be any or a combination of the following alternatives:

- Purchase additional equipment.
- Hire additional resources.
- Utilize overtime.
- Add additional shifts.
- Outsource or contract with an outside operation to produce product.

■ Relieve for breaks, lunches, and meetings, so as to never let the constraint sit idle.

If the constraint is external to the operation, your options are obviously different. For example, suppose the constraint is market demand or a lack of sales. Clearly, this means that you have excess capacity, so in this case activities will always be geared toward increasing the competitive factors that result in increased sales. These activities include improvements in cost, lead times, quality, customer service, and flexibility.

No matter whether the constraint is internal or external to the organization, elevating the constraint usually always means spending more money. It also means that you have done everything possible to squeeze the most out of the constraint before you spend the money. It is important to remember that different alternatives cost more or less than others, so whichever one you choose must be chosen after careful deliberation and analysis of the entire system. Sometimes alternatives are more attractive than others in ways that cannot be measured financially. For example, if breaking a constraint results in a process that is easier to manage, this might be the best alternative as long as TH increases.

Considering the Alternatives

Your choice of alternatives must be made after careful consideration and analysis of the entire system. You know that when you eventually break the constraint, a new constraint will immediately appear. It is for this reason that in the first step of the UIC you must identify both the current and the next constraint. That is, you should have identified the next, most limiting operation, no matter whether it is internal or external to the organization. Your choice of alternatives for breaking the current constraint must necessarily consider the impact on and interaction with the next constraint. Let us consider several examples. In each example, you assume that the market is not the constraint and that you can sell any additional products produced.

Consider the simple five-operation process in Figure 12.1. If you consider only the current capacity of each process step, it is clear that operation B is the capacity constraint because its capacity is less than that in all the other steps. Suppose you have completed steps 1a through 3c of UIC and these are the capacities after improvements. It should be clear that before any additional improvements in TH can occur, you must elevate operation B in Figure 12.1.

Because the market demand for its product is 14 parts/hour, the improvement team has come up with a plan to increase the capacity of operation B from its current 10 parts/hour to 20 parts/hour. The plan involves the purchase of an

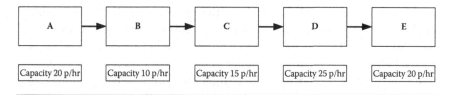

Figure 12.1 Simple Five-Step Process.

additional machine for operation B. The team reasons that if the profit on each part, assuming no scraps, is $10, the additional profit per hour is 20 parts/hour × $10/part, or $200/hour. Because the cost of the new machine is $200,000, the team concludes that the ROI is approximately 125 workdays, or approximately 25 weeks. The team presents its recommendation to the steering committee and it is rejected. Why did it get rejected?

Although with the purchase of this machine the capacity of the current constraint would be increased from 10 parts/hour to 20 parts/hour, the capacity of the line is now constrained by operation C at 15 parts/hour, which is one above the 14 parts/hour of market demand. This implies that the ROI of the equipment is not the 25 weeks calculated by the team but, rather, the time is doubled to approximately 50 weeks. Also, the team did not consider the increase in OE associated with hiring additional resources to run this new machine. Clearly, if the decision had been made to purchase the new machine, it would not have been in the best interests of the company.

The team then decided to look at the expense of working overtime on operation B. The cost per hour for overtime on operation B is 1.5 times the hourly rate of the operator, which in this case was $15.00/hour. The team reasoned that in order to break this constraint, the process has to produce the equivalent of 5 extra parts/hour, because the next slowest operation is operation C, at 15 parts/hour, which is equal to market demand. The process operates for 8 hours/day, so the total number of parts that must be produced on overtime would be a total of 40. Because the current capacity of the constraint is 10 parts/hour, an additional four hours of overtime per day would be required to effectively increase the capacity of operation B. The cost of this overtime would be 4 hours × $22.50/hour = $90/day. But what happens to profit? We already stated that profit is $10/part, so an additional 40 parts/day would result in an additional approximate profit of ($10/part × 40 parts) − ($90/day extra labor charge) = $310/day in additional profit. If we assume that there are 240 working days/year, the total labor cost per year would be 240 days/year × $90/day, or $21,600/year. Thus, by spending $21,600 we are able to generate an additional profit of $310/day × 240 days = $74,400.

Clearly, this is a much better alternative than the purchase of a $200,000 machine, but how long could the company reasonably expect to remain on constant overtime? One month? Six months? What other alternatives might you look at? One alternative is to outsource or subcontract the work to an outside company. Suppose the subcontractor charges $5/part produced, including transportation costs, and is able to produce the additional forty parts required to reduce the deficit to zero parts. Again, assume that you use the subcontractor 240 days/year. The total cost to the company would be $5/part × 40 parts/day × 240 days/year, or $48,000/year. Because you are making $10/part in profit, your profit on these 40 additional parts/day would be ($10/part) – ($5/part) = $5/part. This translates into an additional annual profit of $5/part × 40 parts/day × 240 days/year, or $48,000/year. Obviously, this extra profit is not as good as working overtime to satisfy the market demand, but from a people perspective, it is better than using constant overtime. Are there any other alternatives?

Let us look at the process again. In Figure 12.2, I have included an additional bit of information that might help you with your decision. Notice that in the constraint operation, you are currently losing 2 parts/hour, or about one-half of the needed capacity improvement, to scrap. The team has come up with a way of reducing this scrap level to zero, but it requires that the process be slowed down to an effective average capacity of 9.5 parts/hour. Is this a good decision?

Obviously, if you gain 2 parts/hour in scrap avoidance by reducing the effective capacity by 0.5 part/hour, there is a net gain of 1.5 parts/hour, thus making it a good decision. It does not get you to the needed 4 parts/hour to satisfy market demand, but it gets you closer. In terms of profitability, the extra 1.5 parts/hour provides you with 1.5 parts/hour × $10/part, or an additional $15 in profit/hour. On an annual basis, this translates to approximately $30,000/year in additional profits, and this does not include the savings associated with the 2 scraps/hour.

The calculations used in the preceding discussions could probably be questioned or even seen as incomplete, but the point of these exercises is that there are different ways and combinations of ways to break the constraint. The key is to think through and make rational decisions on the best way to do so.

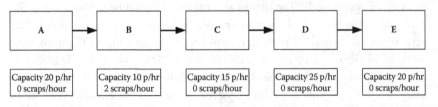

Figure 12.2   Five-Step Process with Scraps Added.

Remember, when you break the current constraint, a new constraint will immediately appear, so you must be ready when this happens. Always consider the entire process, including the most likely next constraint when making capacity or TH improvement decisions.

Chapter 13

Sustaining the Gains with Protective Controls

In a literal sense *control* means to check, test, or verify by some kind of evidence. Thus, a control is any device or means that serves to check or verify the existence of something by collecting evidence. To *protect* can be interpreted to mean to preserve. Thus, a *protective control* is any device or means that serves to preserve something by collecting evidence of the existence of something. In UIC, the aim of a protective control is to check or verify that the gains you have made are being preserved. In essence, a protective control is a check to guard against backsliding.

You may be wondering why I am so concerned about backsliding. Keep in mind that the entire premise of the UIC is that the focus of your efforts is always on the constraint operation. Thus, when you break one constraint, your improvement efforts move from one operation to a completely different one. As a result of this change in focus, there is a natural tendency for the old operation to revert to where it was unless some type of protective control is administered. You have worked very hard to get to this point, and you simply cannot afford to lose all or even some of the gains that have been made.

Reviewing Common Protective Controls

So just what might the protective control look like? The answer is that it depends. If, for example, gains were made as a result of reducing scrap and rework, the protective control might be a simple control chart that guards against the root cause of the scrap or rework returning. Or maybe the gains were made by reducing machine downtime in the constraint. In this case you may have implemented PM and you want to ensure that the maintenance controls are completed according to schedule. In this case maybe your control is a combination of PM schedule compliance and a run chart monitoring the level of unplanned downtime. The key to this step is that you want to protect and preserve the gains you have made in the current constraint once you have broken it. Let us get more specific on these things called protective controls.

Because typically it is not one thing you do that results in breaking the constraint, you need some kind of control that protects all that you have done. For example, suppose in your effort to break the current constraint, you accomplish the following six activities:

- Created a manufacturing cell
- Implemented a DBR scheduling system
- Eliminated a defect that was negatively impacting the line throughput
- Implemented visual status flags
- Reduced changeover time
- Reduced equipment downtime

Each one of the activities contributed something to your successful constraint breakage efforts, so you want to protect each of these from slipping back to the old way of doing business. You could develop a separate measure for each one of these and monitor each for compliance. For example, in the case of the DBR system, you could monitor the amount of WIP in front of the constraint or the total amount of WIP in the line, or even the number of times holes were created in the buffer. Or, in the case of the changeover reduction time, you could plot the time required for changeovers compared to the average changeover time. You could actually create a run chart or control chart for both of these, couldn't you? Although both of these examples represent good control mechanisms and you should always monitor them versus time, what I have also found to be a very effective tool is a *process audit* that monitors all the things you accomplished in a single control. The process audit consists of a major category, a brief description of the function of the activity, and a series of specific questions that are asked to gain an understanding of how well a process is being performed within the production line. Let us look at an example.

Flag Audits

In Chapter 11, I discussed one company in which I implemented a system of simple flags to help the supervisor or leader know the real-time status of her process. The purpose or function of the flag system was twofold. First, it was used to visually display the real-time status of each individual workstation so that the supervisor or leader could be alerted to any potential or existing problems within the process. Second, the flag system was used in conjunction with a delay identification system to continuously record, prioritize, and reduce the amount of downtime or time consumed by delays due to things like material shortages and quality issues. The color of the flag displayed determined the actual status of each individual workstation. A list of all colors used and their meanings is summarized as follows:

- **Green** is used to indicate that everything is okay. The start date and time and the completion date and time are placed on the flag, with the start date and time being the date and time the part was started and the due date being the date and time the part is to be completed.
- **Blue** is used to indicate that the part is complete and is ready to move to the next step in the production process. Nothing is written on the blue flag.
- **White** is used to indicate that the part is in a cure state (grout or cement drying) but not yet complete, and there is no operator currently working on the part. When the drying time will be complete is written on the flag.
- **Yellow** is used when an operator needs something. The operator records the specific need on the flag.
- **Red** indicates that work has stopped on the part. Nothing is written on the red flag.
- **Red and white striped** indicates that the part is ready (and waiting) for QA inspection. Nothing is written on this flag.
- **No flag** indicates that the part has not been started. All materials are available for the part and it can be started at any time.

So, for example, if a green flag is posted at the workstation, everything in the workstation is progressing according to schedule. By contrast, if a red flag is present, all work has stopped in this workstation and corrective action is necessary before the station can restart. This flag system facilitated the supervisor's job, in that he or she could walk the entire production line and know at a glance where problems were, where potential problems were likely to occur (i.e., yellow flags), where a part needed to be inspected (i.e., red-and-white-striped flag), and which tags were completed and ready to be moved to the next workstation (i.e., blue flags).

Pacing Sheets

In conjunction with the flag system, a *pacing sheet* was developed and kept at each workstation that reflected any downtime that had occurred. The pacing sheet included a description of the downtime and the amount of downtime that had occurred. This information was summarized on a dynamic Pareto chart posted on the line's communications board and was updated immediately after the downtime was corrected, and then daily by the workstation operator. This system (i.e., the flag system, pacing sheets, and Pareto charts) provided a visual display of what was happening in the work cell and facilitated continued maintenance of low downtime. The key to this system's success was that the operators were using it in the manner intended, so what was needed was a way to monitor how well the operators were in fact using the system. We developed a process audit with a list of specific questions that required proof of what was actually happening. Figure 13.1 is a portion of process audit developed for this purpose.

Ref #	Flag System Implementation Audit	Yes	No	Leader or Supervisor	Corrective Action	Due Date
	The function of the flag system is to continuously drive down the amount of downtime or time consumed by delays such as material shortages, quality issues and non-production-oriented activities. Flag presence should match the recorded downtime issues on pacing sheets or standard work sheets.					
1	Is there a status flag present at each step of the manufacturing process?					
2	Is there evidence of corrective action activity for any red or yellow flags?					

Figure 13.1 Flag Audit.

3	Is the Quality organization aware of and responding to any quality flags raised? When was Quality flag raised? _____:____ resolved____:__? Quality rep contacted:____ by production rep:_____					
4	Do day 1,2,3 flags indicate complete time? Are operators falling behind? Do flags match pacing sheet? Do flags match pacing sheet?					
5	Is cure time complete indicated on white flag? Does it match spec?					
6	For blue flag (material transfer) is there evidence of transfer in a timely manner? Next destination identified? Time in transfer tracked?					
7	For each red or yellow flag present, is there an entry on pacing sheet and Pareto chart for the delay?					
8	Is supervisor aware of flag status at each station and has assembled a reaction plan?					
9	Is area ME aware of flag status and was time delay initiated for any yellow, red flags present? Reaction plan?					
10	Is leader aware of any pace delays in area? Action plan assembled for staffing to correct/ prevent cycle time delay?					

Figure 13.1 (Continued.)

Random audits of the individual workstations were performed by the department supervisor, the line leader, the shop manager, or the process engineer assigned to the production line. At one point even the vice president of operations performed audits. These audits proved to be very effective as long as they were not scheduled in advance, workstations were chosen at random, and the results were not used to "beat up" the process personnel.

Other Types of Audits

In addition to the flag system process audit, other areas in which process audits were developed and used included things like standard work instruction audits, cycle time audits, problem-solving audits, and so on. In each case specific questions were developed according to the audit function that zeroed in on the specific function of the audit.

Each question's response was assigned a point value of 1 if compliance was achieved or 0 if there was not full compliance. The response values were summed and then a percent compliance was calculated and plotted on a run chart for the total audit, as illustrated in Figure 13.2.

Process audits can be very effective protective control devices, and this one was no exception. However, unless the audits are taken seriously by everyone involved, they will simply become a futile paperwork exercise. By this I mean that their level of importance must be such that when performance begins to fall off (i.e., fall below a specific target level) quantifiable corrective actions must be taken to reverse the negative trend. This importance is strictly a function of leadership in that the results of the audits must be considered as viable performance measures and corrective action must be mandated when performance falls below the target level. If this happens on a consistent basis, the gains achieved through UIC will be maintained and performance will continue to improve. If it does not happen, do not even bother!

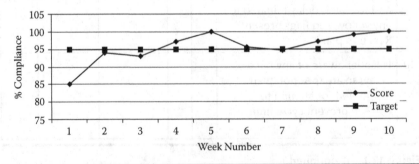

Figure 13.2   Process Audit Score by Week.

Chapter 14

System Constraints and Problems

In previous chapters, I focus on identifying the physical constraints in a manufacturing process, but what if the constraint is not located inside the process? What if the constraint is policy related or something nonphysical, such as an efficiency metric? In this chapter, I discuss different types of constraints, how to identify them, and what to do about them. The good news is that all the key concepts and principles you have learned from UIC still apply.

Types of Constraints

Dettmer explains that "identifying and breaking constraints becomes a little easier if there is an orderly way to classify them."[55] Dettmer tells us that there are seven basic types of constraints:

- Market
- Resource/capacity
- Material
- Supplier/vendor
- Financial
- Knowledge/competence
- Policy

Let us look at each of these in a bit more detail.

Market Constraints

This type of constraint exists when the demand for a product or service is less than the capacity to produce or deliver the product or service. That is, the company has not developed a competitive edge to realize enough orders for its product or service.

Marketplace constraints come about simply because the company is unable to differentiate itself from its competition. So how can a company differentiate itself? Quite simply, there are four primary factors associated with having or not having a competitive edge.

Quality

Quality, in its most basic form, is a measure of how well a product conforms to design standards. It is clear that Japanese manufacturers like Toyota and Honda are the world's recognized leaders when it comes to producing the highest-quality products, but it is also clear that this was not always the case. You probably know the history here, when Dr. Deming went to Japan and taught the Japanese how to become competitive.

The secret to becoming quality competitive is: first, designing quality into the products; second, the complete eradication of special cause variation; and third, developing processes that are in control and capable. It is not rocket science, but so few companies focus on these three success elements for creating products and services that differentiate them in the marketplace. If you want more orders, the first step is to distinguish yourself from the competition from a quality perspective.

On-Time Delivery

On-time delivery requires that you produce products to the rate at which customers expect them. This means that you must have product flow within your facility that is better than that of your competition. The basics involve focusing on and improving the physical constraint that exists within your facility; removing wasted time within your processes (both physical and nonphysical); and eradicating things like downtime, quality problems, variation, and all the other things that cause your processes to be inconsistent. It also involves reducing unnecessary inventory that lengthens cycle times and hides defects. You must create consistent, reliable processes that do not impede your ability to produce and ship on time.

Customer Service

Customer service simply means that you are responsive to the needs of your customer base. Customers must feel comfortable that if their market changes, their supply base will be able to change right along with them. If the customer has an immediate need for more product, the supplier that separates itself in terms of response time will become the supplier of choice. This means that your manufacturing lead times must be short enough to respond to the ever-changing demands of the market. This only comes by creating processes with exceptional flow. It is important to remember that the greater the amount of WIP inventory, the longer the lead time to produce.

Cost

Cost is perhaps the greatest differentiator of all in a down market. But having said this, low cost without the other three factors in place will not guarantee you more orders. Low costs are only achieved by removing waste and OE within the company. In order to be the lowest cost provider in the marketplace, companies must clearly manage all parts of the business. The quality of the products must be superior, with little scrap and rework. The quantity of raw materials must low enough to minimize the carrying costs. The amount of labor required to produce the product must be optimal, with little or no overtime. The cost of expedited shipments must be minimized. All these factors and more make up the cost of the product or service. If the costs are lower than the competition's, cost can be a differentiator, but not without the other three factors, quality, on-time delivery, and customer service.

Resource/Capacity Constraints

This type of constraint exists when the ability to produce or deliver the product or service is less than the demands of the marketplace. That is, the orders are available, but the company has insufficient capacity to deliver.

Resource/capacity constraints are, quite simply, not enough operators, equipment, cash, knowledge, or reliable vendors to satisfy the demands of the market. But do not be misled with this one. There is typically an irresistible urge to run off and either hire additional people or purchase additional machines, but quite often there is no need to do this. Most often the problem is associated with not squeezing the maximum amount of TH out of the physical constraint that exists within the operation.

Before you spend money, follow the UIC and create more capacity. "But how?" you may be wondering. Your process is full of waste and variation, so use the tools discussed in this book and squeeze out more capacity before you try to buy your way out of it.

Material Constraints

This type of constraint occurs because the company is unable to obtain the essential materials in the quantity or quality needed to satisfy the demand of the marketplace.

Material constraints are very real for production managers, and I cannot tell you how often I have heard managers lament that if they just had the materials, they could make the products. In fact, over the years this has been such a problem that material replenishment systems like MRP were invented to ensure material availability. However, as you know, even with MRP and its various iterations, material shortages (constraints) are still a common occurrence. Even MRP cannot predict scrap, or defects, or equipment downtime, or human-related causes like sickness. I once consulted for a company that produced buses that was always missing due dates. Although this company had many other problems, one of the biggest problems involved the excessive time required to procure parts and materials. By creating a VSM, we were able to pinpoint the major source of material delays as the company's purchase order (PO) process. We reconfigured the PO process and implemented pull systems and were able to reduce the overall procurement time by 65 percent. In reality, a material constraint is a subset of a resource/capacity constraint.

Supplier/Vendor Constraints

This type of constraint arises because of an inconsistent supplier or because of excessive lead times in responding to orders. This type of constraint is closely related to material constraints, and the net effect of this type of constraint is that because the raw materials are late arriving, products cannot be built and shipped on schedule. A supplier/vendor constraint is also a subset of a resource/capacity constraint. Let us look at an example.

I once worked in a company that designed, manufactured, and installed truck bodies. The company was losing market share, and I was asked to look into why this was happening. I created a VSM and identified the constraint as being the order entry system. All orders had to pass through engineering to receive a build quote before the company would provide a quote to the customer. The VSM indicated that the average time spent in engineering had increased to forty calendar days. As a result of this delay, customers were simply going elsewhere. Through value analysis and problem-solving techniques, we were able to reduce the engineering lead time from forty days to an average of forty-eight hours.

Because the quality of our products was superior and the cycle time through production was the best in the industry, we were able to increase market share to levels never before seen. All this occurred by identifying one constraint.

In reality then, there are two types of constraints that limit a company's ability to make money now or in the future: the marketplace (not enough orders) and the capacity to satisfy the marketplace (lack of capacity to deliver existing orders). Each of these two types of constraints is diametrically opposite and requires a completely different focus.

Financial Constraints

This type of constraint occurs when a company has inadequate cash flow. Financial constraints are not that common, but they are every bit as penalizing as the others when they exist. This type of constraint is often associated with a lack of available cash needed to purchase raw materials for future orders. Under this scenario companies typically must wait to receive payment for an existing order before taking on any new orders. Again, this type of constraint is a subset of a resource/capacity constraint.

An example of this type of constraint is an accounts receivable process. I was part of a team that transformed an accounts receivable process by reducing the billing process time by approximately 60 percent. In doing so, this company's cash flow rate improved by a proportionate amount.

Knowledge/Competence Constraints

This type of constraint exists because the knowledge or skills needed to improve business performance or perform at a higher level is not available within the company. Once again, this type of constraint is a subset of a resource/capacity constraint.

A good example of this type of constraint is when a company purchases a new type of equipment but fails to develop the infrastructure and knowledge on the equipment itself. Things like the development of a PM system and simple breakdown maintenance are needed to overcome this type of constraint. Without this knowledge or competence, the equipment remains down much longer than it should.

Policy Constraints

Last, but certainly not least, is the policy constraint. A policy constraint includes any written or unwritten policy, law, rule, or business practice that gets in the way of moving you closer to your goal of making more money now and in the future. In fact, Dettmer tells us, "In most cases, a policy is most likely behind a constraint from any of the first six categories. For this reason, TOC assigns a very high importance to policy analysis."[56] The most common examples of policy constraints include the use of operator efficiency or machine utilization or purchase price variance to measure and manage performance.

When companies use operator efficiency as a performance metric, typically there is a push to maximize it in all steps of the process. What typically happens as a result of this misguided focus is that the production floor becomes loaded with inventory, lead times become lengthened, and TH is encumbered. In reality, measuring operator efficiency makes sense only in the constraint operation. In spite of this, many companies continue to use operator efficiency as a performance metric in each of the individual process steps.

Organizational Problems

In studying organizations, we find that there are three basic types of problems that must be dealt with. Problems can be chronic, change related, or a hybrid of the two.

- Chronic problems are those that have seemingly been around forever and have defied all previous attempts at resolution. Chronic problems are very often associated with things like product defects or equipment downtime.
- Change-related problems, on the other hand, are characterized by their sudden onset and can usually be traced to a change made somewhere within the organization or process.
- Hybrid problems are a combination of chronic and change-related problems in that a chronic problem suddenly becomes worse.

All three of these problems are typically associated with the physical world or physical processes and require a systematic approach for resolution.

Although physical world problems can be solved using a systematic process, what about more complex problems related to systems and organizations or the policies within them? How do you determine that these types of problems exist, and then how do you go about solving them? Although it has been said that a well-defined problem is already half-solved, the problem must surely be identified first. H. William Dettmer, in his book *Breaking the Constraints to World Class Performance*, says, "Before we can effectively solve a complex system problem, we must thoroughly understand the cause and effect behind the reality of our current situation."[57]

An Overview of Logical Problem Solving

It is relatively easy to identify or locate physical constraints, but constraints related to systems and policies can be somewhat difficult or even frustrating. It is difficult because there are three things that conspire to work against breaking a constraint. First, most people have trouble identifying exactly what policy might be causing the constraint, and second, many times policy constraints are located outside your own area and typically require someone else to change the policy. This second reason is probably normal simply because nobody likes to admit that something he is doing is the cause of poor performance. Because of this, the person responsible seems to be in denial and requires some form of proof as to the need to change the constraining policy. The final barrier is normal human resistance to change. Changing the status quo is difficult unless a strong and compelling case is made where the conclusion is obvious.

In Eli Goldratt's sequel to *The Goal*, titled *It's Not Luck*, he introduces problem-solving methodologies referred to as *thinking process tools* (TPTs). The most important tool, in terms of problem identification, is the *current reality tree* (CRT). In his book, Goldratt introduces his logical thinking process and then teaches us that good managers must answer three important questions in order to be successful:

■ What to change
■ What to change to
■ How to make the change happen

As part of the logical thinking process, Goldratt introduces a set of tools used to identify the root causes of negative symptoms or *undesirable effects* (UDEs) that exist within organizations. Goldratt believes that there are generally only a few core problems that create most of the UDEs, and if you can identify these core problems (i.e., what to change) and find their root causes and eliminate them, most of the UDEs will disappear. Let us talk a bit more about UDEs and how you can identify and understand them.

In order to understand what UDEs are, you must first understand that they must be considered in the context of an organization's goals, necessary conditions, and performance metrics. For example, suppose the organization's goal is to make money now and in the future, and its necessary conditions are things like keeping its employees happy and secure, keeping customer satisfaction high, and achieving superior quality and on-time delivery. Further suppose that the organization measures its performance by things like on-time delivery, some kind of productivity measurement, the cost to produce products, a customer satisfaction index, and quality through ppm defective. Any organizational effect that moves the organization away from its goal or violates one of the necessary conditions or drives a performance metric in a negative direction with respect to its target is considered undesirable. Think for a minute about what UDEs might exist in your company.

The tool Goldratt developed to expose system-type problems or policy constraints is referred to as the CRT. The CRT is used to discover organizational problems, or UDEs, and then work backward to identify at least one root cause that leads to most of the UDEs.

Solving for Root Causes

Dettmer defines a root cause as "the lowest cause in a chain of cause and effect at which we have some capability to cause the break."[58] His point is that the cause-and-effect chain could continue indefinitely, but unless the cause lies within the scope and control of the organization, it will not be solved. I happen to believe Dettmer's definition of a root cause is the finest characterization I have ever observed. Dettmer further explains that two characteristics apply to root causes:

- It is the lowest point at which human intervention can change or break the cause.
- It is within your capability to unilaterally control, or influence, changes to the cause.

The CRT begins with identifying UDEs or negative symptoms existing within an organization that let you know that a *core problem* exists. Core problems are unique in that if the root cause or causes can be found, they can usually be traced to an exceptionally large percentage of the UDEs. Actually, Dettmer suggests that this percentage could be as high as 70 percent and sometimes higher. Dettmer refers to a CRT as a "snapshot of reality as it exists at a particular moment in time." Dettmer further explains, "As with a photograph, it's not really reality itself, just a picture of reality, and, like a photo, it encloses only what we choose to aim at through the camera's viewfinder."[59]

By aiming your "logical camera" at the UDEs and their root causes, you are essentially eliminating all the details that do not relate to them. In other words, the CRT helps you focus in on and pinpoint core problems. There are several different versions of the CRT available in the literature on the subject, but they all provide the same end product, at least one actionable core problem. Some CRTs are very detailed, while others are more general in nature.

The example I will present in this chapter is a company that was having a problem generating enough TH (i.e., capacity constraint). It had plenty of orders but was unable to produce enough parts to satisfy the market demand. It is clear to me that many of the problems organizations encounter on a daily basis are really interconnected, systems-related problems. It is further clear that by focusing on these core problems, organizations can essentially kill multiple birds with a few stones.

Constructing a Current Reality Tree (CRT)

It was not my intention to present an in-depth discussion of either TOC or CRTs, but because I have presented how to utilize the CRT, it seems appropriate to discuss the basics of how to prepare one. To demonstrate this, I will present a simple example that I developed following the recommended steps for creating a CRT according to Dettmer. The company involved here produces flexible tanks used to hold and transport volatile organic liquids. This company had serious problems generating enough TH to satisfy the volume and delivery requirements of its customers. By creating a CRT, this company was able to pinpoint specific system problems that were constraining its TH and then take actions to alleviate the problem. The following are the steps used to create this CRT, as developed by Dettmer.

Define the System Boundaries, Goals, Necessary Conditions, and Performance Measures

Because we are talking about a system, it is important that you avoid suboptimization. That is, you must always avoid trying to optimize individual processes and assuming that if you do so, you will have optimized the system. This assumption or belief that the sum individual process step optimizations will result in optimization of the total system is completely invalid.

All organizations exist for some purpose or goal—the end toward which effort is being directed. Usually this goal is to make money now and in the future. The necessary conditions, on the other hand, are vital success factors that must be satisfied as you achieve your goal. The performance measurements are simply those organizational metrics that tell you how the organization is performing as it pursues its goal. The following are the actual boundaries, goals, necessary conditions, and performance measures from our example:

Boundary: Manufacturing and assembly (M&A) area.
Goal: Make money now and in the future.

Necessary conditions:
- Minimize customer returns and complaints.
- Achieve at least 95 percent on-time delivery to all customers.
- Provide a safe, comfortable, and secure work environment for all employees.
- Meet budget profit and loss (P&L) expectations for the board of directors.

Performance measures:
- On-time delivery
- Rework hours per tank
- Sales dollars per labor hour
- Accident rate
- Workstation efficiency
- TH/revenue
- OE

State the System Problem

In order to develop a meaningful problem statement, you should always formulate it as a *why* question. Whatever the biggest issue that you do not like about your system's performance, simply state it as a why question, for example: Why is our TH/revenue so low?

Create a Causes, Negatives, and Whys Table

This is done by first creating three columns and then listing, in the negatives column (center column), the things you do not like about the way your system is currently performing, which include all the things that make your job more difficult to perform. My advice to you is: do not try to solve world hunger. List no more than five to eight negatives; otherwise, the CRT will become unmanageable. Table 14.1 is from our example, and as you can see, there are eight entries listed as negatives in the center column. It is important to remember that each of the negatives should be considered in the context of our problem statement.

Next, sequentially number all the negatives and then explain why you believe the negative is considered so. This is done by asking the question: Why is this negative a bad thing in light of our goal, necessary conditions, or performance measurements? Although Dettmer suggests that if you have multiple whys, you should add a lowercase letter to the appropriate number, I have always added a lowercase letter to the number even if I had only one why, like the example in

Table 14.1   Causes, Negatives, and Whys Table

Causes (What is causing this negative?)	Negatives (What I don't like about the current situation)	Why is this negative bad for our goal, necessary condition, or measurement?
	1. Absenteeism is high and unstable.	
	2. Processes are not stable and predictable.	
	3. Operators don't/won't follow specifications.	
	4. Product build cycle times are excessively long.	
	5. Equipment breaks down frequently.	
	6. Incoming materials are frequently nonconforming.	
	7. QA inspections are inconsistent between inspectors.	
	8. Problems are never really solved.	

Table 14.2. I find that it helps me distinguish the negatives, whys, and causes as I construct the CRT.

Once the why column of the table has been completed, move to the cause column and, for each negative, ask the following question: What is causing this negative? or Why does this negative exist? It is important to remember that there could very well be more than one cause responsible for creating this negative, and if there are, make sure you list them. Table 14.3 includes the negatives, whys, and causes. For each cause, place an uppercase letter beside the appropriate number, again, to distinguish between negatives, causes, and whys. When this table is complete, you are ready to construct your current reality tree. All the causes, negatives, and whys will serve as the initial building blocks for your CRT.

Table 14.2 Causes, Negatives, and Whys Table

Causes (What is causing this negative?)	Negatives (What I don't like about the current situation)	Why is this negative bad for our goal, necessary condition, or measurement?
	1. Absenteeism is high and unstable.	1a. P&A is forced to overstaff operations, which drives up operating expenses.
	2. Processes are not stable and predictable.	2a. Wet cement and grout drive cycle times higher.
	3. Operators don't/won't follow specifications.	3a. Excessive rework causes higher operating expense.
	4. Product build cycle times are excessively long.	4a. Throughput rates are too low, causing late P&A deliveries to customers.
	5. Equipment breaks down frequently.	5a. Cycle times are extended, causing late deliveries to P&A customers.
	6. Incoming materials are frequently nonconforming.	6a. Product cycle times are extended, causing late deliveries to customers.
	7. QA inspections are inconsistent between inspectors.	7a. Excess repairs drive up operating expenses and delay shipments.
	8. Problems are never really solved.	8a. Repetitive defects occur that result in excessive repair time and drive up OE.

Table 14.3 Completed Causes, Negatives, and Whys Table

Causes (What is causing this negative?)	Negatives (What I don't like about the current situation)	Why is this negative bad for our goal, necessary condition, or measurement?
A1. Attendance policy is not enforced by HR or operations.	1. Absenteeism is high and unstable.	1a. P&A is forced to overstaff operations, which drives up operating expenses.
A2. Effective process control system does not exist.	2. Processes are not stable and predictable.	2a. Wet cement and grout drive cycle times higher.
A3. Specifications are vague, not current, and difficult to understand.	3. Operators don't/ won't follow specifications.	3a. Excessive rework causes higher operating expense.
A4. Material dry/cure times are excessively long.	4. Product build cycle times are excessively long.	4a. Throughput rates are too low, causing late P&A deliveries to customers.
A5. PM on key equipment is inconsistent or ineffective.	5. Equipment breaks down frequently.	5a. Cycle times are extended, causing late deliveries to P&A customers.
A6. Suppliers are not always held accountable to produce in-spec material.	6. Incoming materials are frequently nonconforming.	6a. Product cycle times are extended, causing late deliveries to customers.
A7. Clear and concise acceptance standards do not exist.	7. QA inspections are inconsistent between inspectors.	7a. Excess repairs drive up operating expenses and delay shipments.
A8. Most problem-solving efforts focus on treating the symptoms instead of the root cause(s).	8. Problems are never really solved.	8a. Repetitive defects occur that result in excessive repair time and drive up OE.

Convert All Negatives, Whys, and Causes to CRT Entities (Graphic Blocks)

Using the alphanumeric entries from Table 14.3, word your negatives, whys, and causes in such a way that they will fit neatly inside the graphic blocks or boxes. The information inside the block should be complete statements and should leave no ambiguity as to its meaning. Figure 14.1 is an example of what your graphic blocks should resemble. Note that the information is a complete statement and its content leaves no doubt about what is negative.

Identify and Designate the Undesirable Effects (UDEs)

After you have converted all the negatives, whys, and causes into graphic blocks, it is time to determine which of the negatives and whys are UDEs. UDEs are those whys and negatives that are negative in relation to the organization's goal or necessary conditions or the key measures of progress toward achievement of the goal. Normally, all the whys will be considered UDEs, and probably some of the negatives will be as well. In some cases even some of the root causes could be considered UDEs. The key point to remember is whether or not the contents of the graphic block would be considered negative at face value or detrimental to achievement of the system's goal. If they are, designate them as UDEs. Once they are designated as UDEs, assuming you are using drawing software (like Visio), mark the UDEs in some fashion so as to make them visual. In my example, I have changed the wall thickness of the graphic block to designate which of them are UDEs.

Group the Graphic Blocks into Clusters

To quote Dettmer, "From this point on, building the CRT is going to be very much like assembling a jigsaw puzzle with the graphic blocks being the puzzle pieces."[60] Grouping is done by aligning the whys (now a UDE) at the top of the page and the appropriate cause directly beneath the corresponding negative, as shown in Figure 14.2.

Figure 14.3 permits you to group together related graphic blocks. Actually, constructing the CRT is very similar to constructing an affinity diagram, if you are familiar with this tool.

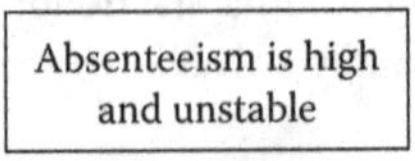

Absenteeism is high and unstable

Figure 14.1 Individual Graphic Box.

7a. Excess repairs
drive up operating
expenses and delay
shipments

A7 Clear and
concise acceptance
standards do not
exist

7. QA inspections
are inconsistent
between inspectors

Figure 14.2   Cluster of Graphic Box.

Connect the Causes, Negatives, and UDEs

Using dotted or dashed lines, connect the negatives individually to each of the UDEs, and then connect the causes to the negatives as demonstrated in Figure 14.3.

Figure 14.4 contains all the connected clusters (a *cluster* is defined as the connected UDEs, negatives, and causes) from our example. Note that the UDEs are designated by thicker walls on the graphic blocks.

Group Related Clusters Together

In this step, you need to search for clusters that appear to be related in some way and then place them near each other. From our example, we see that UDE 7a states that "excess repairs drive up OEs and delay shipments." That is closely related to UDE 8a: "Repetitive defects occur that result in excessive repair time and drive up OE." Thus, you look for connection points between the two clusters. In this particular example, the connection point appears to be at the UDE level, so you place a dotted line to connect the two clusters at the connection point, as shown in Figure 14.5.

Figure 14.3 Connected Graphic Boxes.

In a similar fashion, you search for other related clusters and connection points and then connect them. This activity is not as simple as it may sound because much thought must go into how the clusters are related and where the connection point is located. My recommendation is that if you are not sure, seek out other opinions or do more research. Figure 14.6 displays how the clusters are related from our example. Do not worry about how pretty your grouped cluster arrangement is; just try to connect them in a way that is legitimate and makes sense. It is always a good idea to seek out an objective opinion to make sure what you have constructed makes sense.

As you can see in Figure 14.6, there are three separate grouped clusters. As you continue building your CRT, it is not unusual for the final CRT to show linkages between each cluster as you add additional cause-and-effect relationships. Remember, what you will eventually discover is that only a few core problems will exist, and when these few are solved, many of the UDEs will simply go away.

Scrutinize and Finalize the Connections

When constructing the CRT, Dettmer emphasizes the need to use the *categories of legitimate reservation* (CLR) to solidify the logic of each causal connection.

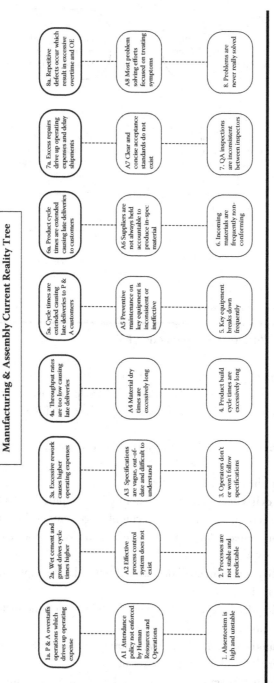

Figure 14.4   Complete Set of Connected Clusters.

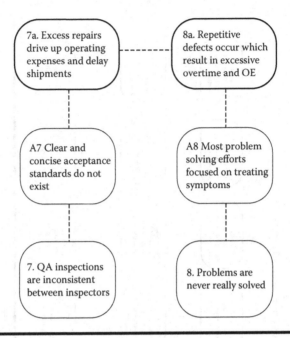

Figure 14.5 Clusters with Connection Point.

The CLRs help you construct your own logical relationships, and enable you to evaluate the logic of others. That is, the CLRs help you avoid errors in logic as you construct your CRT. Dettmer lists eight different CLRs:

- **Clarity:** Be certain that the individual words used are understood, that there is comprehension of the idea, and that there is a clear connection between the cause and the effect.
- **Entity existence:** When constructing the graphic blocks (entities), you must be certain that the text is a complete grammatical sentence, that you have not created a compound sentence, and that the idea contained in the sentence is valid.
- **Causality existence:** Cause-and-effect relationships must be direct and unavoidable.
- **Cause insufficiency:** Be certain you have identified and included all major contributing causes.
- **Additional cause:** Each time you observe or imagine an effect, you must consider all possible independent causes.
- **Cause–effect reversal:** Do not mistake an effect for a cause.

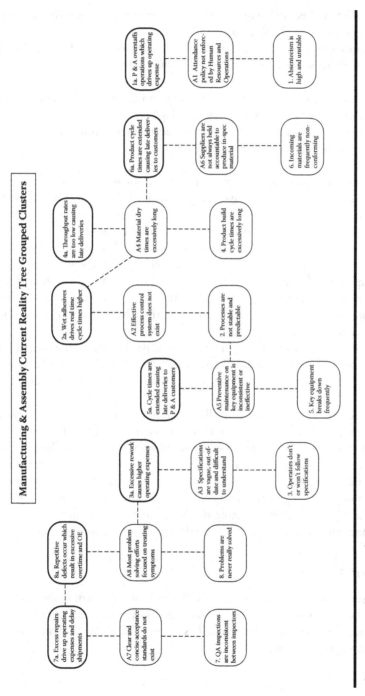

Figure 14.6   All Grouped Clusters.

■ **Predicted effect existence:** Most of the time causes have multiple effects, so make certain all effects are considered.

■ **Tautology:** Do not take the effect as unequivocal proof alone that the cause exists without considering other alternatives.

These eight CLR act as the rules of engagement as you construct your CRTs, so be certain to use them as you check your logic.

Dettmer explains that you must pick a cluster and, beginning with the cause at the bottom, ask three basic questions:

■ Could this cause by itself create that effect, or would it need help from another cause that you have not yet acknowledged? If there is another contributing cause, place it in a graphic block beside the original cause, add an ellipse, and pass both causes through the ellipse.

■ Is there a step (graphic block) missing between this cause and that effect that would better explain what is happening? If there is, create a new graphic block and insert it between the cause and the effect, and then recheck both connections for cause sufficiency. That is, does it need help from another dependent cause to create the effect, or is it a stand-alone, independent cause?

■ Is there another independent cause that could produce the same effect, without any assistance from the one already listed? If there is, create another graphic block and insert it beside the original cause and connect it to the effect.

Dettmer recommends the use of ellipses to show cause sufficiency or bow ties to show magnitudinal effects when they are needed. Magnitudinal effects are similar in nature to interactions in designed experiments (DOEs). That is, there may be several independent causes creating an effect, but when more than one is present at the same time, the effect is actually amplified. Once you are satisfied that a connection is logically sound enough to survive the criticism of someone else, make it permanent by changing the dotted lines to solid lines. Continue in this manner until all connections are considered to be solid and incontrovertible.

Look for Additional Causes

As additional causes and connections are determined, add them to the CRT and solidify the logical connection as demonstrated in Figure 14.7. You are able to distinguish the additional causes added as the graphic blocks without numbers or letters assigned to them.

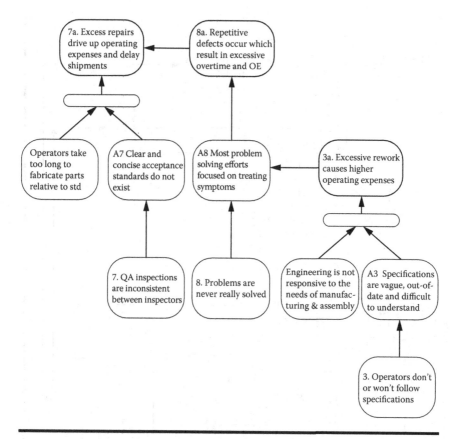

Figure 14.7 Logical Connections.

Figure 14.8 is the completed version of the CRT, with highlighted UDEs, ellipses, and connecting errors. The clusters in the CRT have been tested according to the CLR, so you are now ready for the next step.

Redesignate UDEs

Now that all the clusters are joined into a tree and new causes have been added, it is time to review everything you have done, starting with your UDEs. It is entirely possible that some of the UDEs that you considered to be UDEs might not seem undesirable any longer. Or, as you have added new graphic blocks to the tree, there could be new effects that are considered undesirable. Dettmer advises you to ask two basic questions as you're revisiting the CRT:

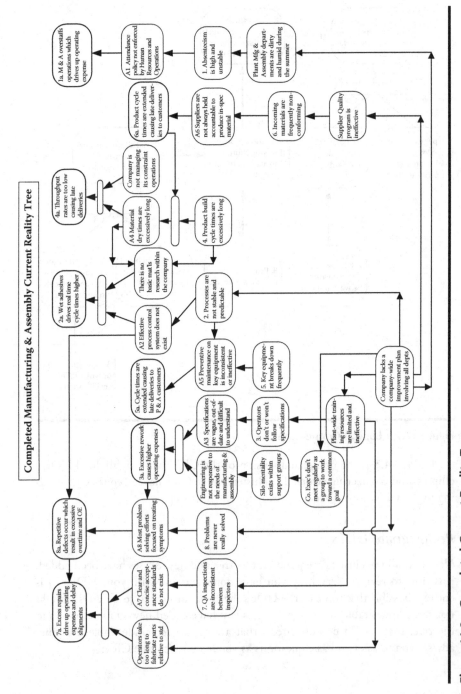

Figure 14.8 Completed Current Reality Tree.

- Are all of my original UDEs bad enough to still be considered undesirable? If they are, do not change their designation. If they are not, remove them.
- Have I added any new effects that might now qualify as undesirable using the same guidelines I used to identify the original ones? If there are, incorporate them into the tree.

Look for Negative Reinforcing Loops (NRLs)

A negative reinforcing loop is a scenario where a negative effect of some cause reinforces the cause. For example, suppose an inspector records a defect, based upon his or her interpretation of an ambiguous acceptance standard, and he or she is praised for doing so. Because the inspector was praised, the behavior one might expect to see from this inspector is interpreting other ambiguous acceptance standards so as to find a new defect. It could be that this condition has been acceptable for years, but because the first event (i.e., finding the first defect) was positively reinforced, the apparent defect might now be looked at differently. Although not common, a good place to look for these NRLs are situations where effects seem to be disproportionately magnified.

Identify All Root Causes and a Core Problem

In this step, you are interested in identifying the root causes upon which you can take action and, with any luck, identify a single core problem. Remember Dettmer's definition of root causes? A *root cause* is the lowest cause in a chain of cause and effect, at which we have some capability to cause the break. This means it is the lowest point at which human intervention can change or break a cause that is within your capability to control or influence. That is, you have no control over things like the weather because it is outside your capability to control or influence.

A core problem, on the other hand, is a unique kind of root cause because it can be traced to an extraordinarily large number of UDEs (maybe as high as 70 percent). If you are fortunate enough to have located a core problem, just imagine what would happen to your system's problems if you were to resolve it. In one fell swoop, you could eliminate most of your UDEs, so it is important to be methodical in the development of your CRT. But having said this, what if the core problem is beyond your scope of influence or control? If it is, elevate it. I have not met many leaders who would not be interested in solving a core problem when the potential results are so enormous.

In Figure 14.8, there are actually two core problems identified. The company lacks a comprehensive improvement plan that involves most of the other departments in the company and the company's attendance policy is not followed. If you were to attack these two problems, there is a good chance that most of the UDEs identified would simply go away. The silos could be broken, specifications could be updated and be less vague, excessive rework could be reduced, problems could be solved, attendance could be reduced, and so on.

Trim Nonessential Graphic Blocks

Personally, I do not believe this step is critical because it does not change the outcome. But if you have rendered some branches of your CRT neutral, Dettmer recommends that, for housekeeping purposes, you should eliminate them.

Choose the Root Cause to Attack

If there is a core problem to solve, clearly, you should attack it. But suppose there isn't one? Which root cause should you assail? Dettmer provides three rules to guide you in this selection:

■ The one with the highest probability of your being able to influence
■ The one that accounts for the greatest number of UDEs
■ The one that accounts for the most precarious UDE

In my opinion, it is always better to attack the problem that is causing the most serious UDE for several reasons. First, the positive impact on the organization will be felt and realized immediately. Second, by solving this problem, it could serve as a rallying point to achieve future buy-in for this approach to problem identification and resolution. Third, if you have chosen the root cause that has the largest financial impact on the organization, it may very well be used to fund other solutions to other, more complex root causes that might require a capital expenditure. Finally, leaders want to see results as quickly as possible.

There are two key core problems to solve. The first one involves the lack of a comprehensive improvement plan that ties together all the individual groups working to achieve the goals of the company. The real problem, as it related to TH, was the excessively long cure times of the various adhesives used to produce the tanks. The second problem related to the specifications supplied by the engineering group. This problem was not so much that the specifications did not exist but, rather, a problem associated with updating the specifications to reflect better ways of producing products as these new ways were developed. If this company could solve both the specification clarity and update problem and discover ways to reduce the long cure times, both should automatically result in significant TH gains simply because rework and cycle times would be reduced. Thus, the question becomes one of coming up with simple solutions to these two core problems.

Resolving Conflicts

Now that you have a completed CRT and have identified and selected the root causes or core problem to attack, what's next? Just how do you go about attacking a system's problem or a policy constraint? You do so by developing simple breakthrough ideas and solutions. But with every problem there are conflicts that seem to get in the way of your ideas for problem resolution.

Types of Conflict

There are three primary types of conflict that you must deal with as you work to resolve problems or, more specifically, the system's problems and policy constraints. The first conflict is one where one force is pulling you to do one thing, but an equal and opposite force pulls in the other direction. Dettmer refers to this type of conflict as *opposite conditions*. The second type of conflict is one in which you are forced to choose between different alternatives, which Dettmer calls, quite appropriately, "different alternatives."[61] The third type of conflict is what I refer to as the *hidden agenda* conflict. In a hidden agenda conflict, there is generally a personality involved in which there is a desire or inherent need to hold onto some kind of power.

In attempting to resolve conflicts, it is important to recognize that there are three types of resolution that can be achieved: *win-win, win-lose,* or *compromise*. Of the three possibilities, you should always attempt to achieve a win-win solution, but sometimes it is not practical. In a win-lose situation, one side typically gets just about everything it wanted while the other side gets very little. This type of solution serves to create antagonistic or hostile attitudes, and your chances of success are diminished because the losing side might attempt to sabotage your solution—not openly but, rather, covertly or surreptitiously. In the case of a compromise, generally the solution ends up being suboptimized because you are attempting to satisfy most of the requirements of both parties engaged in the conflict. Having said this, a compromise is better than a win-lose or imposed solution, but remember, it generally results in a suboptimized solution. The solution for a hidden agenda conflict is much like what happens in a win-lose conflict in that someone works against you behind the scenes in hopes of holding on to his or her apparent power. So how do you resolve conflicts?

Conflict Resolution Diagram (CRD)

Goldratt developed a tool he refers to as a CRD or *evaporating cloud*.[62] The CRD identifies and demonstrates the relationship between the key elements of a conflict and then suggests ways to resolve it. (Note: For a detailed description of how to create and use a CRD, read Dettmer's *Breaking the Constraints to World Class Performance*.) The diagram includes the system objective, necessary but not sufficient requirements that lead to it, and the prerequisites needed to satisfy them. Figure 14.9 provides the basic structure of the evaporating cloud.

The CRD was developed by Goldratt to achieve at least eight different purposes:[63]

- To confirm that the conflict exists and that it is real
- To identify the conflict associated with the problem
- To identify all the assumptions between the problem and conflict
- To provide a comprehensive answer as to why the problem is present
- To create solutions that could result in win-win situations
- To create innovative solutions to problems
- To provide a resolution of the conflict
- To avoid compromising situations

Figure 14.10 is an example of a CRD from our example company. In this example, the conflict was between the M&A department and engineering, with the objective being minimal rework of products. M&A had a requirement for their operators to follow the shop floor specifications, while at the same time engineering had a requirement to focus more resources on new

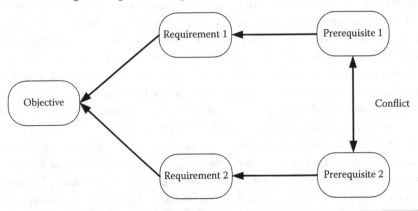

Figure 14.9   Evaporating Cloud Structure.

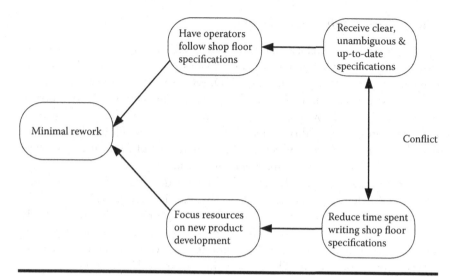

Figure 14.10 Evaporating Cloud Example.

product development. M&A's prerequisite was to receive clear, unambiguous, and up-to-date specifications from engineering, while engineering needed to reduce the time spent writing and updating shop floor specifications so that they could focus more resources on new product development, and herein was the conflict. The requirements are not in conflict with each other, but the prerequisites certainly are.

The key to breaking conflicts is the assumptions surrounding a conflict, so it is imperative that you understand what they are. The assumption of the M&A department was that engineering did not care about the quality of the specifications they were delivering to M&A, while the engineering group's assumption was that M&A was asking for specifications that were just too specific. There was a third assumption that stated that additional manpower could not be hired by either group. Once the two departments came together and understood the other's requirements, prerequisites, and assumptions, the conflict was resolved. The engineers had been writing the specifications, but because they had very little clerical help, it was difficult to keep them up-to-date as better methods were found. At the same time, there were new products on the horizon that needed to be engineered. The conflict was resolved when M&A offered to supply some existing clerical support to engineering to relieve some of the burden of updating the specifications. The solution was simple and the conflict was resolved.

The Future Reality Tree (FRT)

Now that you have developed a CRT and resolved one of the conflicts with an evaporating cloud, what should you do? Obviously, what you would like to have happen is to remove all or many of the UDEs and solve core problems. One tool you can use to do this is an *FRT*. FRTs are used to map out your future opportunities. You do this by first inserting an idea or *injection* that you developed to break your current reality problem or core conflict. An FRT helps you look into the future so you see and test the future outcomes of your cause-and-effect analysis before you actually implement any new ideas.

In its simplest form, an FRT could be envisioned as your current reality with all the UDEs changed to desirable effects. By injecting new ideas into the CRT, you can see how your idea might change your current reality from the UDEs in the present to desirable outcomes in the future. The FRT is a tool for gaining a warm and fuzzy feeling about the solutions you are intending to implement. How do you construct an FRT? Once again, we turn to Dettmer for assistance, as discussed in the following sections.

Define the Desired Effects

The first step is to look at each UDE, envision the mirror image or opposite effect for each UDE, and write it in the form of a simple sentence.

For example, from the CRT, there were eight UDEs, as follows:

- 1a: M&A overstaffs operations, which drives up OEs.
- 2a: Wet adhesives drive real-time cycle times higher.
- 3a: Excessive rework causes higher OEs.
- 4a: TH rates are too low, causing late deliveries.
- 5a: Cycle times are extended, causing late deliveries to M&A customers.
- 6a: Product cycle times are extended, causing late deliveries to customers.
- 7a: Excess repairs drive up OEs and delay shipments.
- 8a: Repetitive defects occur that result in excessive repair time and drive up OE.

In Figure 14.11 you see the original UDEs and the mirror images, desirable effects (DEs), that we created. As you can see, the desirable effects are all stated as positives and are the diametric opposites of the UDEs contained in the CRT. For example, UDE 2a states that wet adhesives drive cycle times higher, while the corresponding desirable effect states that adhesive cure times have little impact on cycle times.

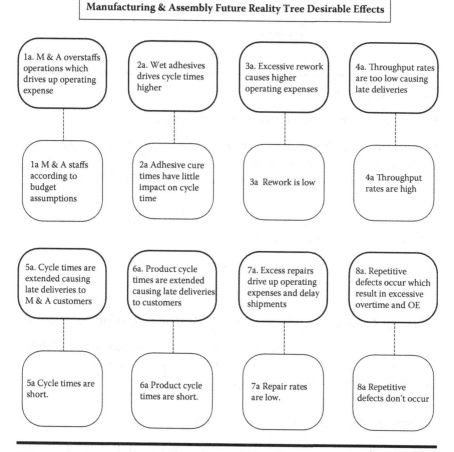

Figure 14.11   Future Reality Tree Step One.

Formulate the Basic Injection of the FRT

Because the common theme of the CRT involves things that drive up cycle times and therefore lower TH rates, you want an injection that reflects this common theme. Figure 14.12 reflects the basic injection.

It is important to remember that at this point this injection is simply a statement of what you would like to be and says nothing about how you intend to execute or implement it. Place the injection near the bottom of the page and leave room between it and the desirable effects for things like intermediate effects and maybe other injections. The FRT at this point looks like Figure 14.13.

> We have an improvement plan in place that focuses all departments on cycle time reductions that result in throughput increases.

Figure 14.12   Basic Injection.

Incorporate Any Other Elements Already Developed

Dettmer recommends that "if you started with a CRT, look for statements about existing reality that will be pertinent in the future." He also tells us, "If you have a conflict resolution diagram, you also have an injection you developed with it."[64]

Start Filling in the Gaps between the Desirable Effects and the Basic Injections

Think about what might be the outcomes of putting this change (injection) into effect.

Look for Opportunities to Build in Positive Reinforcing Loops

Dettmer tells us to "remember that the best solution is one that is self-sustaining and to look for places where one of the effects might loop back down one or more levels to amplify an effect lower in the tree."[65]

Search for Possible Negative Branches

Dettmer explains that "this is one of the most critical steps of all."[66] What Dettmer is warning us about is that you must be certain that the potential solution to the core problems will give you the results you wanted, but you must also guard against creating new problems or ones that are more damaging to the organization.

A Few Reminders about FRTs

As you construct your FRT, remember that it serves two basic purposes:

■ First, it permits you to verify, ahead of time, that the action or actions you would like to take to resolve the core problem(s) will produce the results you expected.
■ Second, the FRT enables you to identify, again in advance, any potentially adverse new consequences your actions might have on the organization.

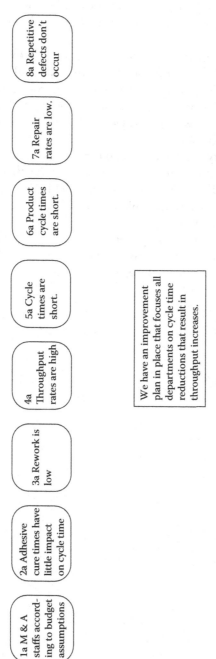

Figure 14.13 Future Reality Tree with Injection.

This allows you to either rethink your solutions or take other actions that will minimize the impact or eliminate them altogether.

The FRT allows you the opportunity to test the effectiveness of your actions before you invest time in them so as to avoid wasteful use of your limited resources. And for the companies that have limited resources, this is an important benefit. The CRT answers the question of what to change, and the FRT answers the question of what to change to. Figure 14.14 is the completed FRT from our example company.

This FRT is a very simplistic one, and I encourage you to obtain more details on how to construct one by reading Dettmer's *Breaking the Constraints to World Class Performance.* The basic concept behind the FRT is to start by identifying all the desirable effects, developing an injection, deciding upon the desired effects, and then filling in the blanks until your FRT is complete. There will probably be negative branches, or potentially damaging effects, that come to mind as you construct your own FRT, so be prepared to deal with them. In my example, there were not any of these.

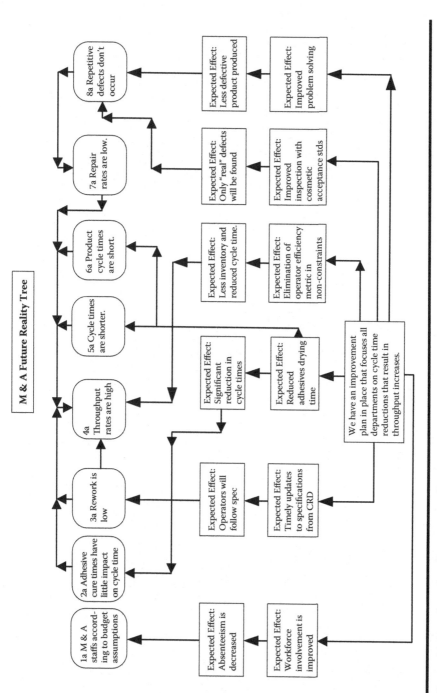

Figure 14.14   Completed Future Reality Tree.

Chapter 15

Establishing the Environment for Change

In the first fourteen chapters of this book, I have laid out UIC and have tried to convince you of its value for your company. If I have convinced you, you probably are wondering about the best way to get started. "Do I go out and just start at step 1a of UIC?" The answer is no, because if you did that, you would almost immediately begin hitting barriers and obstacles that would limit your success or maybe even cause you to question the validity of this cycle of improvement. If not step 1a, then what?

Let us first consider the question of what you are attempting to do. I started this book by stating that the basic goal of all for-profit organizations is to make money now and in the future. If you are already making money, your goal might be better stated as to make *more* money now and *more* money in the future. If this is your goal, the question I would ask myself is: "What is preventing me from making more money now and more money in the future?" My experience tells me that there is a host of things that prevent companies from making more money.

In its most basic form, making money involves generating revenue that is greater than what it costs to generate it. Thus, if OEs are too high and you are not generating enough revenue, you will not make money. The question is: Just how do you generate more revenue? Assume for a moment that you have more orders than you have capacity to fill them. Because you are unable to satisfy market demand, it follows that your TH is too low. If your TH is too low, then your cycle times must be too long. Then the key to generating more revenue must be reducing cycle times. How do you reduce cycle times? Let us first look again at Little's law.

Little's Law

Given that Little's law states that cycle time equals WIP divided by TH (i.e., CT = WIP ÷ TH), it should be clear that reducing cycle time implies reducing WIP as long as TH remains constant. Thus, if you have large amounts of WIP, clearly, you have an opportunity to reduce cycle time. But what if you do not have large amounts of WIP in your plant? (I'm betting you do, though). How else might you reduce cycle times?

You know that cycle time is equal to the sum of all P/Ts for each process step. You also know that cycle time is the sum of all value-added time plus all non-value-added time in the total process. Thus, if you want to decrease cycle time, you have three choices:

- Reduce value-added time
- Reduce non-value-added time
- Do some of both

One thing you know to be true is that non-value-added time far and away accounts for the largest percentage of total cycle time in all processes. This would imply that if you significantly reduce non-value-added time in your process, you could significantly reduce cycle time, which would in turn significantly improve your TH and revenue. So what are these non-value-added times that I am referring to?

Just think about which activities add value versus those that do not. Let us make a list:

- **Transport time:** Moving product from point A to point B.
- **Setup time:** Converting a process from one configuration to another.
- **Queue time:** Time spent waiting to be processed.
- **Process batch time:** Time waiting within a batch.
- **Move batch time:** Time waiting to move a batch to the next operation, which could also include time in storage.
- **Wait-to-match time:** Time waiting for another component to be ready for assembly.
- **Drying time:** Time waiting for things like adhesives to become ready to be assembled.
- **Inspection time:** Time waiting for products to be inspected.

There might be others you could add to the list, but for now assume this is your list. Which of these items add value? Clearly, none of them do, so they would all be classified as non-value-added. There obviously are things you could do to reduce each one of these. For example, process batch time is driven by the process batch size, so you could do two things that would reduce this time. You could optimize the batch size that you produce and, in conjunction with this, reduce the time required for setup. In doing these two things, you would probably also reduce the move batch time and maybe even the wait-to-match time. Clearly, these actions would reduce the overall cycle time.

But even if you were successful in reducing cycle time, you would not realize a single piece of TH unless you reduced the P/T and non-value-added time of the operation that is constraining the TH, the constraint. Any attempts to reduce P/Ts in operations that are not constraining TH are quite simply wasted effort.

The key to making more money now and in the future is, in reality, tied to two single beliefs, *focus* and *leverage*. In TOC terminology these two beliefs of leverage and focus are fundamental to the idea of *exploiting* the constraint. If you want to increase your TH, there is only one effective way to accomplish this. You must leverage the operation that is limiting your TH, your constraint operation. And how do you leverage your constraining operation? You do so by focusing your available resources on your constraint and reducing the non-value-added and value-added times within the current cycle time. It is really that simple.

Prerequisite Beliefs

In the previous section I told you not to just jump right into the UIC and begin the improvement process. If your entire operation is able to accept the prerequisite beliefs of constraint leverage and focus, you have taken the first step. When I say the entire operation, I am referring to everyone. All the individual departments, functional groups, and employees in your organization must become focused on the leveraging power of the constraining operation. If you cannot do that, there simply is no need to continue. Accounting, purchasing, engineering, sales and marketing, production, production control, quality, and maintenance all must be aligned and in total agreement. Unless and until all functional groups within your organization are singing from the same sheet of music, you simply will not make any progress.

Recognizing the Power of Leverage and Focus

The first prerequisite is that your entire organization must accept the idea that the key to improvement is recognizing the power of leverage and focus. That is, in order to increase TH, you must leverage your constraint operation by focusing all of your resources on it.

Subordinating Everything to the Constraint

The second belief that must be accepted by your entire organization is *subordination*. Subordination simply means that every decision made and every action taken by the entire organization must be done so based on its impact on the constraining resource. And when I say the entire organization, I mean everyone! Accounting must provide real-time decision-making information to the organization and not hold onto financial measures that are based on what happened last month. Accounting must also eliminate outdated performance metrics like utilization and efficiency in nonconstraint operations because they mean absolutely nothing. All these two metrics really do is create an environment that fosters and promotes overproduction, resulting in higher carrying costs, extended lead times, and excess inventory.

Purchasing must order parts and materials based upon the rate of consumption at the constraint and stop ordering in large quantities or only on the basis of lowest cost to satisfy another outdated performance metric, purchase price variance. Sales and marketing must understand that unless and until the current constraint is broken, they must not make hollow promises on delivery dates in order to obtain more orders to supplement their sales commissions. Engineering must respond quickly to the needs of production to ensure timely delivery and updates to specifications. Maintenance must always prioritize their work based upon the needs of the constraining operation, including preventive and reactive maintenance activities. If there is an inspection station that impacts the constraint TH, inspectors (if they exist) must always provide timely and accurate inspections so as to never cause delays that negatively impact the flow of materials into and out of the constraint. Finally, production control must stop scheduling the plant, based on forecasts that you know are wrong, using the outdated algorithms contained within the MRP system.

If your entire organization believes in and is ready to subordinate to the constraint, you have taken the second step. If your organization is like so many others where individual departments exist as silos, letting go of the apparent control that they now have will be a difficult pill to swallow but one that is absolutely necessary. If you are not ready, do not proceed any further.

Continuously Improving

The third belief that must be accepted by the entire organization is that improvement is never-ending. UIC is predicated on the fact that once a constraint is broken, a new one will appear immediately, so all organizational resources must be prepared to shift to it and subordinate actions and decisions toward the cycle of breaking the new constraint. This cyclical process has no end, so be prepared to accept the idea of always getting better.

Involving Everyone

The fourth belief that the organization must accept is one of involvement of the entire workforce. If you are like many other companies, you have probably been taught that improving profits means reducing expenses. And reducing expenses has typically involved reducing the size of the labor force. This is exactly opposite the behavior that is needed to successfully navigate through the UIC. Why would anyone be willing to participate in improving the operation to the point that he loses his job? So if, in the past, you are a company that used layoffs as a way of reducing or controlling expenses, you are doomed to failure. You must accept the fact that the key to making money now is increasing TH, and without everyone's involvement, it simply will not happen. If you cannot accept this belief, stop here.

As you identify the constraint and subordinate the rest of the organization to the constraint, there will be idle time at the nonconstraints. If you are like many organizations that use total system efficiency and utilization as key performance metrics, you will see both of them predictably decline. You are normally trying to drive efficiencies and utilizations higher and higher at each of the individual operations under the mistaken assumption that the total efficiency of the system is the sum of the individual efficiencies. In a TOC environment the only efficiencies or utilizations that really matter are those measured in the constraint operation. You may even be using workpiece incentives in an effort to get your operators to produce more, and I am sure many of you are using variances as a key performance metric.

Abandoning Outdated Metrics

Efficiencies, utilizations, incentives, and variances are all counterproductive. Thus, the fifth belief in preparing for the implementation of the UIC that must be accepted is abandoning outdated performance metrics, incentives, and variances. If you are unwilling to do this, do not attempt to use the UIC.

Reducing Waste and Variation

The sixth and seventh beliefs that must be accepted involve *waste* and *variation*. You must accept the premise that every process contains both excessive amounts of waste and variation that are waiting to be identified, removed, and reduced. No matter how perfect you might believe your process is, believe me, it has variation and it is full of wasteful activities. Your job will be to locate, reduce, and hopefully eliminate the major sources of both. Variation corrupts a process, rendering it inconsistent and unpredictable. Without consistency and control you will not be able to plan and deliver products to your customers in the timeframe you have promised. Waste drives up both OE and inventory, so improvements in both of these go directly to the bottom line as you improve the TH of your process and, more specifically, your constraining operation. Yes, you will observe waste in your nonconstraint operations, but for now focus your resources only on the constraint.

Embracing Problem Solving

The eighth belief that your organization must embrace is that problems must be addressed instead of being swept under the carpet. You can no longer accept temporary fixes to your problems, and believe me, problems will be uncovered as you progress through the UIC. If you are like many companies, there are problems that have been hidden with excessive amounts of inventory used to guard against their negative effects. This way of thinking can no longer be accepted. Your organization must be committed to determining the root cause of problems and implementing effective and sustainable solutions or the UIC will not work for you.

Accepting That Constraints Can Be External or Internal

The ninth belief that your organization must accept if you are to be successful involves the type and location of the constraint. Constraints can be either internal or external to your organization, and they can be either physical or policy related. If they are external, this typically means that you have more capacity than you have orders. If this is the case, you must use your improved process to leverage this constraint. That is, your improved process will result in less lead time, which your sales team can use to leverage more sales. If you have excess capacity, your sales team can even quote a lower sales cost to leverage additional sales. Think about it: as long as your expenses or truly variable costs are less than the sales price, you are adding more money directly to your bottom line. Yes, the margins will be lower than normal, but it all flows to your company's bottom line. If your constraint is found to be a policy constraint, you know it involves a conflict that must be resolved. You now have the tools to resolve conflict, so you must be ready to use them. All of what is involved in UIC requires out-of-the-box thinking for your organization.

Embracing Systems Thinking

The tenth and final belief is the understanding that the organization is a chain of dependent functions that requires *systems thinking* rather than individual thinking. There are interdependencies that exist within the organization, with all functions playing a role in the final outcome. Unless and until individual functions cease from protecting their own turf and begin collaborating as a team, real and sustainable progress will not be achieved.

Let us review the ten prerequisite beliefs that your organization must be prepared to accept if you are to successfully implement and navigate through UIC:

- Believing that leveraging the constraint and focusing your resources on the constraint is the key to improved profitability
- Believing that it is imperative to subordinate all nonconstraints to the constraint
- Believing that improving your process is a never-ending cycle
- Believing that involving your total workforce is critical to success
- Believing that abandoning outdated performance metrics like efficiency and utilization, reward or incentive programs, and variances is essential to moving forward
- Believing that excessive waste is in your process and that it must be removed
- Believing that excessive variation is in your process and that it must be reduced
- Believing that problems and conflicts must be addressed and solved
- Believing that constraints can be internal, external, physical, or policy, or any combination of the four
- Believing that the organization is a chain of dependent functions and that systems thinking must replace individual thinking

If your organization has truly accepted these ten prerequisite beliefs and all that goes with them, you are ready to begin this exciting journey that has no destination. But simply saying you believe something can be hollow and empty. It is your day-to-day actions that matter most. Review these ten prerequisite beliefs as a group on a regular basis and hold people and yourself accountable to them. Post them for everyone to see. Utilizing UIC and true acceptance of and employment of these ten beliefs will set the stage for levels of success you never believed were possible.

Endnotes

1. Womack, James P., and Daniel T. Jones, *Lean Thinking—Banish Waste and Create Wealth in Your Corporation* (New York: Free Press, 2003).
2. Liker, Jeffrey K., and David Meier, *The Toyota Way Fieldbook—A Practical Guide for Implementing Toyota's 4Ps* (New York: McGraw-Hill, 2006).
3. Womack and Jones, *Lean Thinking*.
4. Harry, Mikel, and Richard Schroeder, *Six Sigma: The Breakthrough Management Strategy Revolutionizing the World's Top Corporations* (New York: Doubleday, 2000).
5. Pande, Peter S., Robert P. Newman, and Roland R. Cavanaugh, *The Six Sigma Way—How GE, Motorola, and Other Top Companies Are Honing Their Performance* (New York: McGraw-Hill, 2000).
6. Harry, Mikel, and Richard Schroeder, *Six Sigma: The Breakthrough Management Strategy Revolutionizing the World's Top Corporations* (New York: Doubleday, 2000).
7. Wells, Herbert G., *Mankind in the Making* (1904).
8. Goldratt, Eliyahu M., *The Goal* (Great Barrington, MA: North River Press, 1986).
9. Dettmer, H. William, *Goldratt's Theory of Constraints: A System's Approach to Continuous Improvement* (Milwaukee: Quality Press, 1996).
10. Thompson, Steven W., "Lean, TOC or Six Sigma: Which Tune Should a Company Dance To?" *Lean Directions*, Society of Manufacturing Engineers, August 11, 2003.
11. Liker and Meier, *The Toyota Way Fieldbook*.
12. Lean Enterprise Institute, 2004 and 2005 Surveys on Lean Manufacturing.
13. Premo, Jason P., *Please Help! My Lean Is Broken*, Institute of Industrial Engineers.
14. Survey by Celerant Consulting, December 2004.
15. Smith, Debra, *The Measurement Nightmare: How the Theory of Constraints Can Resolve Conflicting Strategies, Policies, and Measures* (Boca Raton, FL: CRC Press, 2000).
16. Pirasteh, Reza M., and Kimberly S. Farah, "The Top Elements of TOC, Lean and Six Sigma Make Beautiful Music Together," *APICS*, May 2006.
17. Ibid.
18. Standard, Charles, and Dale Davis, *Running Today's Factory: A Proven Strategy for Lean Manufacturing* (Cincinnati: Hanser Gardner Publications, 1999).
19. Ibid.

20. Smith, *The Measurement Nightmare*.
21. Dettmer, H. William, *Breaking the Constraints to World Class Improvement* (Milwaukee: Quality Press, 1998).
22. Rother, Mike, and John Shook, *Learning to See—Value Stream Mapping to Create Value and Eliminate Muda* (Brookline, MA: The Lean Enterprise Institute, 1999).
23. Ibid.
24. Ibid.
25. Smith, *The Measurement Nightmare*.
26. Standard and Davis, *Running Today's Factory*.
27. Umble, Michael, and Mokshagundam Srikanth, *Synchronous Manufacturing—Principles for World Class Excellence* (Wallingford, CT: Spectrum Publishing, 1987).
28. Womack and Jones, *Lean Thinking*.
29. Deming, W. Edwards, *Out of the Crisis* (Cambridge, MA: MIT Center for Advanced Engineering Study, 1986).
30. Shewhart, W. A., *Economic Control of Quality of Manufactured Product* (Princeton, NJ: D. Van Nostrand Company, 1931).
31. Taguchi, G., E. A. Elsayed, and T. Hsiang, *Quality Engineering in Production Systems* (New York: McGraw-Hill, 1989).
32. Standard and Davis, *Running Today's Factory*.
33. Hopp, Wallace J., and Mark L. Spearman, *Factory Physics: Foundations of Manufacturing Management*, 2nd ed. (New York: McGraw-Hill, 2001).
34. Ibid.
35. Davis, John W., *Fast Track to Waste-Free Manufacturing—Straight Talk from a Plant Manager* (Portland, OR: Productivity Press, 1999).
36. Ibid.
37. Standard and Davis, *Running Today's Factory*.
38. Hopp and Spearman, *Factory Physics*.
39. Ibid.
40. Nakajima, Seiichi, *TPM Development Program—Implementing Total Productive Maintenance* (Cambridge, MA: Productivity Press, 1989).
41. Ibid.
42. Ibid.
43. Hopp and Spearman, *Factory Physics*.
44. Standard and Davis, *Running Today's Factory*.
45. Scholtes, Peter, *The Team Handbook—How to Use Teams to Improve Quality* (Madison, WI: Joiner Associates, 1988).
46. Ibid.
47. Smith, *The Measurement Nightmare*.
48. Dettmer, *Breaking the Constraints*.
49. Hopp and Spearman, *Factory Physics*.
50. Ibid.
51. Ibid.
52. Ibid.
53. Ibid
54. Ibid.

55. Dettmer, *Breaking the Constraints.*
56. Ibid.
57. Ibid.
58. Ibid.
59. Ibid.
60. Ibid.
61. Ibid.
62. Goldratt, Eliyahu M., *The Goal.*
63. Ibid.
64. Dettmer, *Breaking the Constraints.*
65. Ibid.
66. Ibid.

About the Author

Bob Sproull is an experienced manufacturing executive with a distinguished track record of achieving improvement goals in manufacturing, quality, product development, and engineering. He gained his experience in industries ranging from low-volume custom products (truck bodies) to process industries (tires) to service industries (mail services). He is a nationally known speaker and author, specializing in exploiting problem-solving and statistical techniques, especially implementing an integrated version of Lean, Six Sigma, and TOC.

Sproull has served as a consultant to private equity firms, where he performs due diligence assessments and executes manufacturing turnarounds. Sproull has also served as vice president of quality and engineering at Morgan Corporation, a $200 million, seven-facility manufacturer of truck bodies. In addition, while serving as general manager of American Sunroof, he executed a brilliant facility turnaround that significantly improved bottom-line results in a short timeframe. Sproull has also held technical positions at Michelin Tire and Xerox Corporation, where he implemented the company's first SPC program on consumables. He is currently applying his initiative in an MRO organization in the defense industry.

Sproull's first book, *Process Problem Solving: A Guide to Maintenance and Operations Teams* (Productivity Press, 2001), provides manufacturing workers the essential training and skills they need to understand the root causes of manufacturing problems. Sproull is a Six Sigma Black Belt and an expert in Lean and TOC. You can contact him via his Web site at www.sproullconsulting.com.

Index

Printed in the United States
by Baker & Taylor Publisher Services